THE GREAT GERMAN ESCAPE

THE GREAT
GERMAN ESCAPE

*Uprising of Hitler's Nazis in Britain's
POW Camps*

CHARLES WHITING

Pen & Sword
MILITARY

First published in Great Britain in 1992 as *The March On London*
and reprinted in this format in 2009 and 2010 by
PEN & SWORD MILITARY
Pen & Sword Books Ltd
47 Church Street
Barnsley
South Yorkshire
S70 2AS

ISBN 978 1 84884 032 4

Typeset and printed in Great Britain by
CPI Antony Rowe, Chippenham, Wiltshire

Pen & Sword Books Ltd incorporates the Imprints of Pen & Sword Aviation,
Pen & Sword Family History, Pen & Sword Maritime, Pen & Sword Military, Wharncliffe
Local History, Pen & Sword Select, Pen & Sword Military Classics, Leo Cooper,
Remember When, Seaforth Publishing and Frontline Publishing

For a complete list of Pen & Sword titles please contact
PEN & SWORD BOOKS LIMITED
47 Church Street, Barnsley, South Yorkshire, S70 2AS, England
E-mail: enquiries@pen-and-sword.co.uk
Website: www.pen-and-sword.co.uk

CONTENTS

Another aspect of the Germans' thorough plans was the amazing scheme, somehow transmitted to Britain, for a break by all German prisoners of war. By all odds the most Wellsian phase of the German war of nerves, it has still not been completely explained. We do know that German prisoners began organizing for a mass break; that they plotted to seize arsenals, obtain tanks and actually prepare the way for German landings in England.

Captain Robert Merriam (official historian to the US Ninth Army in the Second World War)

No escape story of the Second World War was more daring in concept, more fantastic, more ambitious, more hopelessly fanatical than that of the prisoners of Devizes. It began with a bold master-plan for a mass break-out of German POWs from prison camps in wartime Britain.

Colonel Alexander Scotland (head of the British POW Interrogation Service in the Second World War)

ACKNOWLEDGEMENTS

The author would like to thank the following individuals and institutions for the great assistance they have given him with this book: Mr R. Brinkworth; Mrs M. Charles; Mr R. Dyke; Mrs L. Painter (Devizes); Mr R. Beckton; Mr A. Stewart (Sheffield); Mr A. Jacques (Eden Camp, Malton); the various gentlemen of The Old Prisoner-of-War Camp, Thirkleby, North Yorkshire; Mr T. Dickinson of the New York City Public Library System; Kreisverwaltung Monschau, Germany; Mil. Forschungsamt, Freiburg i.B, Germany; Monseiur Fagnoul, St Vith, Belgium; plus the *Manchester Evening News*.

I would like to take this opportunity to thank all the many readers who have contacted me since my husband died in 2007. He was a very prolific writer as you are aware and his knowledge of military history was phenomenal. I have chosen this book for a reprint because 'it's a cracking story' and one where he was the first writer to acquire new evidence of the German POWs plan to march on London.

Gill Whiting

INTRODUCTION

They are not fools, however much we try to persuade ourselves to the contrary. But supposing they had got some tremendous sacred sanction — some holy thing, some book or gospel...something which would cast over the whole ugly mechanism of the German war the glamour of the old torrential raids.

John Buchan

In March, 1945, with only two months of the war to run, some sixty British, French and Belgian officers, plus one Pole, were kicking their heels impatiently at Dormie House at Wentworth, the mock-Tudor premises of Sunningdale golf course. They were all highly experienced members of the SOE, (Special Operations Executive) who had parachuted into Occupied Europe repeatedly to organize resistance to the Germans. The women among them had set up escape routes and had acted as wireless operators. Others had kidnapped a German general in Crete, smuggled arms into Albania, transported V-l and V-2 secrets right across Germany back to Britain. Most of them wore the bright upturned wings and parachute of men and women who had made three or more operational jumps into enemy territory.

A week or two before, the authorities had become alarmed at the fate of Allied POWs in German hands. In London, they knew from the MI9 network in POW camps that the Germans had moved the great majority of British and American prisoners to the narrow section of land in Central Germany still under Nazi control. From there the POWs, according to their own secret reports back home, expected to be moved to the Bavarian and Austrian Alps, where it was assumed that the fanatical Nazi rearguard would make its last stand.

In particular, the Allied authorities were worried about the fate of the *Prominenten,* as the Germans called their most important prisoners. What would the Nazis do with them when they realized the war was lost? Would they use them to blackmail the victorious Allies into concessions? Or would they shoot them out of hand as a last act of spite? Allied Intelligence already knew that Hitler had declared vehemently, *'Erschiesst sie alle!'* (Shoot the lot of them).

Now, as the Allies prepared to cross the Rhine and write the final chapter in the history of Hitler's vaunted 'Thousand-Year Reich', the authorities agonized over the problem of the *Prominenten.* They included an American ambassador's son, a senior US air force general, Earl Haig's only son, a close relative of Field-Marshal Alexander and the nephew of King George VI himself, the present Lord Harewood. Could they let people of such importance be shot by the Nazis?

In the first week of that March, the authorities decided they couldn't. Hastily an irregular force called the Special Allied Airborne Reconnaissance Force (SAARF) was set up. Under the command of a fierce brigadier of formidable demeanour, known behind his back as 'Crasher', SAARF was to consist of twenty three-man teams: an officer, an NCO and a signaller with an easily hidden transmitter set. When the time came, each team would set off from the nearby airfield to be dropped after dark near its target prisoner-of-war camp. Dressed in tattered uniforms, they would hide in the nearest wood, spy out the land, and then join an *Arbeitskommando,* a POW working party. When the *Arbeitskommando* returned to camp in the late afternoon, they would go with it and report to the SBO, the Senior British Officer in the camp. With his help they would open up radio contact with the nearest Allied troops. These would then paradrop arms and supplies to the POWs, while the air force gave air cover, flying over the camp until the POWs had subdued their guards and taken control. Then it would be up to the armed POWs to defend themselves against any German attempt to cart them off to the 'National Redoubt' in the Bavarian and Austrian Alps.

Captain Patrick Leigh Fermor, one of the most experienced members of the SAARF unit, was given permission to break the secrecy of the operation to interview Colonel Miles Reid, who had not long been repatriated from Colditz, where many of the *Prominenten* were imprisoned.

Colonel Reid 'exploded. Had we heard nothing of the impregnability of the fortress, no idea of the thoroughness and the rigour of the checks and counter-checks? There was absolutely no hope of the plan succeeding. We would all be goners.'* The next day Colonel Reid went to

* Introduction by Patrick Leigh Fermor to *Into Colditz* by Miles Reid, Michael Russell, 1983.

see the brigadier in charge of the airborne operation. A long and heated discussion followed. Bitter words were exchanged. 'They both emerged scowling,' Leigh Fermor recalled years afterwards. He watched stony-faced as Colonel Reid snorted angrily at the red-faced brigadier: 'I'll go to Churchill if necessary!'

In the end the scheme was called off. The Allies were already beginning to overrun the POW camps in Germany. Instead of trying to shoot their prisoners, the German guards were fleeing before the Allied advance and leaving the POWs to liberate themselves. *SS Obergruppenführer* Gottlob ('Praise God') Berger, head of the German POW system, whom one of his *Prominenten* prisoners described as 'more venal than fanatic', had decided by then to save his own skin. He wouldn't shoot them as Hitler had ordered.

So the threat was averted. The SAARF never did go into action. But if the threat had not been averted by events and by Berger's desire to wheedle himself into Allied good graces while there was still time, there would have been little chance of Colonel Reid being able to change Churchill's mind about the operation. The Prime Minister would have ordered it to go ahead, despite all the dangers, for he knew something that none of the others involved in the SAARF scheme knew. A similar plan for prisoners-of-war to arm themselves and take over their camps, with support from an airborne operation, had been conceived three months before in the heart of the Empire — and it had very nearly succeeded.

In that winter of 1944 when Allied authorities had thought that Hitler's Reich was on its knees — one more blow and it would collapse — the Germans achieved a surprise which was superior to any of the Intelligence coups which the Allies pulled off in the Second World War. Naturally the Anglo-Americans, particularly the British, were proud of those great deception schemes, 'Bodyguard', 'Fortitude', the 'Double-Cross' scheme, etc, with which they fooled the Germans about Allied intentions. But between October and December, 1944, the Germans were able to raise, train and emplace a massive assault army of 600,000 men with all their equipment, not twenty-odd miles across the English Channel, as had been the case with Allies before D-Day, but a mere two hundred yards away on the other side of the front line in the Belgian Ardennes.

But even that achievement paled in comparison with the brilliance of their forward Intelligence operation. A handful of German parachutists dropped behind Allied lines and a dozen or so 'jeep-teams' of Germans dressed in American uniforms, who did the same, created an unprecedented spy scare.

Just as in May, 1940, when the Wehrmacht had first moved westwards, the scare spread from the front to the rear areas and then to the civilian populations of the Allied countries. Once again the long refugee columns began to roll. Thousands of soldiers and military police patrolled every crossroads and bridge looking for infiltrators, while civilian police searched for disguised German parachutists. And every village *gendarme* knew they came in the guise of an innocent nun. Europe was gripped by a spy mania; as Jean Cocteau put it, the general public 'spied nuns doing up their garters behind every bush'.

But the Germans, always thought so stolid and unimaginative, pulled off an even greater coup within the framework of these covert operations on the Continent. Unknown to the long-suffering British public in that week in December leading up to the last Christmas of the war, the whole of the country had been placed on military alert. Not because of the new threat emerging on the Continent, but because of the threat from within Britain itself.

Throughout the Second World War there had been a potentially lethal Trojan Horse inside Britain: the vast numbers of German prisoners-of-war spread throughout the Kingdom. From Comrie in northern Scotland down to Devizes in Wiltshire to the far south, from Colchester on the East Coast to Bridgend on the West, every racecourse of any note held German POWs, as did football grounds. There were German POW camps in or near most large cities — Hull, York, Sheffield, Wolverhampton, Swansea, Southampton, Ayr... The Germans were everywhere, over a quarter of a million of them. Fit, virile young men, most in their late teens or early twenties, a goodly number of them fanatical National Socialists (at least while Germany was winning), they were guarded by the sick and the old: British soldiers who were too old or unfit for active service overseas.

Now, in December 1944, as the crisis loomed on the Continent, what would these young men do if they were armed and given a plan which transcended mere individual escaping? What if that POW operation was timed to coincide with the last great German counter-attack in the West at a time when Britain was virtually denuded of fighting troops? And what if these desperate young men, who were prepared to fight to the last for their homeland, were given the promise of an airborne landing by German forces in Britain: the vital support they would need if they were to capture their primary objective — London?

The Great German Escape is the story of that abortive mass escape of 1944 and the covert operations on the Continent which went with it. For over a half a century it has never been revealed in full. The reason why is easy to explain. For it is not a pleasant story, but one of betrayal, treachery, and in the end lynch justice. No story is pleasant which details just how wilfully and carelessly the lives of young and patriotic men were

4

thrown away. But that Christmas, the last of the Second World War, when so many young men died, there were few pleasant stories.

BOOK ONE

The paratroops are so valuable to me that I am only going to use them if it's worthwhile. The Army managed Poland without them. I am not going to reveal the secret of the new weapon prematurely.

Adolf Hitler to General Student, October, 1939

1

THE BARON AND THE SIXTH PARA

*Never surrender. For you it is either victory or death: there
is no other alternative. This is a point of honour.*
Baron von der Heydte to the men of the 6th Para, 1944

ONE

By nine o'clock that June morning the Baron knew that his regiment was
doomed unless he acted decisively — and independently. For the Baron
had no illusions about the manner in which the German High Command
would conduct the coming battle. The Generals were completely under the
thumb of the Führer and Hitler would order the ground to be held at all
costs. Climbing the tower of the church at Côme du Mont, he peered
through his glasses at the awesome panorama laid out before him,
impressed by the sheer size of the enemy invasion fleet: it seemed to
stretch to infinity. Thousands of ships lay at anchor off the coast, protected
by hundreds of barrage balloons tethered above them in the sky like fat
grey elephants. Angry flashes ripped the heavens apart and signal rockets
hissed into the sky on all sides; and all the while countless invasion barges,
a white bone in their teeth, headed for the Normandy shore.

For a moment the Baron was reminded of the Wannsee on a fine
summer's day. Only on this particular June day, there would be no
pleasure out there on the water, only violence and sudden death.

The Baron, commander of the German Sixth Parachute Regiment,
swung his binoculars round to the left, ignoring the salvo of 15-inch shells
that had just straddled the French village. Here the coast was shrouded, as
if cut off from the rest of the area by a grey-brown curtain of smoke. He
adjusted his glasses. In vain. He could not penetrate the fog of war. More
and more Allied shells were falling, each throwing up another huge
mushroom of black smoke. In the end he gave up and lowered his
binoculars, his face thoughtful. He guessed what was happening there to
the left. That was the enemy *schwerpunkt*. It was there that they were
coming ashore in their thousands, trying to break through Hitler's vaunted
Atlantikwall, which was no wall at all, simply a series of pillboxes and
obstacles, for the most part manned by third-rate troops.

But Baron Freiherr von der Heydte knew his duty. He came from the Bavarian *Altadel,* the old aristocracy which had been fighting Germany's battles for her since the eleventh century. It was there, where the black smoke billowed into the sky, that he would march to the sound of the guns to do battle with the invaders. But brave and efficient as he was, the Baron knew that if he carried out the Führer's order to yield not a metre of ground to the enemy, his regiment would be wiped out. Still the Baron did not hesitate for long. He had seen nearly ten years of service, first in the cavalry and then in the paratroops. He knew that a soldier who hesitated was probably doomed from the start. He called his signaller over and rapped out his orders. His headquarters was to come up to St Côme du Mont immediately. Once there, the Sixth Parachute Regiment would attack.

At that moment the Sixth Para, which had become a kind of personal legion for von der Heydte, was deployed at the door at the narrowest point of the Cotentin Peninsula, into which the Americans were now beginning to pour. Marshal Erwin Rommel, who was now in overall command in France, had always envisaged that the Sixth Para would act as a kind of bolt to that door once the *Amis* had landed. He had reasoned that the 3,000-strong regiment, regarded as the best in the whole of parachute corps, would be able to hold the enemy until the armour rolled up from further inland and drove them back into the sea.

At that moment, nine o'clock on the morning of Tuesday 6 June, 1944, the Baron was not so sanguine. Since dawn his efficient listening service had been picking up American radio signals, presumably from enemy airborne troops already landed, demanding heavy weapons, medics, more ammunition and reinforcements — and all these radio messages back to the American headquarters somewhere in England were in clear. But although the *Amis* must have dropped in force in the Cotentin, they were obviously finding it hard going.

By six o'clock that morning the Baron's forward patrols had already brought in their first *Ami* paratroop prisoners, 'all of them two metres tall', as the *Fallschirmjäger* reported, with blackened faces, heads shaven like Mohawk Indians and with the badge of a screaming eagle on their shoulders. The Baron had known immediately who they were. That eagle badge belonged to the US 101st Airborne Division, which meant this was not an isolated raid but a full-scale invasion.

The Baron had questioned them himself in his excellent English, of which he was very proud. He liked to ask POWs if they trusted their commanding officer; he felt that their answers helped him to assess a unit by revealing the morale of its fighting men. But this morning the Baron had been disappointed. The new prisoners with their shaven heads —

10

'white walls' he found out they called their strange haircuts, (by analogy with white wall automobile tyres, popular in the States at that time) — were for the most part very confident. They had learned their lessons well, despite the frivolous slogans and pictures of pin-up girls painted on their flight overalls and the somewhat optimistic boasts, such as '*See You in Paree!*' They gave him little beyond the name, rank and age, as military tradition laid down. He had their pockets searched for maps, letters, etc., but found nothing save that they were lavishly equipped with everything from lavatory paper to water purification tablets.

At seven o'clock, desperate to know more of the enemy's tactical set-up in that smoke-covered area where now there was an almost constant sound of artillery shelling and the persistent whine and thump of heavy mortar fire, the Baron sent out further patrols to bring in more *Ami* prisoners — and fast.

Corporal Anton Wuensch was the first to see the *Ami* chute hanging from a tree. It was blue and below it swung a heavy canvas container. He crouched warily and listened to the snap and crackle of small arms not far away. Next to him his second-in-command *Gefreiter* Richter looked at the dangling container. 'Probably ammo,' he whispered to Wuensch. 'Might be grub,' said a third member of the patrol named Wendt. 'God, I'm hungry...'

Wuensch ignored him, though his stomach was rumbling too. Their task was find prisoners for the Baron; still, the container might hold something useful. On his belly he squirmed forward and, wary of booby traps, tied two stick grenades to the trunk of the tree from which the chute hung, then pulled the pins. A muffled crump, a creak of breaking wood. The next instant the tree came crashing down in a shower of leaves and smoke. For a moment Wuensch cocked his head to one side to listen for any suspicious noise. There was none. No one had noticed. Hastily he and the others of his patrol doubled forward to examine the container which was now on the ground.

Wendt was there first and suddenly he croaked, hoarse with emotion, 'My God — it *is* grub!'

For the next half hour the seven men of Wuensch's patrol completely forgot their mission as they gorged themselves on the contents of the *Amis'* supply container, the 'food bomb', as it was called by the men of the Sixth Para. There were cans of orange juice, Hershey bars, cigarettes made of real Virginia tobacco, not the coarse black stinking Marhoka rubbish they had grown used to in these last years of the war, and food the like of which they had not seen in months. Indeed, Wendt was now eating raw powdered Nescafé, washed down with thick creamy condensed milk.

11

'I don't know what it is,' he chortled, 'but it tastes wonderful!'

After a while, however, Wuensch, conscious that the Baron was waiting for them, decided that they'd better set off again. Minutes later there was a flat dry crack like the sound a twig makes underfoot. One of Wuensch's men moaned softly and pitched forward, dead, shot neatly through the temple. '*Sniper!*' Wuensch yelled.

His men needed no urging to dive for cover, for already other bullets were whipping the air all around them; snapping and tugging at their uniforms, they fell to the ground, unslinging their weapons as they did so.

'*Schau!*' one of his little patrol hissed. 'Ten o'clock. Bunch of trees. I'm sure I saw him up there.'

Wuensch took out his field glasses and, shading them so that they did not reflect any light, searched the area carefully. There it was. A slight movement in the branches of one of the trees. The *Ami* was up there. For what seemed a long time he remained frozen in the same position, checking whether he was right or not. Again the branches moved. He raised his rifle and took first pressure, knuckle white as he curled his finger around the trigger. He saw the man's legs, then through the foliage glimpsed his upper body. Wuensch hesitated no longer. He pulled the trigger. The rifle butt slammed into his shoulder. He fired again — and again. As his men cheered their section leader's aim, the body of the American sniper slowly slithered out of the tree and slumped to the ground.

Throwing aside all caution, the paras doubled forward and stared down at Wuensch's victim. 'He was dark-haired and he was very handsome,' Wuensch remembered years later, 'and very young. There was a trickle of blood at the side of his mouth.'

Richter bent down and went through the dead man's pockets. He found a wallet with the usual sort of photographs that they would soon learn all *Amis* carried with them. One, Wuensch remembered, 'showed the soldier sitting next to a girl and we all concluded that maybe it was his wife'. Another was a snapshot 'of the young man and the girl sitting on a verandah, with a family, presumably his family'.

Richter started to stuff the photos and a letter he had found into his pocket. When Wuensch asked him why, Richter explained that he would send it to the address on the envelope after the war. Wuensch tapped his forehead to indicate the other man was crazy. 'We may be captured by the *Amis*', he growled, 'and if they find this stuff on you...' He drew one finger across his throat to indicate what the Americans would do. 'Leave it for the medics,' he said. 'Let's get out here.'

As the little patrol moved out, Wuensch stayed behind for a few moments, staring down at the dead *Ami,* lying limp and still 'like a dog which has been run over'. Then he shivered and hurried after the rest.

So Wuensch's patrol did not bring in any further US prisoners for the Baron to interrogate. But by now he needed them no longer. He had made up his mind what was going on in the smoke-shrouded Cotentin Peninsula. He called the Chief-of-Staff of the German 84th Corps, to which the Sixth Parachute Regiment belonged, and told him that this was the real thing: this was the long-expected Allied invasion of France. The Chief-of-Staff agreed. He said, however, that first reports from Berlin suggested that the Führer thought this was a mere feint: the real invasion would come in further north around Calais where the Channel was at its narrowest.

The Baron slammed the phone down in a rage. What did he care what the Fuhrer thought? He had long since broken with Hitler, though Hitler's War had brought him fame, promotion and those military decorations in which he gloried. Three months before, Field-Marshal Rommel had visited Sixth Para HQ. After dinner he had asked the Baron, 'Are you sure of your regiment, *Herr Oberst*?'

'Absolutely, *Herr Feldmarschall*,' he had answered, guessing what Rommel meant.

But the 'Desert Fox' had persisted. 'You are sure of *every* man? If need be, would they obey you *alone*?'

The Baron had nodded and Rommel had concluded with the significant words, 'We want a lot of units like yours.'

Then the Baron had known with absolute clarity that his Supreme Commander, Rommel, was in the same plot to deal with Hitler as was his cousin, Colonel Claus von Stauffenberg.*

Since that fateful dinner with Rommel, the Baron had kept his own council, knowing that not only his own life but those of his 3,000 paras depended upon his judgement and military cunning. Therefore, without waiting for the 84th Corps to take a decision, he made his own. He was not going to play a defensive role and wait tamely to be chewed up by the Allies' planes and guns. He would chance an attack. With luck he would be able to deal with the enemy paratroops to his immediate front before they had time to organize. He had dropped on Crete himself back in 1941; he well knew how disorganized paratroops were in the first few hours after landing. Speed was of the essence and an immediate, hard counter-strike. Within ten minutes of having made his decision, the Baron acted. He sent his first battalion off in the direction of Ste Marie du Mont. His second followed, heading for Turqueville, where a third-rate infantry unit made up of ex-Russian POWs under the command of German officers and

_____

* Von Stauffenberg had tried to kill Hitler by planting a bomb at his HQ in July, 1944.

NCOs and the 795th Georgian Battalion, another renegade outfit, were already under attack, and breaking. His third battalion he kept close to his own HQ as the regimental reserve.

At first everything went much better than the Baron had anticipated when he had first seen that awesome enemy armada out to sea and had told himself that nothing could stand up to such overwhelming strength and power. At midday a dispatch rider, covered in dust, rushed into the courtyard of the Baron's HQ to report, 'First Battalion has reached Ste Marie du Mont, *Herr Oberst!*' Under the rimless helmet, the Baron's lean face broke into a wintry smile. Ste Marie was only a few kilometres from the coast. With a bit more luck his First would break through cleanly by the late afternoon.

A little later he was informed that his Second had penetrated to Turqueville and was helping to shore up the defences there, forcing the ex-Russian POWs, who had little desire to die for Hitler fighting against Americans, to stay in their positions at gunpoint. Now the Second Battalion was preparing to move on from Turqueville to Ste Mère-Eglise, where large-scale enemy airborne landings were reported to have taken place. But the Baron warned against going into the village itself. The Second should wheel around the place and advance across the causeway between the flooded fields of the area and go straight for the coast, only six and a half kilometres away.

Captain Mager, in charge of the Second, agreed to his CO's suggestion and then signed off, leaving the Baron to wait anxiously for further news of the Battalion's progress.

None came at first; then the rapid crackle of small-arms fire and the high-pitched hysterical hiss of German MG 42s followed by the heavy ponderous return fire of American machine guns told him enough. His Second Battalion had run into trouble.

It had. As Captain Mager's men attempted to cross the causeway towards the coast, his left flank had come under heavy American fire. The *Amis* of the 82nd Airborne's 507th Regiment had dug themselves in on the outskirts of Mère-Eglise. Now the paras were going down, wounded and killed all along the line of march, with others going to ground to return the enemy fire. Mager was a veteran of ground fighting in Russia. He knew his lightly armed paras were not equipped for protracted action. They were trained for swift decisive actions of short duration; he could not let them get bogged down like this. Swiftly he ordered a change of plan. The Second Battalion would wheel round and make a frontal attack on the village and capture it before resuming its drive on the coast. It was a fatal decision.

Mager's men attacked in open order across the bare fields, tough keen young men in their camouflage smocks, every man a volunteer, full of pride that they belonged to the elite Sixth. But the men of the 82nd Airborne, waiting for them in their foxholes on the outskirts of the village, were equally proud, aware that they belonged to a division that had jumped twice in combat. They, too, were all volunteers.

Almost immediately the American paratroopers opened up. Tracer skidded across the fields, bare of any cover. Bazooka rockets followed, trailing a series of fiery-red sparks. The Germans began to fall at once, spinning round with the impact of the slugs, clutching suddenly shattered shoulders and arms, or falling flat on their faces without even a single cry, dead before they hit the ground. Within five minutes Captain Mager was forced to call it off.

An hour later he tried again. This time he came in from the flank. But the fields there were just as bare of cover as the other ones had been and again the 'All Americans', as they called themselves (because the Division was supposed to be recruited from every state in the Union), were waiting for the Sixth once more. Again after five minutes the attack fizzled out without result, save for the fact that yet more young men lay prone and motionless in the sodden fields in front of the village.

As darkness fell over the battlefield Captain Mager, angry and frustrated as he was, gave up. He ordered his tired paras to dig in. Hastily they set to work with their entrenching tools, as out to sea the cannon of the great invasion armada continued to boom. 'We'll take it in the morning,' they told each other as they sweated over their holes. 'Tomorrow.'

But they never would take St. Mère-Église. On the morrow the destruction of the Baron's Sixth Parachute Regiment would begin.

TWO

Oberst der Fallschirmtruppe Baron von der Heydte, known to his admiring men as 'the Baron', came from a long line of Bavarian Catholic aristocrats. He and his family were related to most of the great families of Europe, and in a very roundabout way, through the Wittelbachs, the Bavarian royal house, to the British royal family itself. With his long, ascetic face and pronounced front teeth, he would have looked just as much at home wearing a crusader's helmet as his ancestors had once done as he did wearing the rimless helmet of the German paratrooper.

15

Born on 30 March, 1907, in Munich, the son of a Bavarian cavalry officer and a French mother, he left his Munich Gymnasium to do two years with the Reichswehr, until, in 1927, he was discharged in order to study law at the Universities of Innsbruck, Graz and Berlin. After his doctorate, he became an assistant to Professor Kelsen at Cologne University. Unfortunately his chief was both a Jew and a Social Democrat, not a winning combination in the new Nazi Reich; in due course the Professor was fired and emigrated. As was customary in German academic circles, when the Professor went, the assistant went too.

Professor Kelsen disappeared, but 'the Baron' landed on his feet, as he always would do. He secured an American Carnegie Foundation Scholarship, financed by the estate of a Scottish businessman who had made his fortune in the United States. It looked as if von der Heydte was all set to become the professor of international law which one day he did indeed become. But that was in the distant future. In late 1934 Germany was in the throes of the 'national re-awakening', as the new Führer called it. The law, national and later international, was thrown out of the window. As a consequence, von der Heydte decided that his future, as the scion of a long line of soldiers, lay with the military. He decided to join the newly created Wehrmacht, which was expanding rapidly and badly needed officers. So he joined the 15th Cavalry Regiment, stationed in Catholic and arch-conservative Paderborn where it was being retrained as an anti-tank unit.

After the war von der Heydte described his decision to join the Wehrmacht as a kind of 'inner emigration' as the Germans called it: an attempt to distance himself from the Nazis by 'emigrating' into the apolitical Army. But that was afterwards. In fact, von der Heydte was at that time involved in National Socialist politics. At the university he had been a member of the 'Brownshirts', the student SA organization, as well as of the ultra-right-wing Catholic organization, led by Franz von Papen, which helped Hitler to power. As his interrogator, Major Milton Shulman, said of von der Heydte in 1945,

> [He] belonged to that softly spoken, extremely intelligent class
> of Germans whose protestations of innocence of everything
> National Socialist almost bit off the tongue they held firmly
> wedged in their cheek. For even while he was disclaiming his
> connections with the Party, he managed to introduce a whole
> subtle stream of Nazi propaganda into his talk.*

One year after the Baron joined the cavalry, his regiment incidentally still retaining its horses, the Wehrmacht formed the most modern arm of the

---

* *Defeat in the West,* Milton Shulman, 1948

service — a parachute regiment. The first officer volunteers were called for, and with typical German thoroughness they were put through a full pilot's course as well as their parachute training; not only could they jump out of a plane but also fly it if necessary.

But as the force expanded, pilot training was dispensed with, though right into the first years of the war German paras were also expected to know how to refuel aircraft, hitch gliders to the towplanes and marshal aircraft for dispersal around an airfield perimeter. By the time von der Heydte volunteered for this new arm, after winning both classes of the Iron Cross in the Battle for France, the training had become standardized. The first three months of the new recruit's training were spent refining infantry skills and learning unarmed combat, plus plenty of physical training. In the course of the latter, the recruit learned aircraft drills and, in particular, the usual head-first dive out of the plane which was used to leave the Junkers 52, the three-engined workhorse of the German Parachute Regiment.

After passing out from this course, the budding para went for a short sixteen-day intensive parachute course. Here the men packed their own chutes (unlike the British practice whereby servicewomen did the job for them) and made six jumps in quick succession (eight in Britain) to win the coveted parachute badge. This was a diving eagle surrounded by a wreath in metal which was worn on the breast pocket of the formal uniform, again unlike the blue-and-white cloth wings that the British para wore on his shoulder. Curiously enough German trainees never made a night jump, an oversight which von der Heydte would regret in years to come.

Fully trained as a parachutist, the Baron quickly worked his way up from company to battalion commander, but he played no part in German airborne operations in Norway or the Low Countries. He was to have his first taste of para combat in May 1941, leading one of the first assaults on the island of Crete.

One month earlier von der Heydte had been in Germany, still training his 3rd Parachute Battalion. Long afterwards he remembered that fine spring morning when he decorated twelve of his young men with their parachute badge and told them:

> Our formation is young. We have not yet any traditions. We
> must create tradition by our actions in the future. It depends
> upon us whether or not the sign of the plunging eagle — the
> badge which unites us — will go down in history as a symbol
> of military honour and valour.

On 20 May, 1941, the Baron found himself dozing in the 'Auntie Ju', as their Junkers 52 transports were called by the German paras, on the way to the island of Crete. But not for long. Roused by his adjutant, a minute later he was preparing to drop at the beginning of one of the most daring airborne operations of the whole war: a combat drop on an isolated island, held by a large garrison, with the whole operation dependent on the German command in Greece being able to supply the assault troops solely by air.

> I stepped to the open door. We were just flying over the beaches. The thin strip of surf, which looked from above like a glinting white ribbon, separated the blue waters from the yellow-green of the shore. The mountains reared up before us, and the planes approaching them looked like giant birds trying to reach their eyries in the rocks.

Then came the order to jump.

> I pushed with hands and feet, throwing my arms forward as if trying to clutch the black cross on the wing. And then the slipstream caught me and I was swirling through space with the air roaring in my ears. A sudden jerk upon the webbing, a pressure on the chest which knocked the breath out of my lungs and then — I looked upwards and saw spread above me the wide-open, motley hood of my parachute. In relation to this giant umbrella I felt small and insignificant.

Baron von der Heydte had made his first combat jump.

Ten days later it was all over. The German paras had achieved the seemingly impossible: they had captured a well-defended island from the air. But the cost had been high. General Kurt Student, father of the German parachute arm, known behind his back as 'Papa', visited his soldiers immediately after the island had fallen and the Baron was shocked at the change in the General's appearance. Almost overnight he had 'visibly altered':

> He seemed much graver, more reserved and older. There was no evidence in his features that he was joyful over the victory — his victory — and proud of the success of his daring scheme. The cost of victory had evidently proved too much for him. Some of the battalions had lost all their officers and in some companies there were only a few men left alive.

'Papa' Student was not the only one concerned at the high losses suffered by the German paras in their capture of Crete. Hitler was, too. He ordered that all parachute operations entailing more than a battalion should cease immediately. With the invasion of Russia soon to begin, the Führer did not want to waste highly skilled infantry in costly attacks such as that on Crete.

The losses suffered by the 7th *Fliegerdivision,* to which the Baron's battalion belonged, were soon made up by men from the depots, many of them as yet without parachute training. By the late autumn of 1941 the Baron found himself fighting as an ordinary infantry battalion commander at the siege of Leningrad. Again losses were high and again they were made up by men without parachute training. Slowly but surely the Seventh Division was becoming an ordinary infantry division and the Baron began to despair. Would he and the remaining 'old hares', the veterans, never again carry out the role they had been trained for?

In 1942 the Baron's hopes were raised when the Division was ordered to Italy. There, together with the Italian Army's own parachute division, the Folgore Division, it was planned to make a mass drop on the island of Malta. This was cancelled at the last minute and the attack was switched to Gibraltar. In the end that assault was called off too, and the 7th *Fliegerdivision,* its name now changed to the 1st Parachute Division, was sent back to Russia as an ordinary infantry division.

The Baron was lucky. He did not go to Russia with the rest of the Division, but was posted to a special parachute brigade, which was scheduled to drop on Cairo once Rommel had gained the upper hand in the Western Desert. This First Paratroop Brigade was commanded by a pugnacious veteran, General Hermann Ramcke, who had started off his long service career in the Kaiser's navy back in the First World War. He had a mouthful of metal teeth, replacing those he had lost in a parachuting accident, and was eager to have a 'crack at the Tommies'. But it wasn't to be. The drop on Cairo was called off and Ramcke's 1st Parachute Brigade went into the line again as ordinary infantry.

Four months later, in the retreat which followed Rommel's defeat at El Alamein, Ramcke's Brigade, which possessed no transport of its own, was cut off and disappeared among the mass of fleeing Germans and Italians. On 4 November, 1942, Rommel officially wrote off the paras and Ramcke's unit was taken out of the Afrika Korps' order of battle. But Rommel had underestimated Ramcke and his officers, such as the Baron. As parachutists they had been trained to exist and function in circumstances where ordinary troops lost their heads and fell into confusion. Three days after they had been written off General Ramcke appeared outside Rommel's bus and threw the surprised 'Desert Fox' an immaculate salute. Rommel acknowledged it, Ramcke flashed a metallic smile and told the C-in-C how his men had ambushed the supply column of a British armoured brigade. Using the Tommies' trucks, they had driven 350 kilometres through the desert to rejoin the Afrika Korps. With him Ramcke had brought back no fewer than 800 of his paras. Not surprisingly, one week later Ramcke was awarded the Oak Leaves to the Knight's Cross for his daring.

But Ramcke's boldness and the bravery of his paras did not impress

Hitler enough for him to give Student permission to carry out further airborne operations. Instead he ordered that more parachute divisions should be set up, two whole corps, but they would not drop from the sky to do battle; instead they would walk in on their own two feet and fight as ordinary infantry.

Thus it was that after service in Crete, Russia, North Africa and Italy, the Baron found himself in France in early 1944, commanding the Sixth Parachute Regiment, which was to be the nucleus of yet another parachute division, the Sixth (it was never formed). As far as possible, the Baron took only volunteers for his regiment, which he tended to regard as a kind of personal fief, and ensured that at least thirty per cent of all new recruits received parachute training — just in case.

Every new recruit was welcomed by the Baron personally. He told the soldier:

> From the moment a man volunteers for the airborne troops and joins my regiment, he enters a new order of humanity. He is ruled by one law only, that of our unit. He must give up personal weaknesses and ambitions and realize that our battle is for the existence of the whole German nation.

The new recruits were also required to learn the 'Decalogue', the Baron's Ten Commandments, the first of which read: '*You are the elite of the German Army. You are to seek out combat and to be ready to endure hardship. Your greatest ambition should be to do battle.*' The tenth commandment stated: '*Never surrender. For you it is either victory or death; there is no other alternative. This is a point of honour.*'

Of course all this was part and parcel of 'unit spirit' which every good outfit attempts to build up, with distinctive uniforms, titles, instant 'traditions'. Many commanders foster these things, not because they believe in them implicitly, but because they know they bind men together, and in the end soldiers fight not for their country but for their unit: the feeling that they must not let their comrades or their unit down.

The Baron was well aware of this. He knew that three types of young men were attracted to his Sixth Parachute Regiment. First came those with 'a love of adventure'. Then there was the sort of man who wanted to join a team: 'He was looking for comradeship.' And thirdly there was 'the idealistic type, the convinced young Nazi who wanted to fight for the Führer and for Germany.' Being the clever man he was, the Baron played on the loyalties and emotions of all three types, while at the same time he always attempted to set an example to his young hopefuls, eager for some desperate glory, by leading from the front.

> All my men were volunteers and that ensured good morale.
> Then, too, I had a very good relationship with my soldiers, a

camaraderie. There was no attack in which I did not participate myself, no order that I didn't give from the front. In the paratroop tradition of modern war, it is essential to observe and command from a forward position. It is impossible to command from the rear. When we parachuted, I jumped with my men. When they patrolled, I patrolled too. If a soldier knows his commander is out there with him, he will attack in a different way. He will have a different attitude, be more aggressive.

As a result, Allied Intelligence could sum up the quality of the Baron's soldiers that summer thus:

In these young, indoctrinated Nazis, fresh from a Luftwaffe that had ceased to exist, their faith in their Führer and their cause had not died....None of them had felt the sickening impact of defeat. They had not given way to despair and hopelessness that now gripped most Germans. Parachutists in name only they were. They had never been taught to jump from an aeroplane. The bulk of them had never received more than three months' (infantry) training. But they possessed two other compensating virtues — youth and faith.*

The Baron's emphasis on the elite quality of his Sixth Parachute Regiment had a strictly military basis. It was to make his young men fight to the utmost and, if necessary, die on the field of battle for the sake of the regiment and their comrades. But some of those young men who were to experience their first battle this June would take the words of the Baron's Tenth Commandment quite literally when it stated, '*Never surrender... Victory or death...*'

They would not surrender. But neither would they find an honourable death on the field of battle. Instead they would have the life squeezed out of them by the English hangman's rope. Long before the Baron died peacefully of old age in his own bed, acclaimed for his military, political and academic achievements, those young men would be mouldering in English earth far away from their beloved Germany.

* Shulman, op. cit.

THREE

'*Halten Sie! Halten Sie!* Defend to the last man... that is all we heard from Hitler,' the Baron complained bitterly after the war. 'It was impossible.'

It was. For three solid days the Baron's paras had been attacking the village of Ste Mère-Église, and each time their attacks were thrown back with heavy losses. At six o'clock on the evening of the third day it seemed as if the paras might at last be successful. Word came into the Baron's makeshift HQ that the *Amis* of the 82nd Airborne Division were pulling out; the pressure was too great for them. The Baron renewed his attacks. But he had not reckoned with Colonel 'Gentleman Jim' Gavin, the 82nd's Assistant Divisional Commander.

Gavin, on the spot, found the defenders very shaky after their commander had just been hospitalized. The regimental executive said the Germans were attacking again and he couldn't hold. But the pale-faced executive officer didn't know Gavin. A veteran of the Sicilian campaign and one of the first Americans to jump into Occupied Europe, Gavin did not believe in withdrawing from ground captured with American blood. He ordered a counter-attack. Everyone who could fight would fight, including himself, he told the executive officer: 'regimental clerks, headquarters people, anyone we could get our hands on with a weapon'. The regimental executive blanched, but dutifully rounded up the rough-and-ready assault force. Meanwhile Gavin posted two of his toughest officers at the rear; they would turn back anyone who tried to retreat and they were empowered to shoot if necessary. Then Gavin personally led the attack against the Baron's paras. Bent double, he started across a cornfield 'when, I suddenly noticed the stalks being cut as though by a giant invisible scythe'. He dropped on all fours, but continued crawling towards the enemy. He came across a platoon of mortarmen intent on withdrawing, but he turned them around and sent them into action once more. Bit by bit the young colonel — soon he would become the US Army's youngest divisional commander — patched up the shaky line and stopped the German attack, just as fresh US troops in the shape of the 90th Infantry Division began to appear on the battlefield to bolster the defence.

That day the Baron realized that his regiment would soon be destroyed if he kept up these incessant, purposeless attacks, and he did not intend to let that happen. He would not sacrifice his precious regiment to Hitler's senseless order to hold ground. So without the knowledge of his corps commander, he started secretly withdrawing his men from the line in the Ste Mère-Eglise area. As he later explained, 'I found a way. I established an aid post for the wounded a safe distance behind the lines and every day I sent men back, wounded or not.'

But time was running out for the Baron's Sixth Parachute Regiment and it seemed that 'hospital alley', as his paras called the escape route to the aid station, was not going to operate swiftly enough for them all to get away. Already the Baron's first Battalion had pulled back to his HQ — *twenty-five men* out of the original 700.

Unshaven, hollow-eyed and exhausted, they slumped over their coffee and cigarettes and told their commander their story: how they had been split into groups by the attacking *Amis* and then wiped out. One third of the battalion had been killed or drowned trying to escape through the swamps. The rest, nearly every one of them wounded more than once, had been captured.

That same day, while enemy guns pounded his positions, an American officer appeared in front of his HQ bearing a dirty white flag — a looted French tablecloth, in fact, stuck at the end of a garden pole. The *Ami* explained that he had a message from General Maxwell Taylor, commanding the other US airborne division, the 'Screaming Eagles' of the 101st Airborne. It was written in German and demanded that the paras should surrender immediately. The Baron, so proud of his English and French, replied in the former, saying that he could not comply with the surrender offer, adding, 'What would you do in my place?'

But that note and the state of his 1st Battalion made up the Baron's mind. By now he had identified three major American units fighting against his Regiment, the 82nd and 101st US Airborne and the 90th US Infantry Division. Well over 30,000 men against what was left of his 3,000. As a pretext for what he planned, he asked for further supplies. HQ 84th Corps replied that 'Parachutists only need knives'. Angrily the Baron signalled, 'parachutists are only human too'. In response, 84th Corps did manage to get a supply column through, bringing with them shells for his mortars, but they were French-made and of a different calibre. The inventive paras nevertheless managed to use them by wrapping each shell in a blanket so that it fitted the tube and fired them off successfully in this manner.

That night of 10/11 June his sentries spotted aircraft above their beleaguered positions. A delighted shout went up. '*Tante Jus*!' ('Auntie Jus!') They were the old familiar Junkers 52 transports, the first German planes they had seen since the start of the Allied invasion.

Minutes later the first containers, swinging below their parachutes, were landing all around. Risking their lives to retrieve them, the paras wriggled out into the damp fields to find that they contained not only small-arms ammunition but, in one case, surprisingly enough, a large pack of 'Parisians', their slang for contraceptives. As the disgusted Baron commented, 'What does Corps HQ expect us to do — fuck our way out?'

That night the Baron started to withdraw his survivors from the Cotentin Peninsula. The Americans were in hot pursuit. They kept up the pressure all night and into the following morning when the Baron decided to make a personal reconnaissance of his front. He hadn't gone far in his open radio car when he was overtaken by a highly-polished staff car bearing the stiff metal pennant of an SS general on its bonnet. The driver signalled him to stop and the Baron found himself confronted by no less a person than *Brigadeführer* Ostendorff, the Commander of the 17th SS Panzergrenadier Battalion 'Goetz von Berlichingen'* and his Chief of Operations.

Heavy-set and cold-eyed, Ostendorff acknowledged the Baron's salute and formal greeting with a wave of one pudgy hand. '*Herr Oberst,*' he said, 'I have been ordered to place you and your regiment under my command.'

The Baron was surprised. 'By whom, sir?' he asked.

'By the Commander of the 84th Corps,' the SS General replied. 'You are to put me in the picture. As soon as the main body of my Division arrives we are to counter-attack. Lost ground must be re-won.' Ostendorff's Division had never fought in action before, but the General was in excellent spirits. 'We'll get that particular little job cleaned up all right, won't we?' he announced.

The Baron was not so optimistic. He said that the *Amis* were tough opponents. Ostendorff, whose combat career so far had been spent on the Eastern Front in Russia, was not impressed. Surely the *Amis* weren't tougher than the Russians, he asked.

'Not tougher,' the Baron replied, 'but considerably better equipped, with a veritable steamroller of tanks and guns.'

With typical arrogance, the SS General refused to believe him. '*Herr Oberstleutnant,*' he interrupted, 'no doubt your parachutists will manage till tomorrow'. And with that he was gone, leaving the Baron fuming with rage.

He returned to his farmhouse headquarters to find that his paras might not even last that long. The Americans were advancing again and it looked very likely that the rest of his Regiment would suffer the same fate as his First Battalion if he did not act swiftly; it was obvious the *Amis* were attempting to encircle him. He was not prepared to risk that eventuality. Without consulting the commanding general of the 17th SS Panzergrenadier Division, he ordered his men to pull back out of the

---

* Goetz von Berlichingen was a German robber knight in the Middle Ages, who became the subject of a play by Goethe in which the poet uses the coarse expression 'kiss my arse'. Gradually the name came to be used as a euphemism for that vulgarity. Hence, the 17th SS Panzergrenadier was 'the Kiss my Arse Division'.

impending trap. And, during the hours of darkness, his paras did just that. Now it was Ostendorff s turn to fume with rage.

The next morning, despite the fact that there was no hope of the SS counter-attack succeeding, Ostendorff s men attacked, supported by the Baron's Second Para Battalion. It was a total failure. The *Amis* were waiting for them. From prepared positions they poured a hail of fire into the advancing ranks of the eighteen-year-old SS youths in their camouflaged tunics.

The SS men went down on all sides. Angry officers and NCOs shrilled their whistles and bellowed orders, trying to keep the mass moving in the face of that terrible fire. Green but brave, those products of Hitler Youth and National Socialist New Order kept on going for a few moments before they, too, joined the dead and dying.

Then they broke. They started fleeing to the rear, tossing away their weapons, scrambling for their lives. The Baron watched them contemptuously. Only his own Second Battalion managed to achieve its objective, but when Ostendorffs boys broke and ran, they, too, were forced to pull back. It was all over.

All the same, the Baron decided he could profit from the flight of the SS. He reasoned they were good boys. All they needed was firm confident leadership and he was certain he could give them it. He needed to make up his losses of the last week's fighting and the SS were going to do it for him. Accordingly he stationed some of his senior NCOs at the crossroads of the routes the SS were using to flee to the rear. They set up tables, looted from the nearest French houses, where the senior NCOs sat licking their pencils in anticipation. Behind them stood a bunch of grinning young paras armed with machine pistols, with stick grenades stuck in their belts and down the sides of their jackboots.

As the first of the young fugitives came stumbling up the road, the NCOs licked the stubs of their pencils more purposefully, as if they were back at some peacetime barracks, ready to take the particulars of a bunch of new recruits. And that, in fact, was what going to happen. As the Baron put it after the war. 'When the SS came to this point, they were given the chance of "volunteering" for the paratroops or being court-martialled. Not surprisingly, they all joined up.'

His ranks filled out with these 'volunteers', the Baron started to pull his battered Regiment back — and then back again. For now the German front was crumbling virtually everywhere, as the Allies poured more and more troops into France. June gave way to July. The Sixth, together with the rest of the Wehrmacht, was still retreating north-eastwards, pounded day after day by the dreaded enemy *Jabos* (fighter bombers). Any German column caught out on the roads in daylight stood very little chance. The enemy Spitfires, Typhoons and Thunderbolts dominated the air over France, waiting in what the enemy pilots called 'cab ranks' to pounce on the German vehicles. Once a German column was spotted, its vehicles were sealed off to front and rear by a few well-placed bombs. Then with the column stalled, the *Jabos* would finish the vehicles off at their leisure, using their deadly rockets and cannon.

One of the Germans caught in the panic-stricken chaos, Karlludwig Opitz, described it thus:

> Vehicles pile up. Cars, heavily laden with officers' gear, honk a way through the jam, twisting past lorries in their effort to make better time. Guns are abandoned and blown up. Heavy tractors stop for lack of fuel: a couple of grenades in the engine and that's that. The huge Mercedes diesels of the workshop company are hit by rockets....Electrical fitting machines, lathes, automatic welders, workshops on wheels, the very best transporters, searchlight trucks with anti-dazzle equipment for night driving, lorryloads of spare parts, dental trucks, a mobile film unit, dredgers, they are all there and the fighters are having a field day. They hedgehop above the road, the engines screeching. Empty ammunition belts fall from them, rockets, grenades, machine-gun bullets, bombs, everything is thrown at the stream of vehicles.

The result of this constant harassment from the air was, in the words of another member of the fleeing German Army, *Generalleutnant* Fritz Bayerlein, 'depression and a feeling of helplessness, weakness and inferiority. Therefore, the morale of a great number of men grew so bad that they, feeling the uselessness of fighting, surrendered, deserted to the enemy ....Only particularly strong-nerved and brave men could endure the bombardment.'

The Baron and his surviving paras were such men. They kept their nerve. Indeed, at one stage the paras turned on their tormentors: twenty of the Baron's paras, supported by a tank from the SS, succeeded in capturing a whole American battalion of 600 men and thirteen officers. Thereafter the Baron attached his regiment to a battle group of the 2nd SS Panzer Division. With the Baron in the lead, guiding the men 'like a Red Indian chief' as one of his paras put it, he directed them down secondary roads at night, moving in single file, while on both sides on the main roads the American armour rumbled forward, unaware of the enemy in their midst.

Somehow the Baron pulled it off. His Regiment succeeded in getting through. But little was left of his proud formation: a few hundred men out of the original 3,000 and most of the survivors were either sick or wounded. Only sixty out of the whole total were unwounded.

At the end of August, 1944, the Baron finally reached the frontiers of the Reich. Here, as he himself recorded after the war,

> I was told that the German Army was not in the control of its commanders. The whole command organization had broken down. Nobody knew to which corps or army he belonged. Most regiments had been sent back to Germany to rebuild. The whole front was quite open, completely unprotected except by local police who were not able to defend. The Germans even had the crazy idea of forming the *Volkssturm* with old men and young boys of less than sixteen who were to fight Allied tanks with shotguns! But you couldn't meet a real soldier anywhere. If Eisenhower, in the beginning of September, had decided to continue the attack into Germany, then the war would have been over.

But Eisenhower didn't, and the war would continue another eight months, with the evil genius Adolf Hitler still pulling a few more aces from his sleeve to confuse and dismay the Western Allies. The Baron and his paras were yet to play their greatest role in the history of airborne warfare in the Second World War.

FOUR

'*Dolle Dinsdag*' — crazy Tuesday. It was 5 September, 1944, the day the Dutch went mad. On that day the Dutch, who had been suffering under German domination for four years, learned from the BBC that the British had captured the Belgian port of Antwerp just across that country's border with Holland and were advancing rapidly on the Dutch frontier. Liberation was at hand!

Spontaneous celebrations erupted everywhere as the dirty, demoralized Germans, looting as they went, departed for their homeland, with the British — or so it seemed to the excited Dutch — at their heels. But while the normally staid Dutch celebrated, dancing in the streets and openly displaying portraits of their exiled Queen framed by ribbons in the national colours, the British decoding centre at Bletchley picked up an Ultra signal which in due course would bring that celebration of impending liberation to a violent end.

The signal was from Berlin to General Student, who, four years before, had virtually conquered Holland single-handed with his one division of paratroops. It ordered him to form a paratroop army, the First Parachute Army. Student was to use all the power at his command to comb the Luftwaffe and his parachute training school to recruit a force of not less than 30,000 men and rush it to Holland. There his men would help to defend the line of the Scheldt estuary and by doing so deny the use of the port of Antwerp to the Allies.

As the nucleus of this new army, Colonel von der Heydte's reinforced regiment, now numbering 4,000 men, was to act as Student's emergency unit. As the Baron recalled after the war,

> My real task was to move quickly from one trouble spot to the next. Student called me his *'Feuerwehr'* [Fire Brigade]. For me it was a good assignment. I had only to attack — and I got everything I wished for. If I said I can't attack without this or this, the next day I got it. To attack is more interesting and it is not as difficult as to defend. Our poor infantry had to come in after me to defend the position I had taken and I would be sent to another trouble spot.

On 8 October, 1944, the Baron arrived with his first two battalions and immediately attacked to retake the Dutch village of Hoogerheide, which had been occupied some time earlier by the Canadians.

Unfortunately for the Canadians of the Royal Regiment of Canada they were advancing at the same time, crossing the morass of inundated polder country, plodding slowly forward through ground mist. They hit the advancing paras head-on. 'The Germans opened up with a murderous fire,' the regimental historian wrote after the war, 'which practically annihilated one of the assaulting platoons and caused heavy casualties among the remainder'.

The Baron's paras were up to their old tricks. One was the feigned act of surrender, a trick they always used with new troops and this was the first time they had fought against the Canadians. Several of them came out of a dyke opposite the Royals' D Company position with their hands up. The Canadians ceased firing, just as the paras had expected. The paras now broke into a wild run, evidently out to outflank D Company's machine guns and capture them. But the company commander, Major Tim Beatty, reacted fast. He yelled an order to his mortarman. Suddenly three-inch mortar bombs were dropping on the running Germans. As Major Beatty recorded after the war, 'that put an end to that'.

All the same, the advance of three Canadian battalions ended that October afternoon as the Baron's paras attacked all along the line, with virtually every Canadian company on the verge of being overrun. By evening the Baron's soldiers had succeeded in pushing to the edge of the village of Hoogerheide. As always his paras were setting their mark on the battlefield.

Two days later, however, the Baron had to break off and attack on another section of the front. An urgent message from General Student revealed that a strong force of Canadians had been observed heading for the village of Woensdrecht. This drive had to be stopped for it was thought to be the point of an all-out Allied attack up the Dutch coast towards Rotterdam. The Baron set off immediately and established his HQ in a brickworks just north of Woensdrecht, from where he could observe all troop movements across the flat polder around the village. As he recalled later: 'I would make my customary evening stroll and could walk just a thousand metres away to the houses over at the top end of the ridge overlooking Woensdrecht. Or, if I wished, I could easily get to the first cluster of farmhouses at Hoogerheide.' He made it all sound so easy, a gentleman officer's kind of battle which could include a leisurely stroll after dinner. In reality, the battle for Woensdrecht was a savage bloody affair, with houses in the village changing hands nearly every day. Little quarter was given or expected. Bodies were booby-trapped. Captured snipers were routinely shot and if a soldier didn't surrender quickly enough for his captors he might end up dead. More than once the Canadians and the paras engaged in hand-to-hand fighting; in one recorded case a para tried to bite out a Canadian's throat.

On 16 October, after the fighting had been going for over a week, the Baron received a disturbing report from one of his company commanders dug in at the edge of Woensdrecht. The young lieutenant had observed some movement in the Canadian positions about 500 metres from the German front line. What did it mean?

Never one to shirk his duty, even though it was two in the morning, the Baron swung himself into the side-car of his motorcycle which he always used when visiting the front and set out to find out what was going on. He reckoned that the Canadians were probably forming up for another attack. His plan was then to withdraw his men to a secondary position and, once the Canadians thought they had achieved their objective cheaply, launch a savage counter-attack on them when they were off-guard. But when he reached his forward positions, 'I saw I was too late. The Canadians had already begun their attack. There was no time for an orderly withdrawal to a secondary position. I gave the order to retreat to those of my men that I could find. My duty was to bring as many as possible back to the prepared positions.'

By dawn the Canadians had taken over the whole village and were congratulating themselves on how easy it had been. Six paras whom the Baron had been unable to warn in time were rooted out of their hiding place in a cellar, and as one of the Canadian officers bent over a wounded para spat in his face. The officer remarked, 'Even in captivity, the beast could snarl'.

Dawn passed and still the damp sombre countryside was dark, as if the very sun was reluctant to illuminate the horrors below. So it was that a young Canadian sentry, posted to watch for any sign of a German counter-attack, made his fatal mistake as he glimpsed the file of men, well strung out, advancing on the Canadian positions. 'Hey,' he sang out cheerfully, 'I didn't know the Americans were fighting here.' He had confused the American steel helmets with the rimless ones of the Baron's paras.

Moments later the full weight of the Baron's counter-attack struck the Canadian positions. The first Canadian company was overrun by the paras who were supported by Mark IV tanks and self-propelled assault guns. The company commander of another company broke down and fled the field; the pressure was too great. Naturally his men broke and started running after him, only to be stopped later by other Canadian officers wielding pistols and threatening to shoot if the men didn't go back into the line. Within the hour all the Canadian companies were heavily engaged and their battalion commander knew it would not be long before his battalion cracked. He yelled into his radio, '*Victor target — scale ten!*' Taking an incredible risk of killing and wounding his own men too, he called for a massive concentration of shellfire to be brought right down on his own positions. Within seconds, there was one great banshee howl and 4,000 shells — some fifty tons of high explosive — came raining out of the sky right on target. For the next three minutes three artillery regiments, three medium and three regiments of anti-aircraft artillery, a total of 312 guns, fired ten rounds per gun.

The result was unbelievable. In an instant the fields all around were transformed into a lunar landscape, pitted with great smoking pits of brown earth, with German tanks and self-propelled guns wrecked and on fire everywhere. The Baron's counter-attack, which he had led personally, had been stopped dead at the price of one Canadian wounded by his own gunfire.

Now the Canadians redoubled their efforts. They were hampered by the fact that they had suffered severe losses in Normandy, but, due to Canada's strange laws, were not receiving nearly enough replacements. (By Canadian law soldiers had to volunteer to go overseas; when the Canadian Government was finally forced to send non-volunteer conscripts overseas, some fifty percent of the first 16,000 promptly deserted before they reached the port of embarkation.) So the sadly depleted Canadian infantry fought Germany's elite with men drawn from

30

the military butchers, policemen, clerks and the barely healed wounded. Anyone who could hold and fire a rifle was thrown into the battle.

Despite the fact that some of the Canadian infantry battalions were below half their nominal strength and only half of them were really trained infantrymen, they started to make progress. The paras seemed to be cracking. They were no longer fighting with the same kind of fanatical determination as before. Some were even surrendering — like Alexander Schmidt, aged nineteen, who had been left behind when his company moved out to guard two machine guns. Alone in the dark and very nervous, as the signal flares indicated that the Canadians would soon be attacking once more, he decided to set off and find his company. After a little while a corporal appeared out of the darkness and joined the scared teenager. The NCO said, 'I know the way, but don't make any fuss'.

As Schmidt recorded afterwards, 'I didn't know then what he meant, but I understood later: he was going to give himself up. As we marched the way he directed in the night all of a sudden we heard "Hands up!". We had marched right into the Canadian lines!'

Schmidt was frisked, had the Canadian pistol taken from him, just as he had taken it from a wounded Canadian the previous day, got into trouble because his pockets were also full of looted Canadian cigarettes and then 'in the morning we were transported to a camp for the rest of the war'.

Schmidt had blundered into captivity, but the Canadians took his surrender as just another example of how weak the German paras' resistance had been in this third week of October. What the Canadians didn't know, however, was that, on the highest order from Berlin, the Baron's men were secretly being pulled out of the line. For there the deep mood of pessimism which had reigned the previous month when the Western Allies had reached the German frontier had changed to one of renewed confidence, even optimism.

On 21 October, 1944, when Schmidt was captured and his comrades of the Sixth disappeared to an unknown location, Colonel Otto Skorzeny was ordered to the Führer's main HQ, the 'Wolf's Lair', to be initiated into the great secret of what was soon to come.

Skorzeny, whom General Eisenhower, the Allied Supreme Commander, described as 'the most dangerous man in Europe', was detested by the Baron and his fellow para officers. The year before, General Student had worked out a careful plan to rescue the Italian dictator from the mountain fastness where his people had imprisoned him after his downfall in July, 1943. It had entailed the use of paras and gliderborne infantry. The operation had been highly successful and

31

Mussolini was rescued. However, Skorzeny of the *SS Jagdkommando* (a kind of German SAS), who had gone in with the gliderborne troops, had spirited Mussolini away in a light plane to Vienna and had claimed the credit for himself. Student and his paras had been left out in the cold.

Now, in a private conversation with Hitler, Skorzeny proudly related how he had just pulled off another successful coup — the kidnapping of the son of the Hungarian dictator, Admiral Horthy. Horthy had been wavering in his loyalty to the German cause and there had been secret talks between the Hungarians and the Russian enemy. By kidnapping Horthy's favourite son, Miklos, and using him as a hostage for his father's loyalty, Skorzeny had succeeded in keeping Hungary in the war on Germany's side.

Hitler listened attentively to Skorzeny's account of his adventures in Budapest, then told him he had been awarded another decoration, the Knight's Cross, for his rescue of Mussolini. Skorzeny prepared to go but the Führer told him to stay. Skorzeny sat down again. For a moment or two Hitler remained silent, as if in doubt as to whether he should disclose his great secret. Then he began, his voice suddenly excited, 'Skorzeny, I am now going to give you the most important job of your whole life. Up to now only a few people know of my plan in which you will play a leading role. In December Germany will launch a great offensive that will be decisive for the future of our country. The world thinks Germany is finished, with only the day and the hour of the funeral to be appointed. I am going to show them how mistaken they are. The corpse will rise and hurl itself in fury at the West. Then we shall see.'

For the next hour Skorzeny listened as Hitler explained that while Germany had been fighting for its very life on its western borders, he had all the time been planning a massive counterblow. Five main operations had come in for detailed examination: a counter-attack into Holland at Venlo, two in central Luxembourg, one at Metz and finally another attack into Alsace. All the pros and cons of these projected attacks had been discussed in depth and now firm conclusions had been reached as to where the attack would go in. Hitler told Skorzeny that his Chief-of-Staff, Colonel-General Jodl, would explain more to him later.

Now, however, Hitler said: 'I have told so much so that you will realize that everything has been considered very carefully and has been well worked out...Now you and your units will play a very important part in this offensive. As an advance guard you will capture one or more bridges on the River Meuse between Liège and Namur.' He paused for a moment before saying softly, 'You will carry out this operation in British or American uniform.'

In his memoirs Skorzeny does not record his reaction to this last statement except to say that he was 'confused'. Perhaps, however, his face revealed his shock at hearing that his men would be going into action dressed in enemy uniform. That meant that if they were captured they could be shot as spies. Hitler went on, 'The enemy has already used that trick. Only a couple of days ago I received news that the Americans dressed in German uniforms during their operations in Aachen. Now in addition to capturing the bridges, you will send out small commando parties in enemy uniform to destroy communications, give false orders, change sign-posts, etc, etc, and generally create confusion in the Allied ranks. And all your preparations have to be completed by the first of December.'

Skorzeny tried to protest that the time would be too short, but Hitler never listened when he was set on an idea. 'I know you will do your best,' he said reassuringly.

Numbly Skorzeny rose and went to meet Jodl. Hitler went with him to the door. There he paused before Skorzeny and the cunning-faced Chief-of Staff went into the operations room. 'But now to the most important thing, Skorzeny,' Hitler snapped briskly. '*Total, absolute secrecy.* Only a very few people know about the offensive.' Skorzeny nodded his understanding. 'In order to conceal your preparations from your troops, stick to the basic cover-plan which we have worked out. Tell them that we are expecting a full-scale enemy attack in the area between Cologne and Bonn. Your preparations are intended to be part of the resistance to that attack.' With that Hitler dismissed him. Skorzeny had been let into the great secret...

Far away in Holland the Baron was mystified that he and his men had been withdrawn when they had been holding the Canadian advance up quite successfully. He did not know what the Führer intended for him. Nor did he know how inextricably his own operation would be tied up with that of the detested Skorzeny. Together the two Colonels would create a tidal wave of panic behind Allied lines.

What neither of them knew was that a third large-scale covert operation was also being planned in Berlin. It would take place in Britain and the men who would lead it were the Baron's paras, now supposedly safely locked away in the country's many prisoner-of-war camps. Its objective would be the seizure of London itself.

2

WHITES, BLACKS AND GREYS

Slow seem'd the sun to move, the hours to roll,
His native home deep imag'd in his soul.

Homer

ONE

By the autumn of 1944, Britain was being swamped by a great mass of
prisoners-of-war. The Wehrmacht, thought the over-confident Allies, was
now virtually beaten. Each day landing barges packed with fresh
prisoners landed from France at ports in the south-east. There hard-faced
military policemen were waiting to shepherd the evil-smelling mob to the
waiting trains.

Obediently they followed the route to captivity, shuffling along in their
dirty uniforms. There seemed to be little discipline left now. Privates
jostled officers and there were angry scuffles for the best seats in the
trains. The redcaps were so contemptuous of the once vaunted *Herrenvolk*
(master race) that they did not even bother to click off the 'safeties' of
their revolvers and Sten guns.

Lousy, depressed, many of them not even German, but coming from
every subject race in Europe (there were even Mongolians among them,
whose language no one seemed able to speak), these thousands of
prisoners were first placed in one of nine 'command cages', one for each
of the nine British Army military commands throughout the United
Kingdom. Usually these camps were set up on racecourses or football
grounds, such as Kempton Park, Doncaster, or the Knavesmire at York.
These sites were thought particularly suitable because they could be
easily guarded and provided accommodation for both captor and captive.
When such places were not available, then the military command simply
enclosed two or three fields with barbed wire and installed watch-towers,
manned by guards armed with Bren guns. Camps like this were set up at
Catterick and Loughborough.

Here the prisoners were interrogated by the Prisoner-of-War
Interrogation Section (PWIS), who tried to obtain military information
from them and at the same time graded them according to the strength of

their belief in the Hitler creed. Those who were thought to be opposed to National Socialism were graded as 'white'; those who were still fervent believers were 'black'; the great majority who had no strong feelings either way were categorized 'grey'.

It was in these command cages that the more interesting prisoners were selected for special interrogation. These might be officers who knew military secrets, Gestapo men who could be connected with war crimes against Allied subjects, or senior officers who had once been close to Hitler and might know something about his further plans. In particular, any prisoner who knew anything about Hitler's terrible new revenge weapons, currently battering London, the V-1s and V-2s, was immediately sent away for special interrogation at the 'London Cage'.

The London Cage was a cream-coloured Georgian building at Number 8, Kensington Palace Gardens. Once the home of a sugar millionaire, it now housed a skilled team of interrogators, many of whom were of German or Austrian Jewish descent, but all of whom spoke fluent German and were well versed in the various ways of getting information out of a prisoner. In addition, the London Cage had an annexe in Richmond Park, a converted mental home.

Although the Cage was run by the military, discipline was not particularly strict, the food was good by wartime standards and the daily routine was somewhat irregular, with prisoners and captors coming and going at all hours. Here there was none of the threatening atmosphere that marked the Gestapo interrogation centre at Number 10, Prinz Albrechtstrasse, Berlin, where prisoners had to turn and face the wall when another prisoner passed in the corridor and the nights were made hideous by the cries of men being tortured.

SS Colonel Alfred Naujocks, the man who always boasted he had started the war,* had been in both, first the Gestapo centre and now the London Cage. Here, he later reported, he was 'reasonably comfortable, well treated and the food was good'. But all the same the London Cage really was a prison. There was barbed wire over the windows, the floors were of solid concrete and each massive door had the usual 'Judas hole' through which the guards, who wore plimsolls so that they could move along the corridor noiselessly, could peer at the inmate at regular intervals. There were no hooks, plugs, switches or cupboards; there was no way the prisoner could hang himself or hide anything. There were also the usual stooges: fellow prisoners who might whisper a conversation with an inmate when food was brought in or who were tossed into a

---

* Naujocks had led the raid on the Gleiwitz Radio Station of 31 August 1939, which Hitler used as an immediate excuse for declaring war on Poland. See Leo Kessler, *Betrayal at Venlo* (Pen & Sword Books, Barnsley, 1990).

prisoner's room late at night 'until a bed is found tomorrow'. The real purpose of these stooges, usually Austrian or German Jews who had fled to Britain before the war, was to worm information out of the prisoner.

Presiding over the London Cage was Colonel Alexander Scotland, the head of the PWIS, who had been in intelligence since the turn of the century. Naujocks called him the 'King of the Cage'. With his white hair and rosy cheeks, he looked like everybody's favourite grandfather, with a firm but kindly manner to match. But after the war Naujocks confessed that he 'felt a little afraid of this man'. And he was right to be. Despite his benign manner, Scotland was extremely shrewd. Moreover, he had seen service in three wars, not only in the British Army but — uniquely — in the German Army too.

Back in 1903, young Alexander Scotland had been trying his hand at business in what was then German South West Africa, when the Hottentots rose up in armed revolt against their German colonial masters. Scotland was asked to help supply the German troops in the bitter four-year war that followed, and, to ensure his safety while travelling about, he was given a German uniform and a German rifle. He had become a soldier in the Kaiser's army. In the course of those years he was contacted by a British officer and asked if he would 'keep an eye' on the Germans. He agreed. It was his first contact with British Intelligence.

In 1914, still in German South-West Africa, Scotland was arrested by his German friends as a spy. Somehow he escaped and made his way — at his own expense, for in those days only gentlemen were supposed to indulge in Intelligence and gentlemen did not need money — to London, where he was recruited into the Intelligence Corps and sent to France. There his duties at first were routine. He tried to work out the German order-of-battle from prisoners and the morale of the Kaiser's army. But he soon became bored and asked to be transferred to a more exciting post. He got it, running agents in the area of the German-Dutch-Belgian frontier called the *Dreilaendereck* (Three-country-corner) by the Germans and the Maastricht Appendix by the Allies, the area where Holland bulges into Germany and where the locals, all of whom speak the same German *patois* whatever their nationality, had long been engaged in smuggling. Here Scotland ran agents back and forth for nearly two years. More than once he crossed into Germany himself to seek information by mixing with German soldiers in their barracks and places of entertainment, once narrowly escaping capture.

The war ended but if Scotland thought he was finished with Intelligence he was wrong. In the mid-1920s, during visits to Germany, he started to take an interest in the career of the rising radical political leader Adolf Hitler. He was asked in London to pass on what he learned to a certain discreet office in Queen Anne's Gate. So it seemed perfectly natural for him to offer his services once more when the next war began in September, 1939.

Five years later, in 1944, Scotland probably knew more about the German Armed Services than many a German general. He had instituted the Red Cross Form given to every prisoner sent to the London Cage so that he could be registered with the Geneva branch of the International Red Cross. Naturally the form contained more than just a request for the POW's name, rank and next-of-kin. He had introduced the 'sweet and sour' method of interrogation, the brutal, threatening interrogator interchanged with the gentle middle-aged officer (himself) who offered the prisoner tea and sympathy: a shoulder to cry on, with military information coming out with the tears. He had compiled a German order-of-battle so that a new POW would be confronted by an interrogator who knew his CO's name and the name of his mistress, too, if needs be. Why try to hold anything back, old chap? *You see, we already know everything about your unit, don't we?*

He had tricked Franz von Werra, the first German POW to escape from a camp in England in the Second World War. He had bugged the cell of General von Thoma, who revealed what he had known of Germany's top secret missile projects to another German general sharing his cell. He had learned of the plot to kill Hitler. He seemed all-knowing. Yet that October, as he released yet another bunch of paratroopers from the London Cage to the normal camps, 'Schottland', as he was called by his German charges, felt a little uneasy.

These newly captured paras seemed truculent, confident, even arrogant, in contrast with the demoralized wretches who had come through the Cage only two months after the Wehrmacht's collapse in France. That wasn't all. He had a feeling that something was going on in the camps.

At the beginning of the war the Germans had been perfect innocents as far as security was concerned. Pilots had flown with maps, personal diaries, unit patches, all sorts of apparently trivial impedimenta that gave away vital military information. Soldiers had talked freely about the units to which they belonged and the personalities and habits of their officers and commanders. As in civilian life, they just loved to talk about themselves. Now, however, the German prisoners were becoming cagy again, sticking to the old formula of rank, age, next-of-kin. It seemed almost as if security had been tightened up on the other side of the Channel. But why? What had the Wehrmacht to hide at this late stage of the war?

There was also the strange business of the message that Ultra had picked up on the morning of 26 October, 1944, a signal sent to the rear headquarters of Field-Marshal Walter Model's Army Group B, located near Krefeld on the Rhine. It had come directly from the Führer's headquarters in East Prussia and it read:

VERY SECRET. To divisional and army commands only. Officers and men who speak English are wanted for a special mission. The Führer has ordered the formation of a special unit of approximately two-battalion strength, for use on the Western Front in special operations and reconnaissance. Volunteers who are selected will report to *Dienststelle* Skorzeny [Skorzeny's company office] in Friedenthal.

The message was transmitted over the signature of no less a person than Field-Marshal Keitel himself.

In between breaks in routine interrogation, Scotland pondered that strange message. He knew who Skorzeny was, of course; since the SS Colonel's rescue of Mussolini the previous year, he had become famous — or infamous — in British military circles. Churchill had even praised the boldness of his rescue scheme in Parliament. But why did Skorzeny need such a large formation for reconnaissance? What were these special operations? And why did the men have to speak English? Scotland decided he would try to survey the mood of the prisoners under his charge in the ordinary POW camps, to which they were sent once they had passed through the Command Cages and the interrogation centres at the London Cage or its annexe in Richmond. But his survey would not be done through the camp's British Intelligence Officer. That would make it too obvious. The prison camp grapevine would soon learn what the Intelligence Officer was up to, for he was shadowed by the camp's stooges whenever he went into the compound. Once he started asking questions in there, however innocent, the whole camp would know that there was something in the wind.

The administration of POW camps was left basically to the Germans themselves. The British provided the guards, of course, and the services, including food. But it was up to the German *Lagerführer,* who played a similar role to the British Senior Officer in German POW camps, to run the affairs of his German charges. He organized the feeding of the prisoners, the work details, and dealt out justice when conflicts arose between prisoners. Otherwise his main problem was trying to overcome the prisoners' boredom and to suppress the more blatant forms of homosexuality. For the 'English vice', as the Nazis had sneered before the war, was quite common among these healthy young men, who had little to do and were fed twice the rations of the British civilian population (they were fed on the same scale as the British Army and received, for instance, three times the civilian meat ration).

The great majority of the German prisoners saw very little of their British captors save at rollcall and during the routine searches, carried out at irregular intervals. The only ones with any real contact with the British were the *Lagerführer* and his clerk. Any other German approaching a British guard or officer would have been regarded as a potential traitor by his fellow prisoners, especially if he was of the 'black' category: and over the years several suspected traitors had been sentenced to death by kangaroo courts, lynched by their comrades or drowned in the latrines.

Since 1942, when German POWs had first started to arrive in the United Kingdom in large numbers, Scotland had therefore tried to secure the appointment of 'whites' as *Lagerführers*. He reasoned that they would inform the authorities of anything strange taking place inside the camps. Failing that, he had made deliberate attempts to plant clerks in his pay on the *Lagerführer*. These '*Spitzel*', as the German prisoners called them, went in constant fear of discovery, but Scotland moved them around frequently and kept promising them that they would be the first to be sent home once Germany had surrendered. There were even rumours that when the '*Spitzel*' were being transferred from one camp to another their escorts stopped off at certain large towns where they were allowed to enjoy the sexual favours of paid women.* Of course, the strict moralist Colonel Scotland always denied that.

Now as October gave way to November, Scotland discreetly pressed his German contacts within the camps for information. In particular, he wanted to know the reason for the changed mood of the most newly arrived prisoners. By now every POW camp in the country held a few German paratroopers, and they, if they had been captured recently, had to be observed most closely. Why were they so truculent and what news had they brought with them from the front? Scotland knew instinctively that something was going on in the camps. But before he could act he had to know more — and fast.

---

* The Germans used a similar system to suborn British and Allied POWs. They established 'rest camps' for certain prisoners whom they thought weak and pliable, where the prisoners were allowed to sleep with whores. If the POW did not succumb he would then be blackmailed by being accused of having intercourse with a German woman, which was a criminal offence.

Devizes, a market town to the north of Salisbury Plain, had enjoyed a quiet war. It had not suffered the bombing that had been the lot of nearby coastal towns such as Southampton. Nor had it been overrun with evacuees from London and Birmingham. But the war had undoubtedly changed the sleepy old place where the highlight of the week had been the Thursday market.

Throughout the war, soldiers had been coming and going. The county regiment, the Wiltshire Regiment, had marched away from Le Marchant Barracks, the creeper-covered red-brick depot of the unit for several generations, to be replaced by the survivors of Dunkirk, a ragged mob of men, mostly without weapons, from many regiments. They had eventually disappeared back to their own units. But still the soldiers kept coming. The ATS came, the Army's female auxiliaries, and there were so many of them that new Nissen huts had to be specially built for them.

By 1942 the first Americans were beginning to arrive. At first they were service units, who helped to improve existing quarters and build new ones for those who would follow them. In part, these were soldiers of the US 29th Infantry Division, 'the Blue and the Gray', which boasted it had stayed in the UK so long that it would never go overseas now; instead it would stay behind while the invasion went in and 'wipe the bluebird shit off the white cliffs of Dover' (a pun on the popular song of the time). But the 29th Infantry did go overseas in the end and suffered a bloody beating in Normandy.

By midsummer, 1944, however, most of the khaki and olive-drab uniforms of the British and American Armies had vanished from Devizes to be replaced by the dusty field-grey of the beaten Wehrmacht. Daily the same landing barges which brought back American wounded to be tended at the US Army Military Hospital at Waller Camp in Devizes also brought back German POWs. The Germans would be deloused and fed at the Southampton Cage, located on the Western Esplanade, before being forwarded by train to Devizes. There they were led in ranks of six abreast through the side-streets to the wired cages of Le Marchant Camp, now officially known as Camp 23. Once more they were deloused, cleansed, cropped, medically inspected by captured German doctors and fed, then given their prison uniform, dyed a distinctive mauve colour and adorned with bright yellow patches so that no one could fail to recognize them as British prisoners. At a rate of 2,000 a day at the height of the battle for France, they were then categorized and shipped to camps all over Britain, with the worst of the 'blacks' being sent to specially secure camps in the wilds of Scotland.

By the autumn of that year, however, the flood of prisoners to Camp 23 had dwindled to a trickle. Slowly it began to build up its own permanent population of German POWs. Locals afterwards recorded several 'favourite' prisoners. There was 'Hitler' who bore a striking resemblance to his Führer. There was 'Little Hans', a hunchbacked dwarf who was the butt of the guards and his fellow prisoners for he certainly did not fit the Nazi stereotype of the blond, strapping Aryan. There was even a German civilian who at the age of seventy-two had been suddenly given an armband and a rifle over in France and sent to the front. When he arrived at Devizes station, the Railway Transport Officer, seeing the state the old boy was in, rang the camp and asked the duty sergeant to send a truck to pick him up. The Camp Interpreter to whom the call was passed, Captain William Spreckley, asked whether the prisoner was wounded. 'No,' the RTO replied. 'He's not wounded. Just too old to march to the camp.'

Most of the prisoners who now remained at Camp 23 in Devizes were in the 'white' and 'grey' categories: docile and glad to be out of the firing line while the young fanatics back home died for 'Folk, Fatherland and Führer'. But not all. Some of the more recent arrivals belonged to the 'black' category, like Karl Zuehlsdorff, a member of the 17th SS Panzergrenadier Division which had failed so lamentably in that first counter-attack against the *Ami* paras. The one-time grocer's assistant had turned into a hardened killer, who boasted of the many *Amis* he had slain in France before he was wounded and finally captured. Another fanatical 'black' was Sergeant Joachim Goltz, who told anyone prepared to listen that he had volunteered for the premier regiment of the SS, *die Adolf Hitler Leibstandarte* (the Adolf Hitler Bodyguard), at the age of sixteen and had fought in Russia before he was captured in France at the Falaise débácle in July, 1944.

In all, the 'blacks' numbered perhaps twenty prisoners, but although they were small in number they managed by threats and blackmail to make an impact on the several hundred other German prisoners in Camp 23. However, the 'blacks' were faced by a formidable trio of fellow Germans in the shape of the *Lagerführer,* Walter Meier, a burly tough soldier, his assistant Mueller, a former cruiser-weight boxer, and the camp's mystery man, *Feldwebel* Wolfgang Rosterg.

Wolfgang 'Bint' Rosterg was the scion of a wealthy German family. His father was a senior manager with the great German chemical cartel IG Farben and according to gossip in the camp the Rosterg family had a holiday villa near Hitler's own country home at Berchtesgaden. Before the war the family had sent Rosterg to London to learn about the chemical business and for a while, living in a bed-sit in St Pancras, Rosterg worked for the British chemical manufacturers F. W. Berk as a trainee. According to one of that firm's senior executives, Mr Edgar Berk, Rosterg was 'a real Nazi in those days'.

But something had changed Rosterg. Now the pugnacious thirty-year-old, who had been born in Lübeck on the Baltic coast, had little good to say about Hitler and National Socialism. In the years since he had left F. W. Berk he had travelled widely and had learned several European languages. Apart from fluent English, he spoke some French, Polish, Magyar and Latvian. Thus he was very useful to the camp's clerk-of-works, Jim Gaiger, and helped him to give instructions to the multi-national work force responsible for Camp 23's maintenance. Naturally Rosterg, who had access to the outside through Gaiger, was Scotland's man.

In that first week of November, while Colonel Scotland worried about the strange signal from Keitel and the changed mood of newly captured German prisoners-of-war, a small batch of Germans captured in the fighting on the Scheldt arrived at Camp 23. Most of them were the usual shabby 'stubble-hoppers', as the Germans called their infantry. But one of them stood out among the cowed lines in field-grey assembled in front of Meier and Rosterg, who as camp interpreter was always at hand in case the new arrivals did not speak German. He was *Oberfahnrich* Erich Pallme Koenig, a tall arrogant para barely out of his teens who had been captured by the Canadians while fighting with the Baron's Sixth Parachute Regiment. Koenig was not a real German. The son of a Viennese professor, he had become an ardent member of the Hitler Youth immediately after Austria's *Anschluss* to Germany. Fervent Nazi that he was, he had known what the average German thought of the Austrians. The Austrians, so most Germans maintained, were a weak sloppy people, prone to compromise and to servility, like those Viennese waiters who addressed everyone fawningly as '*Herr Doktor*' in the hope of getting a bigger tip. So the young Koenig had become a super Nazi and patriot — '*mehrpaepstlicher als der Papst*' (more papal than the Pope), as the Germans say. As soon as he was old enough he had volunteered for the toughest unit in the German Army, the elite Sixth Parachute Regiment. Promotion had been rapid; by the age of nineteen Koenig had reached the highest non-commissioned rank — *Oberfahnrich* (roughly, ensign). In the German Army this rank, which would lead eventually to a commission as a second lieutenant, entailed the would-be officer serving six months at the front. Unfortunately Koenig had not completed the six months before being captured by the Canadians and shipped to Camp 23.

Koenig made it quite clear where he stood as a prisoner. Entering Camp 23 he snarled at the first guard he met, 'One day soon I'll be back with a whip and the first person I'll use it on will be you!'

In vain the *Lagerführer,* Walter Meier, tried to appease the tall young para ensign. He explained that rations were good in Camp 23 and Red Cross parcels arrived regularly and were distributed at once. The Tommies, their guards, were humane, unlike the Poles who had guarded the camp for a while earlier on. The Poles had been feared. Meier ended his little homily with, 'You're out of the war now. Make the most of it till it's over.'

Koenig's face remained stony; clearly he did not want to sit out the war behind barbed wire. Just then came the sound of singing and his expression changed instantly. 'A radio?' he asked, though everyone knew radios were banned in POW camps for obvious reasons.

Meier shook his head. Standing next to him, Rosterg, who had been studying the tall young para during the interview with Meier, said. 'Not a radio. It's our camp choir. The Commandant allows us to use the dining room for practice three times a week. The choir is rehearsing for a Christmas concert.'

As the old Austrian carol, 'Stille Nacht, Heilige Nach', flooded the Lagerführer's hut, Koenig's face twisted contemptuously. 'What's the matter with them?' He indicated the direction of the choir with a jerk of his head. 'They should be planning to escape, not to sing hymns.'

As the Lagerführer dismissed Koenig and the rest of the 'new boys' to where other POWs were waiting eagerly for the latest news of the front and home, Rosterg reflected that this cocky young man from Vienna needed watching. After all, the notorious Otto Skorzeny also came from Vienna. These 'comrade laced shoes'* with their Austrian charm, all bowing and scraping, were not always what they seemed to be.

Rosterg was right to be suspicious. Almost from the day he arrived in Camp 23, Koenig assumed leadership of the 'blacks', although they were all older and more experienced than he was. His initial remark, that the choir should be practising how to escape and not how to sing carols, was no idle taunt. He had arrived in the camp determined to escape — and more.

In the Second World War all servicemen, both enemy and Allied, were told what to do if captured. Troops especially at risk, such as aircrew, paras and commandos, were also supplied with escape kits: compasses disguised as buttons, scarves with maps sewn into them, foreign currency, names of safe houses, even Benzedrine tablets to keep them awake for hours on end during their escape. But a few, a very few, on both sides, were trained *not* to escape if they were captured, but to remain in the

* 'Comrade laced shoes' was the contemptuous name given by the German soldier to his counterpart in the Austrian army who had worn laced-up boots instead of the German jackboots.

camps and carry out specific tasks in the enemy country. Just as the Ultra secret was kept under wraps for nearly thirty years after the war because the technology was still being used against new enemies, so there are few details of these unsung heroes available today because the authorities thought the same technique might be used in a new war.

In the case of the British Army, for instance, there were people like Quarter-Master Sergeant John Henry Owen Brown of the Royal Artillery. During his three years in Germany as a POW he reported back to London from various camps and was awarded the MBE after the war for having done so. In 1945 he was instrumental in bringing to trial several British traitors who had worked for the Germans, including John Amery, the renegade son of a British cabinet minister. There was Sergeant 'Dixie' Deans of the RAF, who helped many a POW to escape by bribing and compromising German guards. He was also the head of a very secret organization within the camps which relayed intelligence back to M19 through a system of coded signals inserted into POWs' messages home. The code, based on the page numbers of a certain English-German dictionary, was almost impossible to spot and crack. Moreover, Deans also ran a group *outside* the wire. It was led by the bold and fanatical Sergeant George Grimson who had escaped from the stalag at Heydekrug and contacted the local Polish underground. Instead of trying to board a ship for neutral Sweden as he had originally intended, Grimson stayed with the Poles and, by means of bribes and coercion, built up an escape and espionage organization. Grimson disappeared at the end of the war, but Deans was awarded the MBE for his efforts.

Another part-time agent was Warrant Officer Richard Pape of the RAF who, when he wasn't escaping — and he won the Military Medal for doing so — was sending back intelligence using the racing code of the *Yorkshire Post* for which he had once worked as a journalist. As Pape wrote after the war, 'Whenever I heard of military information which might be of value to British Intelligence, off it went at the first opportunity.'

The Americans had men such as Air Force Sergeant Ralph Ernst, who kept in contact with London from his stalag for two years after being shot down over Germany. He explained long afterwards:

We had a two-tube radio which I modified to receive BBC transmissions on short wave. Secret messages were received in this way. A certain letter from the first word was formed into a message. Each POW camp had a designated call letter. We located German airfields and factories near to us and we sent the location to London. A few weeks later we would discover that our message had been passed on to the RAF because they bombed it.

In Koenig's case, or so it would seem today, he had deliberately allowed himself to be captured — *not* because he had been ordered to spy on his fellow prisoners who had turned traitor, nor in order to obtain information for SS General Schellenberg's intelligence service, but for a far more significant purpose.

Throughout the war the Wehrmacht had been unable to penetrate Britain. There had been no commando-style raids on the British coast, for instance; no daring paradrops such as the British had carried out at Bruneval. Even before D-Day when the Germans had been desperate to find out where the bulk of the Allied invasion force lay, so that they knew where to expect the main thrust, no investigative raid was launched on the south coast of England. As Otto Skorzeny told the author shortly before his death when queried on the subject, 'We wouldn't have had a chance. The Allied defences were impenetrable.'

But now, in the easiest possible way, the Wehrmacht had an agent, perhaps others too, right in the heart of England.

At first Koenig revealed nothing to his new comrades; he merely started to form a little group of 'blacks' who he felt might be able to carry out the master plan when the time came. They included Joachim Goltz and Kurt Zuehlsdorff of the SS, Warrant Officer Hans Klein, who had won both classes of the Iron Cross for bravery in Russia, and a seaman, Josef Mertens, another fanatical young Nazi who constantly proclaimed his desire to avenge the sinking of his ship by the Tommies.

Sometimes the little group talked openly of escape, telling each other tall tales of how other POWs had escaped and how, although no one seemed to have actually fled the accursed island, there was always hope that one day it could be done. Mertens, for example, who had managed to conceal a map of Britain during the search after he had been captured, said he had heard that some German POWs had stowed away in an American landing craft in the Thames. The craft which was going to join a convoy at Plymouth was taken over by the stowaways off Dover. They forced the US skipper to change course and set sail for the nearest point in German-occupied France. Unfortunately, Mertens told his listeners, the German coastal guns opened up and killed everybody on board. Nevertheless, he insisted, this showed that it was possible to escape across the Channel.

Rosterg, who happened to be listening, poured cold water on the story. But, he went on, he knew of one man who had escaped from Devizes. He stole a car and drove to Dover where he found a motorboat. 'But they caught him as he was trying to start the engine and they brought him back. His reward was twenty-eight days in the *Kuehler*.'

45

The other listeners shook their heads sadly. Why risk bread and water in the 'cooler' when no German POW had ever succeeded in getting away? Better to stay in Camp 23 and live on porridge, bully beef and English tea.

But Zuehlsdorff, who had narrowly escaped being shot in France the previous summer when he was captured by the *Maquis,* looked at the others contemptuously. 'It is our *duty* to escape,' he lectured them. 'Remember the special orders we were given before we left the Reich. We must do more than just escape. We are still German soldiers and we must get back into the war — here, in the heart of England.' He leaned forward, lowering his voice as if the guards outside the wire might hear him. 'First we escape. Then we spread terror among the civilians — kill them, capture their arms, tanks and planes. We must march on London.'

Koenig nodded his approval. Those were exactly the words he would have used himself if he had been allowed to do so. But, for the time being, he had to keep silent.

Rosterg looked bored but Zuehlsdorff's face was flushed with excitement. 'We shall form an escape committee immediately. But you —' he looked Rosterg square in the face, 'you will not be present.'

Rosterg nodded casually and noted mentally, 'These men are dangerous. I must watch them.' In doing so, he signed his own death warrant.

THREE

At the first secret meeting, held in the camp's latrines after morning roll-call, *Oberfahnrich* Koenig was nominated head of the escape committee. No one questioned his right, although he was one of the newest arrivals in the camp and the youngest of the would-be escapers. His arrogant manner gave him a natural authority.

At first Koenig let his fellow 'blacks' chat on the general subject of escaping. It was wild, haphazard stuff, based on '*Latrinenparolen*' (latrine-rumours) and guesswork. Then he stepped in. From the way he spoke it was clear that Koenig had been trained for this sort of thing. He explained how, at the beginning of the war, a certain *Oberleutnant* von Werra had made the first of his daring attempts to escape from Grizedale before trying again and nearly managing it from Swanwick Officers' POW Camp. Finally he had escaped from a camp in Canada and had

46

arrived back in the Reich several months later to be awarded the Knight's Cross, although he was technically a Swiss citizen and not a German.

'But we must do better than that. Things have advanced a long way since von Werra's day.' His listeners looked puzzled. What else was there to escaping than escape? Koenig enlightened them — a little. He told them there were probably 200,000 to 250,000 German POWs in British camps by now, mainly guarded by middle-aged Tommies. Churchill had just ordered the call-up of forty-five-year-olds for the infantry, and across the Channel Montgomery had broken up two infantry divisions, the 50th and 59th, to provide replacements for the losses his other divisions had suffered. Churchill was scraping the barrel for manpower; the island was almost denuded of fit soldiers, and here in the midst of it was a Trojan Horse of some quarter of a million German soldiers, fit, trained and young.

Some of his fellow 'blacks' started to look thoughtful as Koenig went on to explain that he knew of at last six other German POW camps in southern England — Tavistock, Lambourne, Kinnerley, Bourton-on-the-Hill, Coleford and Malmesbury — and claimed he could give them a list of fifty others if they wished. 'Our espionage system in England is good,' he declared with a smile.

Koenig was not being exactly honest with his audience. British Intelligence's XX Committee, known as the Double-Cross Committee, a pun on the Roman numeral and the body's actual function, had effectively 'turned' every German agent who had landed in Britain since 1939. Any agent who refused to be 'turned', in other words work for the British, was hanged or shot. But even so, Koenig's superiors knew from repatriated German POWs (there were at least three such transfers made in the Swedish liner *Gripsholm* up to 1944) where some of the camps were located. Others had been found by aerial reconnaissance because at night POW camps in Britain were the only places not totally blacked out. So over the years the Germans had gained a pretty good idea of the location of nearly all the camps throughout the British Isles, in particular in Northern Ireland, where spies from the south, usually IRA men paid by the Germans, were active.

Koenig knew something else, which American Intelligence hoped the Germans did not know. Because US security in the United Kingdom was somewhat sloppy and because Americans in general did not seem able to keep a secret long — after all, they came from a very open society — Berlin had located the sites of the US divisions in Britain waiting to be sent to the fighting front on the Continent. In the main these divisions were based in the general area of Southampton, which had now become the US Army's major port of embarkation. From here since August, 1944, division after division of American troops had sailed for the US's major port of entry, Cherbourg.

Koenig said that although the supply of new US divisions leaving for the front from Southampton was beginning to dry up — the Americans were experiencing the same shortage of infantry replacements as the British — there were two US divisions located within easy reach of Camp 23 at Devizes. One was the US 11th Armored Division, Thunderbolt' as it liked to call itself, which had arrived at Liverpool on 10 October, 1944, and then been sent to the area of British Southern Command. It was waiting to be shipped to Southampton for its trip to Cherbourg at any moment. The other was the US 17th Airborne Division, known as 'Thunder from Heaven'. It had landed in Scotland at about the same time as the 11th Armored. From there it had been sent by train to Dorchester, where the biggest part of the Division's 66th Regiment was stationed, with the rest being billeted in the surrounding district. Again this division was waiting anxiously for the call to arms which would send it to Cherbourg and beyond.

By now Koenig knew from other POWs, mostly 'greys' who were allowed out of Camp 23 on working parties, that the *Amis* were pretty innocent. Their main concern seemed to be the local girls and their security was lax. As the regimental history of the 66th Regiment of the 17th Airborne stated after the war:

> One thing we noticed in particular and secretly enjoyed was the different attitude of the civilians toward us. Back in the States we were looked upon for what we were ... soldiers, but here we were regarded as liberators and heroes. It made us feel pretty good, especially in view of the fact that these civilians themselves had gone through a whole lot more of the war up to that time than we had.

Koenig wanted to exploit the naivety and trust of these green US soldiers. He ended his lecture by stating that it was time a reconnaissance was made of the local Americans. He turned to Rolf Herzig. Slightly older than th rest at twenty-four, Herzig had been a *Gauführer,* a county-organizer in the *Hitlerjugend,* one of those who believed even at this late stage of the war that Hitler could not lose it. Koenig told him, 'I have appointed you to break out of the camp. You must select eight or nine men you can trus implicitly and then, when you are ready, break out.'

Koenig would reveal his plan in due course. For the moment, however, all Herzig had to know was his immediate task: 'There are airfields around the camp. I want them surveyed.'

Both RAF Yatesbury and RAF Melksham were within a ten-mile radius of Devizes.

'Then I want you to find out exactly where the *Amis* are based and what kind of equipment they have. It is particularly important to discover whether they have wheeled transport and tanks.'

Tanks? It was clear from their expressions that the others were wondering what use tanks would be to an escape force. But Koenig was not going to enlighten them on the subject, not yet at least.

Now he gave his final instruction to Herzig. 'Don't wander too far afield. I don't want you returned to another camp when you are caught. I need you back here — with the information you have collected. Now, this is the way we are going to go about it ...'

As the autumn of 1944 gave way to winter, groups like Koenig's were being formed by 'black' category prisoners in virtually every German POW camp throughout the United Kingdom. All of them were planning to make a mass breakout and all of them had further plans to sabotage the Allied war effort. What form that sabotage would take was not yet known. The order would come from higher up. First they must escape.

At Lodge Moor Camp, some five miles from the centre of Sheffield, the escape committee naturally made up of 'blacks' had even persuaded the 'greys' to join in the plot. For there the conditions were so bad that the 'blacks' had found eager support from the majority. Lodge Moor Camp had been built in the First World War and afterwards was condemned to be demolished; with the outbreak of the new war, however, it had been hastily converted into a POW camp, using the same old facilities from the first war. Soon the battered old Nissen huts were full and by the summer of 1944 the ever-increasing number of prisoners were forced to sleep in tents. Early September was wet, with rain almost every day; there were no duckboards for the tents and prisoners had been forced to sleep in the bare mud. The latrines, too, were overflowing. By the beginning of winter conditions had started to improve, but by then it was too late. The 'blacks' were in complete control and the few 'whites' in the camp kept a low profile, reluctant to incur the wrath of the 'black' leadership.

The 'blacks' at Lodge Moor were led by *Feldwebel* Schmittendorf, something of a bully, the man the 'whites' feared most. He was supported by nineteen-year-old Corporal Armin Kuehne, known as 'Doktor Goebbels' by the 'whites' (behind his back of course) because he was small of stature and had as vitriolic a tongue as the real Dr Goebbels, Hitler's Minister of Propaganda. At the drop of the hat, Kuehne would sound off about National Socialism and his beloved Führer who would never be defeated.

Here at Lodge Moor Camp they had already begun tunnelling, ready for the mass escape. Where they were going and why the plotters did not know yet. The details would come later. But they kept working at the flinty soil, toiling away every night when the guards thought they were asleep, disposing of the spoil in the latrines or scattering it in the compound when they did the usual morning circuit, dropping it from sacks concealed inside their trousers and activated by strings that they worked from holes in the pockets. Later, when it all came out, one of the guards was heard to remark, in his broad Yorkshire accent, 'I allus thought t'Germans was playing pocket billiards. A load o' randy boogers.'

The situation was no different at Glen Mill Camp in Oldham in Lancashire. Here a street of terrace houses had been cordoned off by barbed wire, set around the tall red-brick tower and factory of Glen Mill. Built in 1904, the factory had produced cotton right up until the War Office decided that it and the nearby street would be ideal for a POW camp. Thereupon, the middle-aged reservists who made up the camp's guards had sealed the area off from Wellyhole Street, built a low concrete bunker on the rise overlooking the camp and proceeded to put wire and a sentry post on each floor of the mill itself. For the camp administration had been told that the Glen Mill Camp was to house mainly 'blacks', about a thousand of them.

However, an inspecting officer soon ordered Colonel Dennison, the first Camp Commandant, to move the wire and sentry boxes inside the mill itself. When the Commandant protested he was told, 'To make a prison within a prison contravenes the Geneva Convention. We're going to abide by the rules of war even if the Germans don't.'

The first batch of prisoners the camp received, in early 1940, had demonstrated to both the Commandant and the guards that they were indeed going to receive the most intransigent types: they were U-boat sailors, volunteers to a man, tough and self-reliant. They were followed by Luftwaffe crews, again volunteers, hard-bitten and highly trained. They even mutinied when told they were being shipped to Canada. Their ringleaders maintained that the Tommies were deliberately sending them to their deaths before the Führer could rescue them when he invaded; as German U-boats ruled the seas, they hadn't a chance of surviving a trip to Canada. But the problem was quickly solved by the camp's regimental sergeant-major. A formidable man, he marched up to the mutineers' spokesman. 'So you won't go to Canada?' he barked. 'No sir,' the other man answered. The RSM reached back one hamlike fist and punched the German hard. The mutiny collapsed with him.

Other hardliners followed them to Glen Mill Camp, all troublemakers who exploited any slackness on the part of the guards. Several times prisoners at Glen Mill escaped and once, using the *Lagerführer's* own office as the start of a tunnel, a group of the German 'blacks' managed to get out for several days before being recaptured.

But these haphazard operations changed radically when Sergeant Gerald Hanel arrived from the Command Screening Camp at Doncaster. Hanel was 'blacker than black'. A former member of the *Hitlerjugend,* he had joined the German Parachute Regiment at the age of seventeen. A few months later he had had his first taste of combat at the Pyrrhic victory of Crete. He had fought in Russia. He had taken part in the stubborn defence of Cassino, where he was reported dead; his CO had even written a letter of condolence to his mother in Dresden. But the young para was not dead. Cut off as his unit retreated northwards, Hanel did not surrender. Instead, travelling by night and hiding by day, he made his way back to his own lines and received an award for his daring and courage.

But eventually fate caught up with him. In the summer of 1944 he had been driving the commander of the 5th Parachute Division, General Wilke, when the car was surrounded by American troops. The Fifth Para had been ferocious opponents during the fighting in Normandy and the American GIs were not in the best of moods. There had been atrocities on both sides and their first inclination had been to shoot the General and his driver out of hand. But reason prevailed. Hanel got away with a few kicks and blows before being sent back to the nearest cage. They didn't break his nerve. Indeed, he had the gall to ask the *Amis* to help carry the baggage from the General's car — and they did.

Shipped to England, Hanel was interrogated at Kempton Park screening centre. The British had ways of breaking down even the most arrogant prisoners, but the young Saxon paratrooper stood up to it all. His spirit still remained unbroken when he was sent, with a bunch of fifty other paras from the Fifth Parachute Division, to the POW camp at Glen Mill.

By the time Hanel and his fellow paras arrived at Glen Mill the camp had lapsed into virtual anarchy. The British were too busy trying to guard the place with the few middle-aged soldiers at their disposal and left the policing of the place in the hands of the *Lagerführer.* But the latter had lost control. Bully boys roamed the camp, threatening and terrorizing anyone they took a dislike to with their home-made clubs and caps with razor blades sewn into the peaks — one swipe with a cap of that kind and a man's face was scarred for life.

There was the problem of the Russians too. They had escaped certain death in German POW camps (neither Russia nor Germany recognized the Geneva Convention as far as POWs went and literally starved thousands of prisoners to death during the war) by volunteering to fight for the Wehrmacht. In France these Russian battalions had withered away rapidly, the men surrendering in droves to their former allies. These

51

Russians, most of whom could not read or write and had lived at home in the most primitive circumstances, with hole-in-the-ground sanitation and no running water or electricity, were a disruptive element. Even the German bully boys were afraid to tackle them, for they fought back with a savage ferocity that did not stop short of murder.

Hanel and his para comrades had their first experience of the Russians at mealtime in the mess hall. As the POW orderlies brought in the steaming dixies of food from the cookhouse, the Russians rushed forward as one man. Knocking the frightened orderlies to one side, they started scooping out the food with their bare hands and thrusting it down their throats, while the other POWs looked on in disgust. So Hanel decided that this rabble had to be taught a lesson. Next day a dinner-time when the Russians gave a repeat performance, feeding like pigs at the trough, Hanel and his comrades fell on the Russians, kicking and punching them and forcing them away from the dixies so that the orderlies could pick up what was left. A breathless Hanel announced to the other POWs who had been waiting for the outcome of the fight, 'From now on *everyone* will get a fair share of the food.'

A couple of days later the Russians tried to take their revenge. The Germans were planning to give a concert that night for Germans only and it was the Russians' intention to smash up the stage and the decorations before the concert started. But someone leaked the plan. Hanel and his followers were waiting for the Russians. Armed with iron bars and planks through which large sharp nails had been driven, they ambushed the intruders and in the ensuing battle the Russians were decisively beaten.

From then on, Hanel and his comrades ran the camp. They broke the power of the bully boys with savage beatings. 'Whites' were intimidated with threats of beatings and kangaroo courts. Order and discipline were strictly enforced and when the British demanded that their officers should be saluted at all times within the camp, Hanel and his paras saw to it that the red-faced British were met not with a regular military salute but with the extended arm of the 'German greeting' and a barked 'Heil Hitler!' And all the while the paras were plotting to escape from Glen Mill. They, too, knew that something big was in the air.

The situation was little different at Penkridge POW Camp on the main road between Stafford and Wolverhampton. The camp housed mostly 'blacks' and due to the slackness (or kindness) of the commandant, Lieutenant-Colonel Davidson, who went out of his way to improve the lot of his charges, they had become very mutinous and truculent. They had persuaded the few 'greys' in the place to join them in open defiance of authority. For months now they had routinely thrown stones at the camp's loudspeakers when they broadcast the BBC War News. The camp newspaper was thrown away unread by virtually everyone because the 'blacks' claimed that it was just anti-German propaganda. Guards were routinely jeered and baited. And just as at other camps, there was a small nucleus of men actively plotting a mass breakout from the camp, waiting only for the order to go.

One of them, a young naval ensign named Schweissmann, had idly rubbed away the distemper from a wall and had found a map of England beneath it. Hastily he had copied it before the guards discovered what he had done. Now that map had been re-copied and secreted by a small number of naval officers who would guide the escapees. For the plotter group knew that this would not be an ordinary escape. There had to be some strategic purpose to it.

There were even Italians involved in the great plot. Although Italian POWs in Britain had been officially declared 'co-belligerents' when ex-fascist Italy joined the war on the Allied side in late 1943, many prisoners still refused to co-operate with their former captors. In particular the POWs at Doonfoot Ayr Camp, situated where the road going south from Ayr crosses the River Doon, had long been a thorn in the side of their British guards. Classed as 'non-cooperative', a group of them under the command of an Italian paratroop officer (trained, incidentally, by the Baron) were now actively tunnelling their way out of the camp. Ninety-seven were involved in the escape and they planned to go out on Friday 15 December, just before Christmas.

For the first time a date had been set for the great escape.

FOUR

It was an old POW trick, but it worked. Just before noon, when the plotters at Camp 23 in Devizes knew the sentries along the perimeter would be getting slack, wondering when their relief was coming so that they could go to the cookhouse and warm up on this cold winter day, a gang of 'blacks' came out of their huts carrying their grey army-issue blankets. Going as close to the perimeter wire as they dared without arousing suspicion, they started beating their blankets or flapping them up and down like busy housewives, tut-tutting at the amount of dust that seemed to come from them (actually stale bread crumbled up into tiny flecks). After a few minutes of this the sentries looked away; they had seen the whole routine before. As Captain W. M. Spreckley, one of the camp's officers, was wont to remark, The Germans are very *gründlich* [thorough] in everything they do, even beating their blankets.' Captain Spreckley was very proud of his few words of German.

As the sentries turned away, Rolf Herzig, who was smaller than the rest of the blanket-beaters, darted to the perimeter wire. He had come well prepared: a pair of pliers and wire-cutters had been 'organized' (stolen) from Mr Gaiger's workshop. Herzig seized the strand of wire closest to the ground and snipped through it. There was a loud twang, like a bell being struck. Surely the sentries could hear? Apparently not. Herzig cut another wire, then another, and another. Within two or three minutes he had made a gap large enough for a man to crawl through. As a final gesture, he kicked up some earth against the base of the cut wire in order to make it more difficult for the casual observer to spot. Then, praying that no one would notice the cut wire before dusk, around three thirty or so, he hurried back to the rest and picked up his blanket.

'Well done,' said Koenig.

'*Toi, toi, toi*,' a breathless Herzig whispered back, making the German gesture for 'fingers crossed'.

The afternoon passed in anxious anticipation. Time and again their eyes flashed to the section of cut wire while Koenig gave the escapers their final briefing and they pocketed the tins of bully beef and bread which would sustain them during their period outside the wire. But luck was on their side. No one spotted the cut wire, although a sentry walked by the spot twice, while they watched with bated breath. At about two thirty a cold drizzle started and the sentries paced their beat with heads buried deep in their greatcoats; all they could think of was the warm fug of the guardroom.

As usual the interior of the camp was blacked out after dark, though the lights on the perimeter wire were kept lit. This did not mean the POWs were confined to their huts as soon as the blackout was up. They were still allowed to go to the cookhouse for their supper from five to six and use the outside latrines thereafter. But by six thirty they had to be in their huts. With the doors locked on the outside, they could then continue to talk, carve little wooden toys which they sold to the guards for cigarettes, play cards or read until lights out at ten o'clock.

Thus it was that Herzig and the eight other escapers paid their customary visit to the latrines after supper (once the POWs were locked in at night, 'piss-buckets' were their only means of sanitation). But as the others, jangling mess tins and mugs and talking among themselves, were urged back to their huts by the guards, eager to lock up for the night and

54

go off duty, Herzig and his men went to ground. They had already selected their hiding place. A thin layer of plasterboard covered the rafters. That was soon removed and they squeezed themselves in between the rafters and then pulled the board back in place beneath them. Then they waited.

It was the custom of the sergeant of the guard to inspect the latrines one last time before the POWs were locked up for the night. Satisfied that no one was there, he would snap the single catch on the latrine block door and go on his way. Some guards simply put their heads round the door, not wanting to linger any longer than necessary in that smelly place, and bellow: 'All out of the *bogs*!...*Raus now*!...*Los, los*!' Others made a careful examination of the place before closing the latrine up for the night.

On this particular evening the guard was a conscientious man. He walked slowly down the line of 'Crappers', flashing his torch into the darker corners. Above him the nine escapers froze, hardly daring to breathe, praying that he would not flash his torch upwards and spot the plasterboard being held in place at both ends by white-knuckled German fingers. But he continued his slow progress to the door. The lights were clicked off and a second later the door was closed.

Herzig breathed a sigh of relief. Another man broke wind loudly. 'Stop that fart-cannon!' Herzig whispered angrily.

'Sorry,' the man muttered, 'I've been holding on for the last five minutes. I won't do it again.'

'You'd better not,' Herzig threatened, 'or I'll bung a plug up there next time!'

Now the hidden men gave themselves half an hour to let the camp settle down after lock-up. They knew from experience that sometimes the *Lagerführer* would be held up in the outer camp by business with the commandant or the clerk-of-works. Then he would be escorted across the compound to their huts, which would have to be opened and re-locked after him. But that didn't happen very often. What Herzig really feared was that there would be a late entry of fresh prisoners from Southampton. Their arrival would activate the whole camp.

The minutes passed in tense anticipation. The muted singing of the choir died away. The card-players stopped banging their cards down. Silence took over the camp. Another boring day behind the wire was gradually coming to an end.

Herzig made his decision. It was time to move. One by one, the nine POWs dropped to the floor, any noise they might have made being muffled by the thick grey socks they wore over their boots. The door took only moments to break open. That was why the latrines had been picked for the start of their escape. Besides, in the barracks there might have been a traitor, someone in the pay of the Tommies.

One by one they filtered into the freezing darkness outside. Searchlights operated from each of the camp's towers swung constantly back and forth but the spot where Herzig had cut the wire that afternoon was in relative darkness, equidistant between two searchlights. Hurriedly, bent double, they ran towards the gap in the wire. 'Los,' Herzig commanded, pulling apart the strands of severed wire. The first man slipped through, wriggled a couple of metres on his belly, then rose to his feet and melted away into the darkness. Another man followed. Then a third man was through.

Suddenly there was what seemed to be a tremendous noise; something metallic had clattered to the frosty, iron-hard earth. One of the men had dropped a bully-beef tin out of his greatcoat pocket. The escapers froze as a searchlight flicked in their direction, poking the darkness aside with its silver fingers. But the searchlight moved on and they breathed again.

Herzig impatiently urged the last man through the wire. Then he bent and closed the strands of wire as best he could. In the morning their disappearance would be discovered at rollcall, but he didn't want to give away too much of how they had escaped. Koenig had assured him that the whole camp would be going out soon; they needed to keep their secrets to themselves.

For a moment the young German was overcome by the eeriness of being out at night in this alien blacked-out country. Every man's hand was against them. He had always assumed the British were very *korrekt*. But what might happen if they fell into the hands of local civilians? All winter the V-ls and V-2s had been coming down in Southern England, destroying, killing, maiming. Would the British still be *korrekt* now after the mass slaughter from the sky?

Herzig pulled himself together. They had a lot to do in the next few days, but first they had to get through Devizes. He whispered to his men to follow him in single file. A few moments later they had vanished into the night, leaving Camp 23 behind them, silent and shrouded in sleep.

Captain Spreckley, who was duty officer on the following morning, had already noted a certain tension in the air as the POWs lined up for the daily count. Thus he was not overly surprised when the duty sergeant reported to him that nine Jerries were not accounted for. He told the NCO to search the camp, and to check whether the missing men might be out on a working party. As the NCO saluted and doubled away, Captain Spreckley walked casually out of the compound, making no mention of the escape to the *Lagerführer*. He did not want to let the assembled POWs see that he was worried. They had broad grins on their faces already.

Once outside the compound, however, Spreckley sprang into action. He turned out the guard and ordered them to make another count and at the same time check the perimeter wire. Together with Camp 23's adjutant, Captain Dick Hurn, he reported to the commandant, Lieutenant-Colonel John Trelawnay Upton. Upton didn't wait for a recount. He took Spreckley's word for it that there had been a breakout and activated the emergency drill immediately.

The drill entailed alerting the police, the regular army and the local Home Guard. Within half an hour telephones were ringing all over Wiltshire. Roadblocks were being set up. Home Guards and military policemen were checking civilian identity cards. Even US troops were employed to ensure that Southampton Docks were sealed off, for the German escapers who had been brought to Camp 23 from that port might be heading back there now, hoping to smuggle aboard a ship bound for France.

The point of the breakout on the perimeter wire was soon discovered and the hut from which the escapers had come. All the men in that hut were taken to Colonel Upton's office and questioned by the camp interpreter, Captain Craig, a tall, dark Royal Artillery officer, who had been at a boarding school in the German-speaking part of Switzerland, and his assistant, Staff-Sergeant Reis, who had been a publisher in Stuttgart before fleeing in 1938 when the Nazis went on an anti-semitic rampage.

But the German POWs were mostly 'blacks' or 'greys' who were too terrified of reprisals to talk. They had heard and seen nothing. In the end Colonel Upton gave up in disgust. He knew that no one had ever escaped from Britain throughout the war and he saw no reason why Herzig and his companions should do so now. The Colonel was confident that it could be only a matter of hours before the local police returned the escapers to the camp.

Still, there were one or two things about the escape which puzzled him. Why, for instance, had so many of them gone out together? Two men might not arouse attention, but nine of them dressed in the same distinctive battledress most certainly would. And why escape in the first place? Germany was obviously losing the war. Why not wait for it to end when the POWs knew they would be returned to their homeland safe and sound? Finally, if they did succeed in getting across the Channel, the escaped POWs faced a 200 or 300-mile journey across recently liberated territory which was jam-packed with Allied troops. Under those conditions with every man's hand against them, they stood little chance of ever reaching their own country.

Colonel Upton thought it was all very odd. What was even odder was that two days later the escapers returned. They simply appeared at the gates of Camp 23 and demanded to be let in. Admittedly two of the original party had been captured by the local police. But the rest could have continued to do whatever they were doing outside. Why had they given themselves up so tamely?

The *Lagerführer* was brought over to Colonel Upton's office to identify them, then the cross-examination began. Craig asked them why they had surrendered themselves in this manner instead of waiting for re-capture by the troops and police.

Herzig had his answer prepared, for Koenig had briefed him before the escape what he was to say when he came back. He told Craig they had hoped to make their way to the south coast, but all the signposts were down and they soon became lost. He went on: 'We realized there was little hope of getting away and thought the sensible thing was to come back.'

Craig knew that he was lying. For one thing, Herzig must have known that there were no signposts up in Britain. They had been removed in 1940 when the country was threatened with a German invasion. Herzig surely should have seen the lack of signs on his journey by rail from Southampton to Devizes. If he hadn't, the others would have told him. The story of getting lost on the way to the south coast was pretty threadbare too, Craig told himself. Even if Herzig and the others could not find their way by the stars — and most of the Germans who had been in the Hitler Youth knew how to do so — there would have been other ways of navigating their way to the ports. They could have followed the railway line that led to Salisbury, for instance, and from there to Southampton. They could even have pretended to be Poles — there were a lot of them in the Wiltshire area — and asked directions from civilians. Since the arrival of the Americans in 1942 people had got used to foreigners losing themselves. Any civilian asked for directions would probably have given them without a second thought.

But Craig could not shake their story. Tired, hungry and cold as they were, they stuck to it. In the end the Captain gave up and ordered them back to their huts after being fed. The Camp Commandant would sentence them to the usual spell in the 'cooler' in due course. So they returned, bringing with them the vital information that Koenig needed.

3

A MISSION IS PROPOSED

Hitler had moved to the window and stood looking out, hands
tightly clenched behind him. 'I have an instinct for these
things and I know how successful this kind of operation could
be. A handful of brave men daring all.'

Jack Higgins, The Eagle Has Landed

ONE

Colonel-General Kurt Student was forty-eight when he took over
Germany's fledgling parachute arm back in 1938. He had started his long
military career as a cadet of the Imperial German Army, but in 1913 he
had asked to be trained as one of the Army's first pilots. Three years later
he was commanding his own fighter squadron in France, and in spite of
the short life expectancy of the average fighter pilot over the trenches, he
had managed to survive the war.

Although there had seemed little future in the beaten German Army,
limited in 1919 by the Versailles Treaty to 100,000 men, Student had
stayed on. From 1919 to 1929 he served as the sole member of the
Reichswehr's Aviation Section (the *'Versaillesdiktat',* as the Germans
called it, forbade Germany to have planes), 'responsible for two thousand
individual items from raw materials to the finished aeroplane so that in
time of war or when Germany was again allowed to have an air force, the
factories could start turning out planes immediately'. Secretly Student
also arranged for 300 German pilots to be trained in Russia by the Red
Army although the Reichswehr then possessed exactly one plane. Even at
that age Student proved to be a master of subterfuge and deceit.

In 1929 Student returned to the infantry, taking over command of the
2nd Infantry Regiment. In 1933, the year Hitler came to power, he was
promoted to lieutenant-colonel and transferred to the new Air Ministry.
Thereafter promotion had followed rapidly until as a major-general he
was asked to command the Wehrmacht's newest arm, the paratroops.

In 1940 he had been in charge of the mass paradrop which had virtually
conquered Holland within four days. Crete had followed, and the years in
Russia, though now, after being badly wounded in Rotterdam, Student

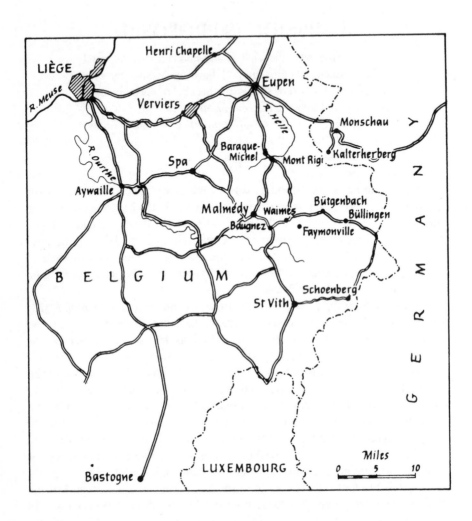

LIÈGE

R. Meuse

Henri Chapelle

Eupen

Verviers

R. Helle

Monschau

Kalterherberg

Baraque-
Michel

Mont Rigi

Spa

R. Ourthe

Aywaille

Malmédy

Waimes

Bütgenbach

Büllingen

Baugnez

Faymonville

BELGIUM

Schoenberg

St Vith

GERMANY

Bastogne

LUXEMBOURG

Miles

0   5   10

mainly fought his battles from behind a desk. However, in September, 1944, he returned once more to active service, albeit briefly. On 17 September he had been at his HQ in Vught, Holland, when, as he recalled after the war:

> I was disturbed at my desk by a roaring in the air of such mounting intensity that I left my study and went on to the balcony. Wherever I looked I saw aircraft: troop carriers and large aircraft towing gliders. An immense stream passed low over the house. I was greatly impressed.

He wished out loud that he had had such a mighty force at his disposal.

After helping to fight against the 'Screaming Eagles' of the US 101st Airborne Division, Student had toyed with the idea of a surprise attack on the Western Allies, two divisions strong. But in that grey winter, with the enemy present on both Germany's frontiers to west and east, the idea had seemed but a vain dream.

By late November, Student, now the commander of the 1st Parachute Army, numbering ten divisions, four of them parachute divisions, at least in name, had been reconciled to fighting a basically defensive battle in Holland. But that had changed abruptly when he was let into the secret of the Führer's last great offensive which would split the Anglo-American armies and throw them back to the Channel. By this means Hitler hoped to relieve Allied pressure on the Reich and prepare the ground for a negotiated peace with the West, which would be far more favourable than the harsh 'unconditional surrender' terms which were all the Allies were prepared to offer at present.

Student had little time for the politics of the offensive. He was strictly a professional soldier. What delighted him was that there was a role for his 1st Parachute Army in the coming offensive and above all that Hitler wanted to include a real parachute operation in the framework of this operation. For the first time since Crete, some of his paras would carry out the role he had originally trained them for — they would jump into battle.

From what little Student knew of Hitler's 'last gamble', as he was calling the proposed counter-offensive, his parachute troops might be called upon to carry out three operations. At least he had been ordered to alert three different parachute units for combat. One was a battalion under the command of Major Mehs, who had been instrumental in rescuing Mussolini in 1943. Though he had no hard details yet, Student thought that this battalion would be used to knock out the Canadian Army HQ at Tilburg which controlled all the Canadian and British divisions in Holland. Another parachute battalion that he had been told to alert was in Holland. The reason for its inclusion was even more obscure to him, though he half-guessed that it was to be used for a long-range objective, perhaps Antwerp. And then there was the third force, to be commanded by 'The Baron', Colonel von der Heydte.

In the first week of December, 1944, Baron von der Heydte, now the commander of the parachute school at Bergen op Zoom in Holland, was summoned to meet General Student at his Dutch headquarters.

Student was in a good mood and received his subordinate warmly. The scar in his forehead (he had been shot by an SS trooper back in 1940, during the invasion of Holland) was glowing as it always did when he was excited. The Baron, who could not salute because his arm, injured in a plane accident in Italy, was tightly strapped to his side in a leather bandage, was ordered to sit down.

Student had sworn a personal oath to Hitler, like all the other senior officers who were to take part in the 'last gamble', that he would not divulge the details. But von der Heydte was far too shrewd an officer not to guess that something big was in the offing. So Student told him that the Führer had decided to undertake a major operation — he said nothing about where — and that as part of this attack there was to be a big paradrop.

The Baron's first guess was that the drop would take place behind Soviet troops surrounding the German bridgehead on the River Vistula in Poland. It seemed logical that the German High Command should try to relieve this sector of the Eastern Front which was under heavy pressure from the Red Army, preparing to march into East Prussia. But he did not tell Student of his guess.

Student continued in his usual brisk, confident manner, explaining that he wanted the Baron not only to assemble this force, but to lead it. The Baron's face brightened momentarily, then fell again when Student told him that for reasons of security he would not be able to take men from his old regiment, the Sixth. Instead, Student assured him, he would be sent the best: a hundred paras, trained and fit, selected from each battalion of the First Parachute Army, 1,200 men in all. Student did allow him, however, to pick his own platoon and company commanders; with that he had to be satisfied.

Finally Student told him to be ready for action by zero five hundred hours on the morning of Thursday, 14 December.

The Baron nodded his understanding and then he was gone, racing back to Bergen op Zoom, his mind buzzing with new plans and ideas. For the first time since May, 1941, he was going to parachute into combat again: that alone was a thrill to him. But there were innumerable problems facing him if he were to meet that deadline. He did not like the idea of 'the hundred best men' picked from each battalion of the parachute divisions under Student's command. He had been in the Wehrmacht since 1935 and he knew the old army game only too well. Divisional commanders might ask for the best men available, but subordinate commanders would have other ideas. They'd use the order as an excuse to get rid of their misfits, the 'barrack-room lawyers', the men with two left feet.

Then there was the question of weapons. A few of the new recoilless cannon were available in the Wehrmacht, but the SS and its own parachute battalions had first claim on them. He would have to make do with his machine guns and mortars. There would be no ground transport either; the Junkers 52s, the old 'Auntie Jus', which would be delivering them to the dropping zone, were not built to carry transport other than bicycles. There were no Gigants in Holland, the huge gliders which could carry everything up to a light tank. No, his battle group would have to advance on foot.

But above all the Baron was anxious to see what sort of men they would send him. The first of them appeared on the morning of 9 December — and the Baron knew that his worst fears had been realized. As he recorded after the war, 'Never during my entire fighting career had I commanded a unit with less fighting spirit. But then who gives up his best soldiers to another unit?' Of the 1,200 men assembled at the end of that day, only 200 had actually jumped into action and they were men of his own Sixth Para Regiment who had 'deserted' from the Regiment in order to join *Herr Baron.*

Swiftly the Baron set to work to knock the men into shape, aided by his own former company and section commanders. Four days after the first drafts had arrived, he had formed four para companies, a signal section, one company of heavy machine guns, a section of mortars and a pioneer company. It was hard work, but he did manage to inspire the dead-beats foisted on him with some of the spirit of the elite Sixth, though he had trouble persuading them to take the mission seriously. For not even he knew what that mission was. However, he had by this time changed his ideas on where the offensive would be launched: it would be in the West now, he had convinced himself, but where in the West he had not the faintest idea.

At the end of those first four days the Baron moved his battle group to the long-time German Army training ground of Sennelager in Westphalia. He had picked Sennelager because it was close to Paderborn airfield, where the Junkers 52 transport squadron which would fly his men into battle was based. The weary half-frozen paras arrived at their destination in the middle of the night — only to be told by the camp commandant that there was no room in the barracks; the camp was bursting at the seams.

Angrily the Baron called the Chief-of-Staff of the Münster Air Region and told him that he needed beds for 1,200 men. His request was turned down. So at four o'clock on a freezing December morning the Baron found himself and his command shivering in the blacked-out streets of the little town of Oerlinghausen, with no one apparently interested in the welfare of the young men who were going to play such an important role in the coming offensive. Fortunately the Baron chanced upon the local chemist who had been a pre-war comrade of his in the cavalry when he had been stationed in the area. The chemist and the Baron set to work, knocking on doors in an attempt to find accommodation for the freezing soldiers. Eventually they succeeded in bedding down all the men. But the Baron's troubles were not yet over. Leaving them to sleep, he drove to Paderborn airfield to meet the commander of the squadron which would fly them to the site of the airdrop. He turned out to be an old acquaintance, Major Erdmann, who had flown the Baron's battalion to Crete in 1941.

Erdmann was the commander of the Stalingrad Squadron, famed for having helped to supply the trapped German Sixth Army at Stalingrad in 1942. An experienced pilot, Erdmann knew all about dropping paras and their supplies, but his crews were completely inexperienced in such work. Most of them had just come from flying school. Erdmann was especially horrified to learn that the drop would take place at night, for none of his pilots had ever done any night supply work. But the two old acquaintances knew better than to question their orders. In spite of grave doubts about the feasibility of the operation, they continued with their planning.

On 13 December Erdmann and the Baron were summoned to the headquarters of the Luftwaffe Commander-in-Chief, Air Fleet West. At last they were informed of their objective. They were not going to fight the Russians, but the Americans. Hitler's last great offensive was to be directed at Antwerp. It would be launched by Model's Army Group, with the Baron's battle group taking orders from Model's HQ.

Deeply worried now, the two officers left Luftwaffe headquarters at Münster and drove straight to the pretty walled town of Münster-Eifel where Field-Marshal Walter Model had his headquarters. They arrived late in the evening to be received by General Krebs, Model's Chief-of-Staff, who, like his master, affected a monocle.

Krebs filled in some of the details of what was expected of *Kampfgruppe von der Heydte.* The paras would help to clear the way for armoured divisions of the Sixth SS Panzer Army, commanded by the veteran Nazi bully-boy and SS general, Sepp Dietrich. They would seize a key crossroads and hold it until the SS tanks linked up with them. At the most they would be on their own for twenty-four hours.

Erdmann and the Baron objected that they needed more time to prepare and train the men. Krebs, a smooth staff officer who had been German military attaché in Moscow and who would soon commit suicide in Hitler's bunker, shrugged off their protests and led them to see his master.

Perhaps the most competent and aggressive of Hitler's surviving field-marshals, Model was roused from his sleep to meet them, and he was not particularly pleased. He was well known for his short fuse and was generally feared by his staff officers, though revered by the frontline soldiers whom he visited every day. Still, he listened to the two subordinate commanders' objections calmly enough. Then, glaring at the Baron through his monocle, he asked him bluntly what chance he gave his paras. 'A ten per cent chance?' he suggested.

'Yes', the Baron replied honestly.

Model nodded. Then it is necessary to make the attempt. The entire offensive has no more than a ten per cent chance of success. It must be done since this offensive is the last remaining chance of concluding the war favourably. If we do not make the most of that ten per cent chance, Germany will be faced with certain defeat.'

The Baron was impressed by such honesty. Besides, Model's logic seemed unassailable. He gave in tamely and allowed himself and his paras to be assigned to Sepp Dietrich's command, knowing in advance he was not going to enjoy serving under the old Party bully boy. And he was right.

TWO

Like his former commander, the Baron, Koenig, in the confines of Camp 23, had also been working feverishly. He knew quite a lot now from Herzig and the other escapers about the British and in particular the American military dispositions in the immediate Wiltshire area. Elements of the US 17th Airborne and the US 11th Armored Divisions were spread around the vicinity, waiting for the call to move to Southampton and take ship for France.

They were green and slack in their security, the escapers reported, and Koenig reasoned that they could be surprised with ease and their vehicles and weapons taken from them. Plenty would be needed, for he had heard through the grapevine which existed between most camps in Britain that 'blacks' in many other camps were similarly prepared to break out. He had heard, too, that all these break-outs had to be co-ordinated with a new offensive in Europe. In the first week of December Koenig did not yet know when that German offensive would start. He guessed it would be soon, however. Urgently he tried to focus on the last details of his bold escape plan.

Unfortunately for the success of his operation, two of those green *Amis* about whom Koenig had waxed so contemptuous to his fellow plotters now appeared at Camp 23. They were Captain Frank Brandstetter and Captain Joe Hoelzl, both with the 17th Airborne Division, both German-Americans and both speaking fluent German. Their task would be to interrogate prisoners once the Division went into action in Europe.

It had been decided by the authorities that these two American officers should be attached to the staff of Camp 23 in order to learn something of interrogation techniques in practice. The Camp Commandant, Colonel Upton, agreed and assigned the two Americans to Captain Craig and his assistant, Staff Sergeant Reis. Together they walked around the camp, observing and listening but giving no sign that they spoke German. Thus it was that they stumbled by sheer accident on the great escape plot.

One day in that first week of December the two Americans entered the *Lagerführer's* office to arrange a working party of POWs. They did not knock; they just walked straight in — and interrupted a full session of the Escape Committee. Koenig was saying, 'The arms store is the key—' when he spotted them and broke off.

Brandstetter and Hoelzl reacted with commendable calm. Neither man indicated that Koenig's words meant anything to him.

Instead they made their request in English to the *Lagerführer* and left a few minutes later. Shortly thereafter they saw Captain Craig and Brandstetter commented: 'I thought the arms store was strictly out of bounds to all prisoners.' He meant the heavily locked storeroom from which rifles were issued to the camp sentries when they went on duty. 'Can you think of a reason why the prisoners should be interested in it?'

Craig could. His face suddenly serious, he answered slowly, There can be only one reason. They must be planning an escape.'

The two Americans looked impressed. This wouldn't be merely an escape but an *armed* break-out, similar to those which had occasionally happened back home when armed convicts had made a jailbreak in the thirties.

Craig's thoughts were spinning. Now he realized that Herzig and the other escaped 'blacks' had surrendered far too tamely. He should have been more suspicious. They weren't the kind to give up because they were lost or hungry. Their escape had had some other purpose behind it. Somehow, he knew instinctively, it was linked to this armed break-out attempt. Warning the Americans to keep the information to themselves, he reported the matter to Colonel Upton and Captain Hum, the adjutant.

Upton and Hum agreed that something serious was afoot. Their immediate response was to activate the listening devices that the Americans had been surreptitiously planting all over the camp, in the *Lagerführer's* office, the washrooms, the latrines, etc. Next they summoned everyone with contact with the 'whites' and authorized them to offer bribes in return for information. Thirdly, Colonel Scotland's man, Sergeant Rosterg, was ordered to keep his ears open for anything he could find on the plot.

Now Craig, Reis, Brandstetter and Hoelzl set about interrogating the nine escapers once more. Herzig was the first to be cross-examined, but he was like a rock. He stuck to his original story in every last detail. The two Americans had more luck. They had one of the escapers named Schmidt brought to a room which they used as an office. US techniques of interrogation were much more imaginative than those of the British. Schmidt was first offered a cigarette. Normally a POW got five a week, none in the 'cooler' where Schmidt was at the time. He accepted it gratefully. Then he was given a mug of steaming hot, well-sugared tea. That too he accepted.

'More comfortable here than outside,' Brandstetter began, meaning the time Schmidt had spent outside the wire during his escape.

Schmidt agreed, 'But a front-line soldier like me prefers action,' he boasted.

Brandstetter reminded himself that Schmidt had returned to Camp 23 voluntarily. Aloud he said, 'But you are out of the war. No more action for you.'

Schmidt looked up from his tea with a smug expression on his face. 'I wouldn't be so sure of that, sir,' he said. 'Our paratroops may liberate us shortly.' Then, after a moment's pause, looking at his two interrogators with that same knowing look on his face, he added: 'Think what would happen if all the prisoners in England were liberated at once!'

Brandstetter and Hoelzl caught each other's eyes. They were new to this game, but the thought of those thousands of fit young Germans running loose in the heart of England was not a very pleasant one.

Schmidt baited the two *Amis* a little more. 'A flying column breaking out of Devizes could seize some tanks from your armoured division,' he said, meaning the US 11th Armored up the road. 'Your local airfields could be captured without much trouble. We Germans know how to wage war, you know. Why, within thirty-six hours, with only a little outside help, we could be attacking London with tanks and planes!'

For a minute the two American interrogators were totally flabbergasted.

67

Was the prisoner off his head? Some did go stir-crazy after years of captivity. Was Schmidt simply trying to get a rise out of the American new boys? Or was there really some kind of plot being hatched here in Camp 23?

Brandstetter recovered himself enough to offer Schmidt another cigarette. The German thanked him politely, saying, 'You do not believe this, but I tell you it is possible.' And that was about all he was prepared to say.

The Americans worked on him a little longer but without further results. When Schmidt was taken away, they went straight to see the Commandant.

'What Schmidt told us, sir,' Hoelzl summed up for Colonel Upton, 'sounds utterly crazy. But how did he know about the 11th Armored up the road? Could it be that they broke out of the camp only to gain information like that?'

Colonel Upton was old but prudent. He had 7,500 prisoners in his charge, guarded by less than a battalion of middle-aged, not very fit soldiers. He could not risk letting that number of Germans loose in an area that was so close to one of the Allies' vital supply ports, Southampton. He ordered security to be tightened even more. In the meantime it was vital to find out what was going on.

The Baron told himself the same, as he drove to the headquarters of the Sixth SS Panzer Army, winding up and down the steep Eifel roads. The villages he passed through were packed with troops and camouflaged vehicles. Tanks and artillery were everywhere and they all looked brand new, as if they had come straight from the Reich's factories — which they had. The sight gave him a little more confidence in his own role in what was to come. He had not seen a German Army so well equipped for battle since the heady days of 1940. But his good mood vanished when he and Erdmann reported to General Sepp Dietrich at his HQ.

Dietrich had begun to drink heavily. He did not like the idea of attacking into Belgium in the depth of winter — indeed, he had tried to protest against the plan to Hitler himself, without any luck — so he took refuge in the bottle. When the Baron and Erdmann reported to him that morning he was already bleary-eyed and slightly drunk.

Almost immediately it was clear that the Bavarian aristocrat and the Bavarian peasant were not going to hit it off, in spite of the efforts of Dietrich's Chief-of-Staff, the elegant and cultivated General Kraemer, to mediate between the two.

'What can you paratroops do anyway?' barked the burly one-time butcher's apprentice.

The Baron replied, 'Give me a mission, General, and then I can evaluate the feasibility.'

Dietrich slapped the map with one huge paw. 'Take that spot.' He slapped the map again. 'Or this one...or that.'

Finally the Baron got a chance to study the objectives which Dietrich had apparently assigned to him. He told Dietrich coldly that he would need a whole division to hold such an area until the armour arrived. Finally they reached a compromise. The Baron and his paras would drop at Baraque Michel, just beyond the highest point in Belgium, Mont Rigi, to take and hold a crucial crossroads leading to the Belgian towns of Verviers, Eupen and Malmédy. There they would hold out until the link-up by the 12th SS Armoured Division, the Hitler Youth, was achieved, barring any attempt by the US V Corps to send in troops.

The jump itself would take place before the great artillery bombardment which would herald the German counter-attack at five thirty on the morning of Saturday, 16 December.

'You will go there and make confusion,' Dietrich added somewhat mysteriously, at least for the Baron.

Kraemer then interrupted his chief. 'It is not von der Heydte who is to make the confusion, *Obergruppenführer*. That is Skorzeny.'

The Baron frowned at Skorzeny's name. What was he doing in this business? But he merely asked Dietrich what kind of opposition he could expect from the Americans.

'I'm not a prophet!' Dietrich snapped. 'You'll learn earlier than I what forces the Americans will employ against you. Besides, behind their lines there are only Jewish hoodlums and bank managers.'

Kraemer, ashamed of his chief, looked at the ceiling in despair; but he said nothing as the Baron talked Dietrich into giving him a liaison and forward artillery team from the 12th SS Division. Airily Dietrich said they would have no parachute training, but that didn't matter; they would jump without training.

That did not please the Baron. Anything might happen with men who had never jumped before. Could he, therefore, have pigeons?

'Pigeons!' Dietrich exploded. 'Pigeons! I'm leading my whole damn army without pigeons. You should be able to lead one battle group without a damn menagerie!'

That ended their one and only meeting. Kraemer led the Baron out to show him what information the Sixth had on the opposition and the proposed dropping zone.

The SS Intelligence knew that facing their 1st SS Panzer Corps, to which the Hitler Youth belonged, were two divisions of the US Army; one had come into the line five weeks before, the other had arrived on the front only a few days before. Both were totally without combat experience. Behind them but not in the line were two infantry divisions of V Corps, which had its headquarters in Eupen. They were the 1st, 'the Big Red One', and the 2nd Infantry, 'the Indian Head' (both named after their divisional patches). They were experienced divisions but had been badly battered in recent fighting. American tactical doctrine was the same as the German. When there was a breakthrough, US tactics were to hold the 'shoulders' and limit the extent of the breakthrough. So when the Sixth SS Panzer Army broke through, those two divisions, the 1st and 2nd US Infantry, would be the ones sent south to hold the 'shoulder'. It would be the Baron's task to stop them using the road network that branched out from Baraque Michel.

It was while he was briefed for the coming paradrop that the Baron discovered that Otto Skorzeny would also be involved in the Sixth's attack. The cover-name given to his own operation was *Unternehmen Stoesser* (Auk) while that of Skorzeny's was *Unternehmen Greif* (Gryphon). By chance, when he asked an SS Intelligence NCO to bring him the papers relating to *Stoesser* to see what information there was on the dropping zone, the sergeant mistakenly handed him papers relating to the *Greif* operation about which the Baron had known nothing up to this moment.

'People clearly wanted to keep Skorzeny's mission from me,' he wrote after the war, 'Only through this NCO's mistake did I learn of the Skorzeny plan.' He asked Dietrich's staff for further details, but they were not forthcoming. The Baron wanted nothing to do with the Viennese parvenu who had betrayed General Student in the Mussolini rescue affair in 1943. Perhaps, too, his lawyer's keen eye saw that an SS Colonel like Skorzeny was going to be in serious trouble with the Allies if they won the war — which the Baron was now sure they would. He was determined that the Skorzeny operation, which also included the use of parachute troops and infiltrators, should not interfere with his own, and protested energetically to General Kraemer. In the end Kraemer agreed that boundaries should be laid down between each zone of operations and that different passwords for each outfit should be issued to prevent confusion on the day.

That was that. Exhausted, the Baron and Major Erdmann set off on the long journey back to Oerlinghausen. But, tired as he was, the Baron could not fall asleep. Erdmann soon nodded off in the back of the car as they rolled through the night for the Rhine and beyond, but the Baron's mind was still spinning. The Skorzeny business had affected him. It seemed the Viennese giant was planning all sorts of weird and wonderful exploits behind the *Ami* lines: Germans dressed as Americans, bearing American weapons and driving American jeeps and trucks; men ranging far ahead of the fighting troops, some supposedly going as far as Paris with a rendezvous arranged at the Café de Paris.

This was not the kind of war Germany usually fought. Admittedly in 1940 they had used a few special troops dressed in Dutch uniforms to seize key crossings over the River Meuse, but that was about it. The Wehrmacht had always left such games to the Tommies, who were forced to use subterfuge and covert operations to make up for their lack of strength in the early days. Now it appeared that, to support the new counter-offensive, a whole Pandora's box of tricks was to be opened up, which would range the width and breadth of Western Europe.

The Baron did not like it one bit.

THREE

Within forty-eight hours of the momentous discovery in Camp 23, it had become clear to the camp's authorities that what the escaper Schmidt had told Brandstetter and Hoelzl at the cross-examination was true. Some kind of ambitious plan was indeed being hatched by the 'blacks' and their aim was not merely to escape.

That first evening, after the POWs had been locked away for the night, Colonel Upton chaired a conference on what had been discovered so far from the listening devices, from the 'whites' and from Sergeant Rosterg. Normally Colonel Upton's office was not blacked out, but now the shutters were closed to help ensure secrecy and an armed sentry was posted outside the door.

The plotters had been very careless. Secrecy has always been difficult for the average German, who tends to tell a stranger his life-story within five minutes of their meeting, and the plotters were no different. Soon Colonel Upton and his little committee knew most of what Koenig had told his fellow conspirators.

On the day picked for the break-out twenty selected toughs, all from the SS and under the command of SS man Joachim Goltz, would assemble in the compound nearest the main gate for the final check of the day. At a given signal they would rush the sentry and seize his weapon, and do the same with any guards coming to his aid, then begin picking off the other guards on the catwalk above and at the same time attempt to knock out the searchlights while others burst open the gate. Meanwhile another group would have broken through to other compounds. With hundreds if not thousands of POWs running loose, the SS would now storm the armoury at the nearby Le Marchant Barracks. All telephone wires would be cut and the cookhouse raided for extra food, while in the confusion another group of volunteers would run across the road to the US military hospital, 'organize' as many vehicles as they could find and take the hospital commandant, Colonel Mack, prisoner. According to the listeners at the hidden microphones, Koenig had said: 'Tell him we shall not touch his hospital, but warn him to have doctors standing by to treat any German casualties.'

Colonel Upton held another conference in his office the following night, and the night after that, until it became a regular event. At each meeting further details would emerge, leaving the Allied officers gasping at the magnitude of the plot. Once the initial break-out had been completed, a machine-gun party would be sent out to take and hold a hill to the east. This hill dominated the cluster of camps at Devizes and also the main road, which was to be blocked, to prevent any counter-attack. Then the plotters would converge on the nearest unit of the US 11th Armored Division.

The 11th Armored was currently in the process of beginning its move through Southampton to Cherbourg, and then on to the Liège area of Belgium where it would join the US First Army. Some officers had already gone to the Continent with the the advance parties, and on 3 December the Divisional Commander ordered that the first elements of the Division should be ready to move on the 10th. Koenig and his fellow plotters intended to exploit the inevitable muddle and bustle surrounding this move by stealing some of the newly arrived 76mm Sherman tanks, as many as they could find drivers for. At the same time an attempt would be made to seize a Mosquito from RAF Yatesbury, eight miles north of Devizes. It was a measure of the plotters' boldness that there were pilots among them who were prepared to risk taking off in a strange plane over the heavily defended southern coast of England. For the listeners had heard Koenig state: 'At least one aircraft must be captured quickly and flown to the Reich. The Führer must know that we are still in the war.'

It all seemed unreal. Here was a group of German POWs planning an armed escape from the camp, with all the risks that this would entail, at a time when their country was virtually defeated anyway. But the proof that the plotters were serious came when they revealed to the hidden microphones that the coded signal for the start of the operation had already been picked: '*Hans drei, Gustav vier*' (Hans three, Gustav four). No one ever discovered whether there was a special significance behind the words.

Contact had already been established with *Feldwebel* Schmittendorf and his assistant, Corporal Arnim Kuehne, at Lodge Moor Camp in Sheffield, where a similar plan for a mass break-out had been devised. Here again the POWs would arm themselves and then make their way gradually south-eastwards, joining escapers from Glen Mill under Para Sergeant Gerald Hanel, and others from Penkridge and from other camps. With a bit of luck on their side, the plotters hoped that when the mass escape began there would be thousands of Germans, armed and perhaps even equipped with tanks, converging on the key objective — London.

As yet Colonel Upton and his officers at Devizes did not know the full extent of the plot; the final objective remained obscure to them. Nevertheless, the enormity of what they did know overwhelmed them. Throughout history, prisoners-of-war have tended to accept their lot meekly. There are always a few, of course, who try to escape, usually driven by an intense personal need for freedom or wish to return to the fray. But this was open revolt, something that had not been attempted since Spartacus roused his fellow slaves in ancient Rome to challenge the authority of their masters. Was it really possible? It all seemed too fantastic.

The first suggestion that an attempt should be made to start an armed revolt by German POWs in the British Isles had come in 1943 from *Oberleutnant* Dr Hermann Goertz — and it had been made, surprisingly enough, while he was in a prison camp.

A barrister by profession, Goertz had volunteered for the German Army in the First World War and had been severely wounded. On his recovery he had joined the German Air Force as an observer, but after thirty-one reconnaissance flights over Russian territory he suffered a nervous breakdown and was taken off flying duties. Thereafter Goertz never really settled down. In 1935 he rejoined the Luftwaffe and in due course volunteered to do some spying in Britain. Taking with him a pretty young girl who rode pillion on his motorbike, he toured RAF bases in southern England, taking secret photographs of planes and installations. He also took copious notes which was rather foolish for a spy, but then Goertz was typical of the enthusiastic amateur. In due course that notebook was discovered and Goertz was arrested and sentenced to four years' imprisonment.

During his stay in prison he got to know several IRA men and soon became familiar with their struggle against the English. By February, 1939, when he was released early for good conduct, Hermann Goertz, now aged forty-nine, had a bee in his bonnet about the IRA. Over the next year or so he tried repeatedly to find someone in authority who would listen to his view of the IRA's value to Germany in her fight against Britain. But as he wrote shortly before his death, The High Command was not very interested in my ideas of using the IRA for sabotage or spying but was more interested in my idea of kindling some sort of rebellion in Ulster against the English.'

Then, in January, 1940, Goertz was transferred from the Luftwaffe to German Intelligence, the Abwehr, where he came under the direct orders of 'Father Christmas', the benign, white-haired head of that organization, Admiral Canaris. The enigmatic Canaris, who played both sides of the field and is reported to have once met his opposite number Sir Stewart Menzies, head of the British Secret Intelligence Service, during the war, knew he had a willing tool in Goertz. He asked him if he would be prepared to parachute into Ireland to act as a liaison officer between the Abwehr and the IRA.

Goertz jumped at the chance. His only request was that he should be given a cyanide pill in case he was caught. His wish was granted. On 5 May, 1940, *Oberleutnant* Goertz, dressed in full Luftwaffe uniform under his overalls and carrying his wartime medals (one wonders who he was going to show them to), dropped and landed safely over Southern Ireland.

For the next eighteen months Goertz tried in vain to persuade the IRA to prepare for the invasion of Ulster. He told them that a special SS unit, No.1 SS Special Service Troop, was waiting in Berlin for orders to jump, ready to aid them in their fight against the English. But nothing much came of his efforts, save that the IRA relieved him of most of the US dollars he had brought with him. In November, 1941, Goertz was arrested by the Irish authorities and placed in Dublin jail for a few weeks, then transferred to Custume Barracks, built by the British Army in the little town of Athlone in central Ireland. It was thought that here Goertz and other IRA detainees would be safer from attempts to rescue them.

In spite of the security arrangements, however, Goertz managed to keep in contact with the outside world via 'patriots', mostly guards he had bribed, and through signals transmitted by the Deutschlandfunk, the German state radio, which he was allowed to listen to because he had claimed a passionate desire to hear good German music. Using the 'patriots', Goertz was able to send an uncensored letter to his IRA friends in Ulster. As he wrote after the war when he was expecting to be sent to Nuremberg to give evidence at the war trials:

> In the autumn of 1944 [he might have meant 1943] I made contact with 'Ulrike', the sabotage and espionage group in Northern Ireland, which had radio contact with Germany. I had already suggested a break-out from Athlone and wished to start a revolt with German prisoners-of-war in Ulster and perpetrate

sabotage attacks. Broadly speaking the plan was approved and I was promised the necessary help.

By a remarkable coincidence, at the same time that Goertz's letter was transmitted via 'Ulrike' to Berlin, the Abwehr also received a report from Spain of a plot to stage an Anglo-American rising against the dictator Franco, who was a Hitler supporter. The intention was to try to rouse the Basques and the Catalonians against Franco, establishing Anglo-American bridgeheads on the coasts through which arms could be run to the rebels. But the core of the plot was to seize the great Falangist internment camp at Miranda del Ebro, where 6,000 Allied servicemen, many of them British, were held under terrible conditions. Most of them were soldiers who had escaped from occupied Europe and tried to flee through Spain to Gibraltar, or even Lisbon, where they might find a passage to England. The Spanish uprising never happened, but it did make those in Berlin reflect on the hundreds of thousands of German POWs in British hands. Could not some use be made of them?

For his contribution to the escape plan Goertz received a promotion. It came in the form of a coded message brought into the internment wing by one of the 'patriots', a sergeant who was well paid for smuggling in messages from 'Ulrike' in Ulster. His cellmate recorded later: 'I was decoding a message with the doctor. When we had finished it we read that the doctor had been promoted to major and that he had been awarded a clasp to his Iron Cross First Class. The doctor only looked at me and then began to cry and sank on to his bed.'

But Goertz was not the man to co-ordinate a mass break-out, and Berlin told him to lie low. He ignored orders and tried to escape, but failed, as he failed in most things in his life. So it was left to the new chief of the Abwehr and the SS's own secret service, the SD, to work out the details of how men could be infiltrated into Britain as POWs and then assume control of the camps to which they were sent. The name of this new secret service chief was Walter Schellenberg.

In the autumn of 1944 Schellenberg, good-looking but with a nasty sabre scar from his student duelling days running down one side of his face, was at the height of his power. Hand-picked by SS General Heydrich before the war, he had rapidly climbed the ladder of promotion in the SS's police and espionage organization. In 1939 he had kidnapped two senior officers of the British SIS in Holland.* A year later he had attempted to kidnap the Duke and Duchess of Windsor in Portugal, before Churchill had them shipped off to Bermuda. Thereafter he had turned his hand to politics, for now that Heydrich had been assassinated, Schellenberg had

---

* For details of this operation see *Betrayal at Venlo,* Leo Kessler, 1990.

become the closest confidant of the head of the SS, Heinrich Himmler. He had made the first covert offers of peace to Russia behind Hitler's back; he had tried to bring Spain into the war on Germany's side; and already by early 1944 he had made his first approaches to the Americans to see if they would agree to peace. Now an SS general in his thirties, he was one of the most powerful men in Nazi Germany.

But Schellenberg, realizing that Germany would probably lose the war, still wanted to act as a possible peace mediator from a position of power. Germany must appear to the Western Allies to have continuing reserves of strength, to be able to fight on if necessary. At all costs Schellenberg wanted to avoid the unconditional surrender that the Allies were calling for.

Schellenberg had been present when Hitler initiated Himmler into the great secret, announcing that he was going to counter-attack in the West. Thereafter the Führer had addressed himself to the younger man, telling Schellenberg to remember that

in this war there can be no compromise, there can only be victory or destruction. And if the German people cannot wrest victory from the enemy, then they shall be destroyed. Yes, then they deserve to perish, for the best of Germany's manhood will have fallen in battle. Germany's end will be horrible and the German people will have deserved it.

As Schellenberg recorded later:

I felt that stark insanity stood there in the middle of the room, and any ties which still bound me to the man fell away at that moment, for he was willing to condemn what was dearest to him, his own people. He willed the destruction of all this to satisfy his vengeful spite.

But Schellenberg in the winter of 1944 had no desire to go down with the sinking ship. Ever since he had become the second most important man in the SS after Himmler, he had taken the greatest care of his own life:

My desk was like a small fortress. Two automatic guns were built into it which could spray the whole room with bullets. All I had to do in an emergency was to press a button and both guns would fire simultaneously. At the same time I could press another button and a siren would summon the guards to surround the building and block every exit.

Schellenberg wanted Hitler's last offensive in the West to succeed, not because he felt any remaining loyalty to the Führer but because a victory there would bring great kudos to his patron, Himmler, whose Sixth SS Panzer Army were leading the attack. Himmler would be the man who took Germany out of the war and Schellenberg would be the man who negotiated peace with the Western Allies. But first there had to be a victory. So, as the coming offensive drew ever closer, hidden in his lair somewhere in the bombed and battered city of Berlin, Schellenberg gave the order to activate the great escape.

FOUR

The Allied senior officers in the grand houses, hotels and châteaux were at peace with themselves this Friday, 15 December. The front-line fighting had diminished since the bad weather set in. Up in the north, Field-Marshal Montgomery, the British Commander, had sent his Chief-of-Staff, the long-suffering Freddie de Guingand, home on much-needed leave and had requested leave for himself so that he could spend Christmas with his son. In the centre, General Hodges, Commanding General of the First US Army, spent the afternoon hosting a party for professional baseball players visiting from the States. Soon he intended to go home to his quarters, a villa two miles from the headquarters town of Spa set in an extensive private estate known as Balmoral. He had a bad cold and wanted to go to bed.

Further back at Eisenhower's HQ at the Petit Trianon in Versailles, a senior general reported to a conference of Allied air commanders that the First Army's attack on the Roer dams had failed to provoke a response from the enemy's panzer reserves and that on the VIII Corps front (where Hitler was soon to strike) there was 'nothing to report'. As for the Supreme Commander himself, Eisenhower was busy planning two celebrations to be held on the morrow: one for the wedding of his favourite orderly, Mickey McKeogh, to a bespectacled WAC sergeant, Pearlie Hargrave; and one for his fifth star. All his old buddies would attend. There'd be plenty of champagne and French cognac, even Scotch whisky which was in short supply elsewhere, and a special treat for himself, for a well-wisher had sent him a bushel of oysters. Now his 'darkies', as the Supreme Commander called his black mess servants, were preparing oysters on the half shell as an entree, to be followed by oyster stew, with fried oysters to conclude the festive meal.

After all, this was the last weekend before Christmas. The Top Brass thought they deserved a rest after a busy year. They had no inkling that on the morrow the enemy would launch a major attack which would cost the

US Army 77,000 men killed, wounded or taken prisoner, and the British another 1,500. The fact that the enemy had managed to assemble two huge tank armies, numbering 600,000 men, under their very noses was later to became a major scandal.

That winter, when everyone thought Hitler was finished, the Germans were about to achieve a surprise which must be ranked with the most brilliant of the wartime Anglo-American deception operations, such as 'Bodyguard', 'Fortitude' and the 'Double-Cross System', and all the rest of those intelligence coups of which the British in particular were — and are — so proud. Between October and December the Germans had managed to assemble, train and re-arm a massive attack force, not on the other side of the Channel, as had been the case with the Allies before the invasion, but a mere two or three hundred yards away on the other side of the front line! And there would be even more surprises in store for the Allies when the offensive got underway, including the great scare that virtually paralysed the rear areas of the Allied front with 'half a million GIs playing cat-and-mouse with each other', as an irate General Bradley would put it later.

However, if the front-line generals were feeling sanguine, over in England the authorities were not. The camp officers at Devizes, perched on what might be a huge time bomb, had already transmitted what they knew of the planned mass break-out to Colonel Scotland at the London Cage. As we know, Scotland had been puzzled and worried for months about what was going on in German POW camps throughout the United Kingdom. Now he had confirmation that there was a serious problem facing the camp authorities. He also had recent information obtained from newly captured German prisoners that English-speaking German parachutists dressed in American uniforms were being assembled for a drop. Later he learned that these men were part of the Skorzeny force, which contained a large number of paras. But that Friday Scotland reasoned that a German paradrop on Britain was being timed to coincide with the mass break-out. Naturally, Scotland told himself that a German airdrop could have no real hope of success; but it could definitely spread disruption in a country denuded of troops and already demoralized, at least in the south, by the persistent V-1 and V-2 attacks.

It was understandable, therefore, that Scotland detailed an officer from his staff to go over to the War Office and inform the authorities what was being planned at Devizes and probably at other German POW camps in Britain. The news was sufficiently alarming for the Chief of the Imperial General Staff himself, Field-Marshal Alan Brooke, to be told.

Brooke, the bird-watching Ulsterman who had raised the British Army from the defeat of Dunkirk to the victory of D-Day, was a cautious man by nature, not given to alarmism. But he realized immediately that an operation like this, combining a mass break-out with a German paradrop, whether it failed or succeeded, would have the gravest consequences. The country was practically empty of fighting troops. The Home Guard had become slack and ill-disciplined; no one had thought their services would still be needed. Brooke decided that the news from Devizes warranted an interruption to the War Cabinet discussion that Friday about the threat of civil war in Greece.

Churchill listened to the news calmly. In his opinion, he said, a German paradrop to aid the mass break-out of prisoners was most unlikely; but with Hitler trapped like a rat in a corner, he might try anything. Consequently Churchill ordered Brooke to cancel all Christmas leave for guards at German POW camps, for this was thought to be the most likely time the Germans would choose to act. At Christmas the nation's guard would be down, and by then there would be only one American division left in Britain, the US 66th Infantry, which was also expected to sail for Cherbourg on Christmas Eve. At the same time all Home Forces, such as they were, plus the Home Guard, were warned to be on the alert.

Satisfied that something practical had been done, Field-Marshal Brooke went back to the War Office to resume his manifold duties, which included trying to appease Montgomery and attempting to get Eisenhower to revise his broad-front strategy. But the paper he was preparing on the subject, to be delivered in three days' time, was interrupted yet again by even more alarming news from Colonel Scotland's office.

Earlier that evening Devizes had reported that the hidden microphones had picked up a statement from Koenig, the ringleader of the break-out plot. He had said that the German offensive in the West, which he had got wind of through newly arrived prisoners from the battles on the German frontier, would start before Christmas. Therefore he had decided that 'Hans drei, Gustav vier' should commence on Saturday 16 December, the same day as the great German counter-attack.

On that icy Friday night preparations were being made everywhere for what was to come. At Oerlinghausen, far from the front, the Baron's paras had finally received their chutes. The Baron himself had been sent a special one by Student personally. Captured from the Russians, it was triangular in shape without the usual vent at the top; this apparently helped to reduce oscillations and made the chute much easier to control. It was particularly useful to the Baron as he was jumping with one hand still strapped up.

On that same night he received another gift: 300 straw dummies, attached to worn-out, old-fashioned chutes. Back in June the Baron had noted the *Amis'* use of dummy parachutists to cause confusion. Now he was going to try the same trick on them — to even greater effect.

Skorzeny's nine 'jeep teams' were already in position. They were dressed as Americans and would pretend to belong to the US 5th Armored Division. On their jeeps they had the letters 'CD', 'XY' and 'Z' painted on the near side of the hood so that they would be recognized by German front-line units. It would be their job to penetrate to the River Meuse bridges, painting white spots on bridges, houses, trees etc to indicate safe routes for the following panzers. But the jeep teams bore more than tubs of white paint with them. Four of the jeeps carried a fortune in Belgian and French francs — thirty millions' worth in brand new notes, all forged by slave workers in Germany's concentration camps.

This vast amount of money would be used to bribe those who had remained in Allied-occupied territory as 'sleepers' the previous September when the Germans had fled France, Belgium and Luxembourg. It was planned to use the money, in particular, to pay the French and Belgian communist unions to stay away from their jobs at ports and railways in the week leading up to Christmas. This, it was thought, would effectively sabotage the Anglo-American supply system to the front from the major ports of Antwerp and Cherbourg.

Across the front line there were other agents in place, some of them Gestapo men already occupying their old quarters where they spied on the unsuspecting *Amis*. At Walferdingen in Luxembourg, for instance, the former local Gestapo agent had simply slipped through the front line and returned to his old room, using the key he had taken with him the previous autumn; no one in the village dared report him to the Americans billeted there.

Much deeper into Belgium, the Germans also had agents already in place at Bastogne, the HQ of General Middleton's VIII Corps, soon to be shattered by the coming offensive. That Friday night the locals reported seeing signal lights and parachute flares all around the city which within days would become the site of the heroic defence of the 'Battered Bastards of Bastogne'.

On the Atlantic coast and along the Channel, the surviving 'fortresses' of the Wehrmacht, such as the trapped German garrisons of Lorient and St Nazaire, cut off from the Reich since August, as well as the only part of the British Empire to come under German occupation, the Channel Islands, plans had also been made to exploit the breakthrough in the far-off Ardennes. Under the fire-eating German Admiral Huffmeier, Commander of the Channel Islands, a force was being readied to land on the French coast. In the Channel, coastal E-boats and U-boats were already on station, being directed from Dunkirk, still in German hands, and perhaps by French and Belgian dockside traitors in Schellenberg's pay. Mini-submarines had been positioned at the mouth of the Thames, ready for action.

Everywhere there was hectic activity. Soldiers, spies and saboteurs were all waiting for that fateful dawn of Saturday, 16 December, 1944.

BOOK TWO

Gentlemen, it is either march or croak.
SS General Kras to his staff, December, 1944

1

ATTACK!

The hour of destiny has struck!
Field-Marshal Gerd von Rundstedt, 16 December, 1944

ONE

One minute after midnight on Saturday, 16 December, the night shift at Bletchley Park was alerted. For weeks now virtually no messages of any importance had come from Germany via the German coding machine, the Enigma, and the decoding experts had started to believe that the war had passed them by. Tired and jaded by the months of intensely concentrated activity since D-Day, they had begun to relax. But suddenly the German Enigma machines were functioning again. Signals and messages were buzzing to and fro after weeks of silence. What was going on?

Tensely the men and women of the night shift waited for the first decode, perhaps half-realizing that the balloon had gone up once more. Then the 'flimsy' bearing the first decode came into the Nissen hut. They grouped round the German translator, standing under the single unshaded bulb, while he put the signal into English. It was from Field-Marshal von Rundstedt, the most able of all Hitler's senior officers, and it was addressed to all his field commanders, to be passed on to all their subordinate units. It read:

> The hour of destiny has struck. Mighty offensive armies face
> the Allies. Everything is at stake. More than mortal deeds are
> required as a holy duty to the Fatherland!

That was what it said; but what did it all mean? What were these 'mighty offensive armies'? What precisely was at stake? What could be happening at a time when Germany was virtually beaten? These were the unspoken questions which ran through the minds of the Bletchley Park staff as dispatch riders prepared to rush the message to Churchill, sixty miles away in London.

What was going on was pretty obvious to the men at the front in the Ardennes. For at exactly five-thirty that Saturday morning, while the Top Brass slept off their hangovers of the previous night, the complete front of the US VIII Corps erupted into fire and flame. The whole weight of the

85

German artillery of three armies, ranging from 16-inch railway guns to 3-inch mortars, descended upon the startled Americans of the four divisions holding the line in the Ardennes. As the morning stillness was ripped apart by that man-made storm, the white-clad German infantry burst from the forests, cheering as they came; and behind them were the tanks, hundreds of them rolling forward like primeval monsters seeking for prey. The great attack had started at last.

For one hour the enormous barrage continued. It cut telephone links, destroyed the front-line bunkers, smashed foxholes. It turned the countryside into a smoking churned-up graveyard.

Then it ceased. For a few minutes there was an echoing silence, while the men in the line, the survivors, tried to collect themselves. Their faces were ashen, their eyes wild with unspoken questions. Then at key points along the front searchlights stabbed the dawn gloom. There they were: the first ghostlike figures in 'spook suits', as the GIs called the winter white camouflage suits. They advanced at a steady, ominous pace, twenty abreast, well spaced out, their weapons carried at the high port. Behind them the tanks started to emerge from the forest, snapping the fir trees like matchwood, showering the infantry packed on their decks with snow.

It was unbelievable. This was the Ghost Front where nothing had happened since the previous September. Most of the VIII Corps had come here to train or rest, not to fight. Nobody had warned them to expect this. Now the Krauts were attacking in their thousands!

But not everywhere was this massive German surprise assault meeting success. Although in the first hours of the new offensive, scores of units broke and hundreds of terrified GIs fled to the rear, creating monumental traffic jams in their haste to escape, at Losheimergraben, directly on the border between Belgium and Germany, a straggle of white-painted, slate-roofed houses set around a customs post, General Engel's 12th Volks-grenadier Division was finding it exceedingly difficult to clear a path for the SS armour which was to follow and exploit the breakthrough. In particular the 12th SS Panzer Division, the Hitler Youth, was stalled, impatiently waiting for its chance to drive through to the Meuse as Dietrich wanted.

The Baron was similarly stalled. Ever since the previous night, his paras, dressed and kitted out for action, had been waiting for transport to take them to the airfield. But as in all armies, there was the occasional bureaucratic muddle. Officially Germany's paratroops came under Luftwaffe jurisdiction, although for years they had been fighting as ground troops under the command of the Wehrmiacht. Since the paras were supplied by the Luftwaffe, the army maintained that it was not their job to provide them with fuel to transport them to the airfield. For its part the Luftwaffe argued that its task had been to supply them with fuel only to reach Oerlinghausen; thereafter they were the army's responsibility.

Confused and angry, hardly able to believe that such things could happen at the start of a vital offensive, the Baron pulled out all the stops in order to get transport for his men. He made repeated telephone calls to anyone in authority he could think of in order to obtain the necessary fuel. In the end he received enough to move 400 men to the airfield where the 'Stalingrad Squadron' was waiting. He also received a visitor in the form of a testy officer from the Judge Advocate's branch of the Wehrmacht.

The officer, obviously a lawyer in civilian life as the Baron's own legal training told him, immediately started to cross-examine the Baron and his officers as to the reasons for the delay. He seemed to suspect that they had deliberately not moved because they didn't want to go to the front. The Baron tried to assure him that they did. To be suspected of cowardice or disloyalty in Germany in that winter of 1944 could be enough for a man to be hanged from the nearest lamp post. Finally the *Kriegsrichter* was convinced and the weary paras set off for the airfield. The Baron, who had had no sleep for two days, thought he'd snatch a few hours before take-off, but he had just reached the airfield when General Kraemer, Dietrich's Chief-of-Staff, rang him. The offensive had not progressed as rapidly as expected in his sector, he began.

The Baron's hopes rose suddenly. Perhaps the ill-conceived paradrop would be cancelled after all?

But Kraemer disappointed him. He went on: 'We have reached only a small portion of our objectives. The enemy is still resisting forward of Elsenborn Ridge Camp in anticipation of reinforcements arriving from the north.' Then came the crunch. 'You will, therefore, drop before dawn tomorrow morning in the area previously agreed with the object of intercepting those reinforcements. Hold on as long as possible.' Now there was a note of pleading in Kraemer's voice. 'Two days as a minimum — and do as much damage as you can to the reinforcements. By the way,' he added as a kind of an afterthought, 'your drop zone has been moved slightly south-eastwards to the Belle Croix crossroads, near Baraque Michel.'

With that Kraemer hung up, leaving the Baron more despondent than ever. A night drop was bad enough with his bunch of deadbeats, jumping into unfamiliar territory of which he knew only that it was high and swampy. Now he was to land, armed only with light weapons, and hold out against enemy armour. For the Baron was sure the enemy would send tanks rushing southwards to stop the SS panzer divisions. And he would have to hold them for *two* days. It was a pretty tall order.

But there was no turning back. For better or worse the mission was on.

87

Good Bavarian Catholic that he was, the Baron telephoned the local priest. Would he come out immediately and give the 'Auntie Jus' and their crews a blessing before they took off. The priest agreed, and the Baron gave a weary sigh. This coming night he would need all the divine intervention he could get. Perhaps God might show a little mercy for his ragtag force, flown into battle for the first time by pilots who were as inexperienced as they were, to hold that remote crossroads against the might of the US Army.

While the Baron and his men prepared for their jump, other paras were already in position waiting to go into action again. They were the veteran Red Berets of the British 6th Airborne Division. They had dropped in Normandy on D-Day and had fought as ordinary infantry for over two months. Then they had been sent back to England for rest, replacements and retraining. By December they were being trained in street fighting and river assaults, using the Thames as a substitute for the Rhine. For that was to be their next objective.

But in the last week of December, 1944, the men of the 6th Division were little interested in 'Exercise Eve', the training for the assault drop over the Rhine. Their hearts and minds were firmly fixed on Christmas. Suddenly, however, all leave was cancelled. The Red Berets were placed on alert. Not until February did they receive that Christmas leave — those who survived.

Now, heavily armed and supported by Daimler and Humber armoured cars, both mounting 37mm cannon, the Red Berets moved in silently to surround the Devizes Camp. In the freezing darkness they watched the dim figure of a POW entering the bath hut, followed a minute later by a second prisoner. An officer hissed an order and the Red Berets moved in, rifles and Stens slung over their shoulders, pickaxe handles in their hands.

The POWs were caught completely by surprise. One of them tried to swallow a piece of paper he was carrying. A sergeant snatched it from his mouth, then the two men were frog-marched to the Commandant's office.

Colonel Upton and the Adjutant, Captain Hurn, were waiting for them. 'A Hitler Order of the Day!' Hum exclaimed in astonishment as he read the German. Hurriedly he translated for the benefit of the others. 'Men of the Freedom Movement. The hour of our liberation is approaching and it is the duty of every German to fight with arms in hand against world Jewry.'

Hurn looked at the two crestfallen prisoners. 'A freedom movement in a prison camp!' he said scornfully, and then turned to the Red Beret NCO. 'Take them to the guardroom, Sergeant.'

Later that night, revolver in hand and accompanied by an armed guard

'Baron Freiherr von der Heydte . . . came from the Bavarian *Altadel,* the old aristocracy' (p. 10).

Where it all started: 'Le Marchant Camp, Devizes, now officially known as Camp 23' (p. 40).

"The London Cage was a cream-coloured Georgian building at No.8, Kensington Palace Gardens" (p.35).

Soldiers of the 'Big Red One' find an abandoned parachute near Mont Rigi.

These two German soldiers, taken prisoner in the Ardennes, indicate
the extreme youth of the reserves upon which Hitler was drawing by the
winter of 1944/45.

Swift justice is meted out to German soldiers found behind the Allied
lines dressed in US uniform.

The prisoner-of-war camp, Thirkleby, North Yorkshire.

Eden Camp, Malton, is now a tourist attraction.

of the Sixth, Hurn entered No. 1 Compound of Camp 23. Usually the compounds were sealed from dusk to dawn. Now everything was on the alert. The guards on the catwalks were ready for trouble. The searchlights swung round and concentrated their beams on the door of a hut nearest the gate. Hurn nodded to one of his sergeants. He aimed a hefty kick at the wooden door, which splintered and flew open.

Huddled round the glowing pot-bellied stove, talking in low voices, the prisoners were startled and confused.

Hurn snapped out two names: Erich Pallme Koenig and Kurt Zuehlsdorff.

Koenig stepped forward, the usual arrogant expression on his face. *'Herr Hauptmann —'* he began.

But Hurn had no time for military courtesies this night. 'Get your kit,' he rasped. 'And you,' he added, as Zuehlsdorff caught his eye.

For a moment the two POWs just stood there. The Red Berets moved forward menacingly. The other POWs moved back to their bunks. They had heard of the Tommy paras; they had a tough reputation.

Sullenly the two Germans started to toss a few bits and pieces into their white kitbags, while the other POWs glowered at the stony-faced paras. Not a word was spoken, but the tension was almost tangible. Something had gone wrong with the escape plan and the Germans knew it.

Hurn barked an order and the paras backed out of the hut with the prisoners. But Hurn was not done yet. He had to arrest more of the conspirators. One hour later he had twenty-eight of the chief plotters locked in two vans, while Mr. Gaiger, the works foreman, set up firehoses in case the POWs attempted to rush the wire. By now the place was ringed by Sherman tanks and armoured cars.

Seeing all the activity, the Commandant of the US military hospital across the way came over to where Colonel Upton stood watching. 'Can't wait for the shooting to start,' the American chortled. 'I've got to be in on this one.'

But there was to be no shooting this night. For the sudden arrest of the ringleaders had turned the POWs' aggression into sulky bewilderment. Even the plotters were infected by the mood. 'What's going on? Where are you taking us?' they kept asking their guards.

The guards had orders not to speak to the prisoners, but one of them could not resist it. After he had been asked for the umpteenth time what was going on, he sneered: 'There's going to be no mass break-out. No capture of an armoured division. You're going somewhere you won't be able to escape from — ever!'

For five of those young Germans, the guard's words were to prove all too true.

89

TWO

While Koenig wondered bitterly what had gone wrong, his former CO, the Baron, was also realizing that his operation had begun to go off course. At midnight the local priest had duly blessed the paras' planes and they had set off in the cumbersome, slow-moving Ju-52s, with the paras singing the fatalistic text of their song, '*Rot Scheint die Sonne*' (Red shines the sun):

When Germany is in danger, there is only one thing for us to do:

To fight, to conquer and believe we shall die.

From our aircraft, my friend, there is no return.

For a while the inexperienced pilots of the 'Stalingrad Squadron' were kept on course by searchlights marking the route from below, but as the Junkers began to approach the battle zone the wind strengthened, with flurries of driving snow. The pilots began to get lost. Up front with Erdmann, the Baron was confident that he at least would find the dropping zone, especially as a Messerschmitt fighter was showing them the way with flares. But what about the others in the rapidly worsening weather?

Sergeant Lingelbach was in one of the other planes. Lingelbach was a veteran parachutist. He had made hundreds of jumps, but only one in combat — over Stavanger in Norway in 1940. Now he sat with his comrades, sunk in thought in the swaying Junkers. The interior of the plane was dark. He felt isolated, anxious. He kept remembering that other combat jump.

Everything had gone off splendidly. Two hours after landing, the paras' own fife-and-drum corps — the High Command had thought of everything — had been playing German *Marschmusik* for the benefit of the local populace. But he doubted if the *Amis* somewhere out there would be patient enough to sit back and be entertained by German military marches; they'd be too busy trying to kill the paras as they came floating down.

The plane swayed alarmingly as it was buffeted by yet another gust of wind. One of the youngsters started to be sick in his helmet. Lingelbach told himself he could do with a stiff drink. He wished he'd filled his water-bottle with good Westphalian *Korn* schnapps instead of weak cold tea.

Suddenly the red light up front began to glow. An officer rapped out the orders. 'Helmets on. Check equipment. Stand by to jump.' Obediently the men followed the routine, tapping each other's chutes to see if they were sitting correctly, as the hatch was opened to let in the icy air. The order had been that they should jump at 800 feet, but Lingelbach thought they were a lot higher than that. He shook his helmeted head; the pilot was just too inexperienced. He waited for the signal to go.

In the lead plane the Baron was also ready to go. Suddenly the Junkers rocked violently. They had been spotted by Allied defences. The air was full of white and red glowing balls, gathering speed rapidly as the shells approached the planes. Behind Erdmann's Junkers, one of the thirteen which had managed to follow him stopped abruptly as if it had run into an invisible wall. Next moment its nose dropped and it plummeted to the ground, a vivid orange torch.

The Baron looked around at his 'stick'. They were visibly shaken. Only two of the ten had jumped in combat before. They were not used to the frightening confusion of an airborne landing under fire. The Baron hid his own feelings and concentrated on trying to find the landing beacon — a brilliant burning cross, consisting of three white lights and one red one, pointing westwards. There it was! They were right on target.

The red light changed to green. The Baron's men shuffled forward, feeling the icy wind buffet their scared faces. The Baron was first to go, as always. Below him at the open door the ground raced by at a dizzy pace, patches of black interspersed by the white of the snow. A hard hand hit his shoulder. 'Los!' the dispatcher cried above the roar of the wind. He went out in a rush. The wind gripped him. It seemed to want to drag him down to his death. He was falling at a tremendous rate. Suddenly there was a loud crack and he gasped as the straps jerked at his chest. Above him the strange Russian chute billowed out and he was drifting down to the ground without oscillations. But there was now a new enemy — the wind. According to the weathermen, the wind velocity at ground level should have been twenty feet per second. In fact it was more like fifty. It took the Baron all his strength to stop himself drifting too far from the DZ.

A thick fir forest swung into sight. He crossed an empty road. Suddenly he lost control. The ground came up to meet him. Next moment he hit it, hard. Briefly he blacked out. A few moments later he came round. He was completely alone.

Sergeant Lingelbach had also made a rough landing, in a fir tree some sixty feet above a ravine. He freed himself and dropped unluckily, hitting the bottom of the ravine. When he tried to move his left arm, he couldn't. He had broken his humerus. He looked around and realized he was alone. The ravine was silent and deserted. But Lingelbach was a resourceful man. He bound the arm close to his body as best he could. It wasn't easy and he was bathed in sweat by the time he was finished, in spite of the freezing cold. Then he set off westwards, where he had seen the mass of his fellow paras coming down. By the first light of the new dawn he came across a patch of flat ground, with trees dotted across it here and there, and from one tree a large piece of parachute was hanging. He recognized the insignia of his own regiment on it, but he took no chances. With his pistol in his hand he advanced cautiously until he spotted a man lying on the ground. It was his comrade Wiertz but Wiertz was worse off than himself: both his legs were broken. Wiertz asked his comrade to put a bullet through his head.

'No,' Lingelbach answered, shocked. 'Are you losing much blood? Let me have a look at you.'

'I've already looked,' the other man answered, 'and poked around, too. There doesn't seem to be any flow of blood. Only my bones are broken.'

Then you can be moved and taken to safety,' Lingelbach said.

Wiertz propped himself up on one elbow. 'Where can I be taken? We were dropped fifty kilometres ahead of our own front.'

Lingelbach tried to reassure him. The offensive was moving fast. The panzer forces would soon arrive.

Wiertz shook his head. 'The armour won't come this way. You saw for yourself that there's no road here. We're out in the wilds. I'll die of cold before they ever find me. To tell the truth, I'd rather get it over quickly. If you won't do me the favour, I'll do it myself.'

'Don't be in such a hurry,' Lingelbach said. 'I'll go and find the others. Probably there'll be an officer among them and when I tell him you're here he'll order something done about it.'

Again Wiertz shook his head. 'He'll order me to be left behind. Our unit mustn't be held up by someone who's out of commission. I'm shooting myself, I tell you. I was waiting to see if there might be any other way out, but there simply isn't.'

'You can't shoot off a gun when we've just landed,' Lingelbach admonished him. 'It would be like an alarm signal.'

That argument seemed to convince the wounded man, though Lingelbach himself wasn't convinced. He wondered, if he ever did find an officer, what that officer would be able to do. But he had been a paratrooper since the beginning and he knew the ten commandments of the Corps, including number two: 'Strive for true comradeship. It is with your comrade's help that you will go to either victory or death.' So he made Wiertz as comfortable as he could, wrapping him in the torn parachute and opening a tin of food for him. Then he set off to find help.

By now the Baron had collected six men: four teenage privates, a young lieutenant and a sergeant with a twisted ankle. This sorry little group of men seemed to be the only ones of the 1,200-strong force to have landed anywhere near the DZ. Trudging through the freezing morning gloom towards their objective, the all-important crossroads, they gradually picked up others. But half an hour later, as they crouched in ditches at both sides of the crossroads, they still numbered less than thirty.

Just then there was the sound of heavy motors grinding down the icy slope from Eupen, where the US V Corps HQ was located. Before the paras, numbed by cold and consequently slow-witted this morning, could react and take cover, the first of the open trucks packed with American infantrymen was upon them.

The Baron tensed for the first shots — but the *Amis* did not fire. Apparently they mistook the scared German paras in their rimless helmets for Allied troops; they merely cheered and waved, happy that their own men were already in position up here in these lonely, rugged heights.

That was the first of many US convoys from the 7th Armored and the 1st Infantry Divisions being rushed south in order to hold the 'shoulder' of the new counter-attack. Miserably the Baron watched them roll past. By now he had 125 men under his command. With 1,200 he would have been able to hold the crossroads, possibly even against armour. Not now, however. All he had to repel the *Amis* was a few machine guns and *panzerfausts,* the German missile launcher. It would mean a pointless massacre of his troops if he attempted anything now.

In the end the Baron decided to withdraw into the marshy fenland while he thought things over. But already he knew in his heart that the operation was a failure. All his efforts, all the self-sacrifice and the undoubted casualties had been for nothing. Tired, uncomfortable, his feet frozen, his stomach rumbling with hunger, the Baron concluded that he now faced a simple choice: retreat to his own line or surrender.

Unknown to the Baron, his abortive operation had already started an unmitigated panic throughout Allied Europe. His paras and the dummies had been scattered over literally hundreds of miles. Their arrival out of the dawn sky was seen by local and Allied troops alike. Rumours began to spread and with each rumour the number of German paras grew. Real or imaginary, they were spotted as far north as Maastricht in Holland and as far south as Verdun in France. Eisenhower's Chief-of-Intelligence, General Strong, issued a statement saying that only 350-400 parachutists had been dropped. No one believed it. Everyone knew the Germans were landing *en masse.*

One of the earliest biographers of General Patton has 'Old Blood and Guts' of the Third Army fighting his way through 'massed German parachutists'.* Eisenhower himself recorded, in his *Story of the War* in 1945, that 'Parties of paratroops were dropped throughout the battle area', implying they had dropped along a 500-mile front. This was, of course, quite untrue, but illustrates the confusion caused by the Baron's drop.

* *The Last Phase,* General Millis, 1946

Nervous US staff officers had already begun to react. Up at V Corps HQ in Eupen, 3,000 armoured infantrymen of the US 3rd Armored Division were placed on alert. From that same HQ a regiment of the US 1st Division was sent southwards to hunt out this great para force which had landed in their midst. Further back, all the US reinforcement depots in Liège were emptied. Clerks, cooks, drivers, everyone was being sent to the outskirts of the Belgian city to defend it against German paratroopers.

Further inland at his great sprawling HQ at Spa, General Hodges, the commander of the whole area, was receiving more and more alarmist reports. The mood of the HQ was jittery. Outside the First Army's offices in the Hotel Britannique, trucks and staff cars were already lining up as panicky staff officers began to throw personal possessions out of the windows to the orderlies below. Soon the 'big bug-out' would begin and General Hodges and his staff would flee westwards, leaving uneaten food on the mess tables and top secret maps on the walls.

Then the local mayor opened the doors of the city's jail and let out thirty Belgians accused of collaborating with the Germans, and ordered that all American and British flags which hung on the trees of the great boulevard be taken down at once. His action was typical of the attitude of the local civilians. Throughout Belgium and deep into France, the news that the Boche were returning, dropping parachutists everywhere, created panic. The flags and the pictures of Churchill, Roosevelt and de Gaulle were snatched down from windows. Parents forbade their children to talk to Allied troops. The black market between Allied soldiers and local civilians came to a sudden end. There was a repetition of the previous summer's sniping at Allied soldiers.

Four years before, the Germans had come by air. Fleets of light aircraft had landed infantry in northern France and Luxembourg, nearly managing to capture the fleeing Grand Duke and Duchess with their treasure. German gliders had landed in Belgium and the troops they contained had captured the supposedly impregnable Fort Eben-Emael outside Liège. Student's paras had conquered Holland almost by themselves. All the civilians who remembered that traumatic summer of 1940 when the West had collapsed in a mere six weeks knew that the first Germans had come by air. Now they were doing it all over again.

Despite the total failure, militarily speaking, of the Baron's paradrop, its psychological effect was tremendous, way beyond the wildest dreams of Schellenberg and the others who had planned Germany's campaign of sabotage, spying and disruption. All along the Ghost Front and deep into the hinterland, even right across the Channel into Britain, it added a new dimension to the confusion caused by the surprise counter-attack. Commanders and men began to see paratroopers stalking through the wintry fields towards them on all sides. Nervous minds played odd tricks on a man. And there was worse to come.

THREE

Surprisingly enough it was the Italians at Doonfoot in Ayrshire who first broke out. They had been burrowing for weeks through the light soil of the area and on Friday, 15 December, they decided it was time to go. During the hours of darkness between Friday and Saturday, while on the other side of the Channel the German counter-attack began, ninety-seven Italian POWs scrambled out to freedom.

Immediately the escape was discovered on that Saturday morning, a news blackout was clamped on Scotland. After what had happened in Devizes that same day, the authorities were understandably anxious. They did not want to cause public alarm by announcing that nearly a hundred Italian soldiers were roaming Scotland, which was virtually devoid of troops. Indeed the authorities were so careful that they merely asked the police to keep a lookout for 'an escaped prisoner', not informing them of the scale of the break-out.

Instead of the civil police, the authorities set the military police, who were armed, unlike the local bobbies, to look for the fugitives. All that cold snowy weekend, as more and more alarmist rumours flooded back to Britain from the fighting front on the Continent, the MPs searched Ayrshire, while local people prepared for Christmas totally unaware that ninety-seven desperate hungry men were at large in the county. As the diary writer of the *Ayrshire Post* would later comment:

> There seemed some doubt on the part of the authorities which was the more serious menace, the German counter-attack in the Ardennes or the escaped prisoners from Doonfoot.... Perhaps the break-out at Doonfoot was as serious as the break-through at Malmédy and since it was necessary not to let the German HQ know where they had got to, it was equally important not to let the prisoners know where they were.

What the diary writer did not know was that the authorities considered the Doonfoot break-out as just another part of the great counter-attack, for now POW camps throughout the country were seething with revolt, the prisoners truculent, aggressive and burning to escape. Through their illegal

95

radios they were receiving news of the battle in Belgium from Dr Goebbels' *Deutschlandfunk*. Although the 'poison dwarf' naturally exaggerated German successes — after all, he was the Minister of Propaganda — there was enough truth in his broadcasts to indicate that the Wehrmacht had shattered a whole US corps and had already driven a sixty-mile breach in the American front.

At Penkridge Camp on the main road between Stafford and Wolverhampton, as soon as the POWs' illegal radio picked up the German newscast stating that the long-awaited break-through had been achieved, discipline almost broke down. Ignoring the threats of the guards, the prisoners assembled in the compound to be addressed by the senior officers. As they saw it, the new offensive signalled a welcome change in Germany's fortunes. Those who were prepared to escape and cause trouble on the outside made their hasty last-minute preparations, based on the map that the young naval cadet Schweissmann had prepared for them. Filling their pockets with tins of corned beef and hard British Army biscuits, they were ready to go after the evening roll-call.

That evening, as the British guard was doubled and a very fierce Alsatian police dog was let loose in the compound, fog started to roll across the flat Midland countryside. It was just what the POW escapers had prayed for. One of the escapers' slipped away from the main body and, under the very noses of the guards, cut the wire in advance. After the evening roll-call the prisoners set up an unholy din. They bellowed choruses of Nazi marching songs, rattled tin plates against the sides of their wooden bunks and stamped their feet in unison. The racket was so loud and frightening that an elderly couple living just outside the perimeter wire asked the camp commandant, Colonel Davidson, to put an armed guard outside their house. Meanwhile, under cover of the din, the thirteen men who were escaping slipped through the hole in the wire and disappeared into the fog.

However, the persistent din had alerted the duty officer. The mainly 'black' camp had been unruly before, but normally the prisoners had got bored with the racket after a while. Now it went on and on. The duty officer decided to find out why. He ordered out the guard and the soldiers with the Alsatian dog entered the fogbound compound to check that the POWs were in their huts. They had to be held off at bayonet point as they attempted to hinder the search, but within the hour it was clear that thirteen prisoners had escaped. At first it was thought they had gone out through a tunnel, but none was found. Attention now focused on the perimeter wire. The Alsatian was taken to sniff the whole length of the wire, while the guards peered through the fog trying to find the gap. But it was the dog which found the hole; the escapers had been unable to cover it up in their haste. A piece of one of the escapers' clothing was held to the Alsatian's muzzle and he took the scent. Like a shot he was off into the fog with his handler, barking with the excitement of the chase. But the escapers had been expecting the dog to be let loose on their trail; they had headed for the nearest stream and waded through the freezing water for some time before getting out again. Now the dog stood on the bank as puzzled as the guards.

Back at the camp the POWs were growing ever more aggressive. All night long they stamped their boots and sang defiant Nazi songs. Dawn came grey and still fogbound. The POWs were ordered out of their huts for the usual roll-call and fatigue parties. They emerged with a new insolence, taunting the guards: 'Tommies, you will never find them! They've gone for good!'

Roll-call took twice the usual time, but the POWs calmed down to accept their breakfast. This might be their last meal for a while. Then, as soon as shovels had been issued for the coaling parties, those who drew the rationed allocation of fuel for each hut, the trouble started once more.

A Luftwaffe officer took charge of them, crying, 'Men with shovels to the front rank! Come on, we've got these Tommies on the run!'

The coaling parties pushed their way through the mob of shouting, jeering prisoners and took up their stance, shovels raised above their heads.

Completely in charge of the mob now, the Luftwaffe officer cried above the din, '*Los*! March to the gate! When I give the command, rush the guards: Let's get it over with *now*!'

But the guards, rattled as they were, were also becoming angry, especially the CSM. Company sergeant-majors, even when they are in charge of a bunch of 3-C's — the medical category which meant the man was not fit for the fighting front — always have a sense of their own dignity and power; this one was no exception. What the hell did the Jerries think they were up to, he asked himself. He was in charge here, not the squareheads.

As the Germans moved forward in military formation, with the shovel-wielders in front, all singing lustily, he yelled in that curious high-pitched, strangled tone affected by senior British NCOs, *'Halt!'*

The POWs paid no attention. They were getting very close. It would be a matter of seconds before they rushed the guards, who were hopelessly outnumbered.

The sergeant-major raised his Sten gun and clicked back the bolt. Without taking his steely gaze off the advancing Germans, he bellowed over his shoulder to the thin line of guards, some of them white-faced with fear, 'Prepare to fire'.

As one they clicked off their safety catches and raised their rifles, but only to chest height. It was obvious they were not going to fire a warning volley into the air, but directly into the POWs.

The sergeant-major, speaking very loudly and clearly so that everyone could hear him above the din, said, 'When I give the word to fire, then *fire!*'

That did it. The POWs realized that the guards really would shoot. Suddenly no one wanted to risk his life for some hare-brained escape scheme. One by one the men with the shovels lowered them, as the Luftwaffe officer who had led them abruptly looked very sheepish. The advance faltered to a stop.

The sergeant-major knew he had won. He snapped, 'Now get back to your work — or I'll put the bloody lot of you inside the cooler!'

Deflated and leaderless, the Germans shambled away, shoulders bent in defeat.

Tension had also been building up at Island Farm Camp in Bridgend, South Wales. There the 2,000 prisoners were dominated by the 'blacks', who had terrorized those they felt too luke-warm in their allegiance to National Socialism. They had beaten up even fellow officers who they suspected of informing on them to the British; for by the end of November, 1944, they had a deep tunnel in progress, through which one of the greatest break-outs of German POWs in Britain would take place.

Now, however, as the news of one German victory after another in the Ardennes came through the camp's clandestine radio, they concentrated on intimidating their guards and the local civilian population, prior to a mass escape. All night long they sang their defiant songs of hate. They howled and yelled and roared like demented creatures. The noise was like that of a foul-tempered football crowd whose team was losing and who were about to go on the rampage.

Colonel Darling, the Commandant, ordered in reinforcements and had extra Bren-gunners posted at strategic sites around the camp. The Roman Catholic chaplain, a prisoner himself, was told by the 'blacks' that they needed his chapel. It would make an ideal spot for the 'congregation' to assemble for the break-out. He refused to let them use it. Somehow he managed to inform the Commandant and the latter had him escorted to the chapel by an armed guard. He was greeted by catcalls, boos and threats. One of the 'blacks' told him, 'You'll suffer for this. The penalty for collaboration is death! You may be a priest but you'll hang just the same!'

Another POW, Otto Iskat, a fifty-year-old 'white' suspected of informing on the coming escape, was tortured and so thoroughly frightened by threats of what the 'blacks' would do to him that he died of heart failure shortly afterwards.

Well aware that something was afoot in Bridgend, Colonel Darling called in the senior local police chief, Superintendent May, to discuss a contingency plan for such an eventuality. Darling had been a prisoner-of-war himself for three years in Germany during the 1914-18 war. He had managed to escape to Holland and returned to the front to fight once more. Darling knew a great deal about tunnels and escapes. He insisted that every day two officers should sound out the floor in each hut, to check for that hollow ring indicating that the concrete had been tampered with. Others of the camp staff were ordered to be constantly on the look-out for telltale soil stains from tunnelling. But all the same there was no coordinated army-police plan for dealing with a break-out.

May suggested that he and his men would be responsible for searching and cordoning off the area within three miles' radius of the camp. This could be done without calling in the army. There was a large female population in Bridgend, brought there to work in the local munition factories, and May didn't want to alarm them by having armed troops searching the streets. Only if there was a mass break-out should the army be called in.

May did add, however, as he expressed it later in an order issued to his policemen, 'It should be recognized that the escaping prisoner has opportunities for sabotage in abundance in this division.'

Colonel Darling agreed with May's suggestion. He told the superintendent that he had good reason to fear a mass break-out for he had already found one tunnel. 'We had a tip that a tunnel had been started in a hut and they found that a slab had been cut out of the hearthstone in front of the stove. When the slab was lifted up we saw the mouth of the tunnel.'

May expressed satisfaction that the prisoners' means of exit had been found, but Darling shook his head and explained that in his experience escape tunnels always went in pairs: 'The prisoners reason that if one tunnel is discovered, the camp staff are so pleased that they do not trouble to look for another. Here in Bridgend they would be wrong. Now we have found one tunnel, we shall at once look for another.'

But on that day Colonel Darling was caught wrong-footed. Instead of waiting for the second tunnel to be completed, through which eventually over fifty POWs would escape, two of the officer prisoners freed the iron bars from the windows of their hut and fashioned them into a crude but effective wire-cutter. This they used to snip through the barbed wire and escaped down Merthyrmawr Road. Colonel Darling did not learn of their escape until they were recaptured at Port Talbot.

Now he was really worried. One tunnel had already been discovered, two POWs had escaped and, because of the unruly behaviour of their fellow prisoners at roll-call, their absence had not been discovered till they were captured miles away. And still his every instinct told him that another tunnel was being dug.

Colonel Darling was not the only man worrying about the quarter of a million POWs that week. Prisoners were on the loose from Ayrshire to the Midlands and South Wales. For the moment their numbers were small, perhaps some 130 men at the most, but trouble was seething in virtually every prisoner-of-war camp. Places like Lodge Moor, Sheffield, and Glen Mill, Oldham, were in what amounted to open revolt, with mass break-outs expected at any moment; and all the while the news from the Continent about what was now being called 'the Rundstedt Offensive' grew steadily bleaker.

Now it was learned by the War Office that the Supreme Commander had asked for the last remaining US combat division in the UK, the 66th Infantry, to be sent to the Continent at once. Eisenhower was desperate for more riflemen to bolster up his sagging front in the Ardennes and had already asked for black GIs to volunteer for duty in the infantry in an army which had been segregated since the turn of the century. The 66th Infantry would sail on Christmas Eve. At the same time the 6th Airborne would be sent to the same theatre of operations to join the corps that Montgomery was assembling to help the Americans there. That meant that the last remaining British combat division would have gone too, leaving the country totally denuded of fighting troops.

It was a situation that thoroughly alarmed the War Office. What if the tall tales of a German paratroop landing in the UK to help the escaping prisoners were true after all? Already Hitler had pulled a surprising number of aces from his sleeve in the Ardennes. What if he really did have an airborne division — there were eight of them in the German Army (compared with two in the British Army in the West and three in the US Army) — ready and waiting for a drop somewhere in the south of England? The War Office was anxious to know the extent and seriousness of the POW threat. The order went over to Colonel Scotland at the London Cage: find out what is going on. Grill the Devizes plotters until they begin to sing — and do it fast.

FOUR

By the afternoon of 18 December the Baron, now commanding some 400 men, together with a score or so wounded, plus thirty American POWs, felt that he was achieving absolutely nothing. *Obersturmführer* Etterich of the 12th SS, who had jumped with him completely untrained to be his field artillery observer, had been unable to contact the 12th's guns with his radio, so that they could bring fire to bear on the road south from Eupen. All day long heavily laden US convoys had been passing that way to the front and all he had been able to do was to ambush lone trucks and dispatch riders. Ammunition and food were running out too, and so far there had been no attempt to re-supply by air.

In the meantime the Baron felt himself threatened on all sides, with little but his few machine guns and mortars to defend himself. A whole regiment, some 3,000-men strong, of the 1st US Infantry Division was out combing the swampy fenlands of the area for him and his men. Each time the paras moved out into the open, there would be the trucks and riflemen of the 'Big Red One' waiting for them. Time and again the Baron's paras had escaped disaster by the skin of their teeth. It would be only a matter of time before the Americans, with their overwhelming strength, launched a full-scale attack and wiped him out.

By now the Americans of the 1st Division knew the Baron's real strength. All day long they had been picking up prisoners from *Kampfgruppe von der Heydte*. Lingelbach, for instance, unable to find an officer, had returned to the wounded Wiertz and, despite the other man's protests, had made a crude sledge of pine branches. Attaching a parachute harness to it, he had dragged his comrade for miles across the frozen wastes until he was captured by the *Amis,* to whom he told his story.

Another two paras had been flushed out by a battalion commander of the 1st, Lieutenant-Colonel Horner, who found that they had captured the staff of the 47th Field Hospital at the Belgian town of Waimes. The staff had included several US female nurses, under the command of Second Lieutenant Mabel Jessop, all fearful of being raped by the tough-looking Germans. Horner had put an end to that and had gained further information which led the 16th Infantry Regiment, conducting the anti-parachute drive, to conclude that the Baron had 700 men under his command.

However, a little later as the same regiment pushed into the town of Faymonville, patrols discovered Germans whom they thought were paras 'wearing American uniforms and using American equipment'. Of course these were Skorzeny's men, not the Baron's, but at the time the Americans did not know that. As the regimental history of the 16th records, 'The knowledge that everyone not personally known to us must be considered suspect had a demoralizing effect. The 16th was careful to warn its men of the possibilities of German deception. Forewarned, they were in better condition to stop any possible depredations of this sort than were those units which were caught unawares.'

Once again the Baron's purely military force of paras became confused with Skorzeny's spies, saboteurs and, as we will learn soon, potential assassins. But on the late afternoon of that Monday the Baron did not know that the confusion between his force and Skorzeny's would lead to even greater panic throughout Western Europe — and for some of his young paras a violent and unjustified death at the hands of American firing squads.

Even if he had known, the matter would have been of little concern to him, for as dusk started to fall, with the horizon flecked here and there by the cherry-red flames of bursting artillery shells, he struck lucky for the first time since he had been informed by General Student that he was to lead the paradrop. A lone US dispatch rider came roaring down the road towards the thin wire that the young paras had stretched between two trees. The American braked hard. Too late. As the machine slewed to the right, the wire caught him directly at his throat. It lifted him, his neck half-severed, right from his seat, leaving his heavily laden motorcycle to crash into the opposite ditch.

The excited paras darted forward to loot the dying dispatch rider. Most of them hadn't eaten or smoked for over twenty-four hours, their iron ration, one bar of chocolate, long gone. They rifled the man's pockets, oblivious to his cries. Death in battle was nothing new to most of them and they had become hardened and brutalized in the great slaughters of the Russian front.

A pack of Lucky Strikes was broken open and cigarettes were tossed from one man to another. The couldn't afford to waste time. The next *Ami* convoy might come down the road at any moment. They found a Hershey bar, dark bitter chocolate which was not much liked by the spoiled GIs. But to the German paras it was the height of luxury. It was broken up and swallowed greedily.

While some of them dragged the machine further into the undergrowth, others started to search the saddlebags for further loot. But there was none: no supplies of food or any of those olive-drab coloured cans of hash. All the looters found was a thick wad of papers bound in a solid folder marked 'Secret'. In disgust they prepared to throw the papers away and vanish into trees once more when a young corporal intervened. He knew the Baron could read English and the papers might just be important. They were.

102

Ten minutes later, after skimming through the first closely-typed page, the Baron realized that his paras had found the operational orders of US General Ridgway's XVIII Airborne Corps.

When the German surprise attack had begun, Ridgway had been rushed from England where he had his HQ, together with his 17th Airborne Division, to take charge of what reinforcements Eisenhower could find to stop the gap in the US VIII's front in the Ardennes. Ridgway now had under command, directly and indirectly, the 106th Infantry Division, surrounded in the hills above the Belgian village of Schoenberg; the 7th Armored Division trapped at St Vith, some ten miles from Schoenberg; the 101st Airborne Division trapped at Bastogne to the rear; with the 82nd Airborne Division somewhere in between, desperately trying to stop the SS panzers penetrating even deeper into Belgium.

So at that moment Ridgway was in charge of the two divisions holding the key network centres of St Vith and Bastogne, which the Germans needed desperately so that they could use the main roads which ran through these towns to send their armour racing westwards for the River Meuse. In addition, Ridgway was also in charge of the one US division, the 82nd Airborne, which was on the offensive, trying to bar the advance of the Sixth SS Panzer Army. On this Monday General Ridgway was the most important Allied soldier, tactically speaking, on the whole Ardennes front.

This the Baron realized almost immediately in his freezing forest hideout. If he could get Ridgway's plans back to his own forces they would prove invaluable to the German commanders, for they indicated Ridgway's moves for the next forty-eight hours. But the Baron calculated that there had to be about fifteen kilometres of enemy-held territory between his present position and the German front line. He knew, too, that the area was packed with US troops, because all day long he had seen their convoys rolling southwards to the front. In addition, there was a whole regiment of American infantry systematically attempting to seal off the high fenlands — and they were shooting first and asking questions afterwards. Anyone trying to get those documents back to the German lines would be embarking on a very risky undertaking. All the same, once in the hands of Field-Marshal Model they might well tip the balance of the whole attack in Germany's favour. Indeed, if this counter-attack succeeded, Hitler might be able to negotiate peace with the Western Allies rather than submit to unconditional surrender.

The Baron hesitated no longer. He asked for volunteers to take the documents back to the German lines. Although he had sent back six messengers to report on his activities the previous day, none of them had made it. Nevertheless, ten or twelve of his paras stepped forward, most of them from his old regiment, the Sixth.

The Baron ran his eyes along the line. None of the volunteers had slept, save for the odd catnap, in the last forty-eight hours and none had eaten more than their iron ration during that period. But all of them were prepared to take the risk of being spotted and shot out of hand by the *Amis.* At that moment he was very proud of his men.

In the end he picked two. They were very much of the same type as Koenig, now waiting to be interrogated once more by Colonel Scotland in far-off London. Both were corporals, barely out of their teens, and both possessed that ruthlessness which the Baron knew they would need if they were going to get past the *Amis.*

'Klein,' he said at last, clasping his good hand on the shoulder of a young soldier whose great height made a mockery of his name *(Klein* means 'small' in German), 'you'll go.'

Klein clicked to attention and snapped, '*Danke, Herr Oberst,*' as if it was an honour to be accepted for such a dangerous mission.

The Baron took a couple of paces towards another corporal whose chest bore the bronze *Nahkampfspange,* the close combat badge, and a black medal indicating he had already been wounded. 'Bruening,' he said, 'you'll go with him.'

Again the corporal clicked to attention and snapped, '*Danke, Herr Oberst.*'

The Baron nodded his own thanks and then told them to change their rifles for machine pistols. 'They're better for close combat work in the forest, though I'm hoping you won't have to use them. Try to circumvent opposition rather than fight it. Now this is our present position — roughly.' With the toe of his rubber-soled jumpboot he drew a line in the snow. 'Up there,' he drew another line, 'is the minor road leading to Monschau. Just south of Monschau,' he marked the spot in the snow once more, 'there are the forward positions of our own troops, holding a quiet sector of the line. Now my suggestion is that you follow that road to Monschau, but keeping within the forest all the while. Just before you start coming down from the hills above Monschau, turn off here' — another mark in the snow — 'and head for Kalterherberg. I'm sure that our people are there. If they aren't, the villagers will know the closest German position to which you can report. *Verstanden?*'

'*Jawohl, Herr Oberst,*' both men replied.

The Baron knew that the men had only a fifty-fifty chance of getting through. It was always like that in war. How many times in the past had he sent similar young men to their death, not allowing his voice to reveal the certainty of their fate?

'I shall now scribble a note for the first officer that you meet,' the Baron continued, trying to sound confident. 'I shall make it clear that he should send the documents to a higher headquarters immediately. I shall also ask that we be relieved or reinforced —'

'And what about a couple of "grub bombs", sir?' one of the Baron's younger officers interrupted. He meant the long containers used for dropping food and other supplies from the air.

The Baron allowed himself a bleak smile. 'Yes, and grub bombs, too,' he said and scribbled quickly on his note pad, while the two young volunteers stared down at the marks he had made in the snow as if they were of great significance.

A few moments later they were ready. They had exchanged their rifles for machine pistols, which they hung across their chests, and were now waiting for the Baron's order for them to leave. He took off his glove and shook each of them by the hand, muttering the old formula, *'Hals und Beinbruch'* (roughly, 'happy landings').

Minutes later the two young volunteers had vanished into the snowbound trees, heading through the forest parallel to the road to Eupen. Skirting around the town, which lay in a deep valley, they would then proceed parallel to the country road which ran from Eupen in a straight line to Monschau.

In silence the paras listened for any sound other than the regular thud of the permanent barrage at the front, where the 12th SS Division was still trying vainly to break through the American line.

Even when the noise came, as he had been expecting it would, the Baron started. There was the sound made by the *Ami* Garand rifle, followed an instant later by the high-pitched burr of the German machine pistol, the Schmeisser. Another joined in. The Baron told himself that Klein and Bruening were still together. The Garand loosed off another burst. The Schmeissers answered once more. The Baron, head cocked to the wind, thought he half heard a yell, perhaps of pain. The Schmeissers fired once more. This time there was no reply from that unknown *Ami* firing his Garand.

In the following silence the Baron strained every nerve trying to imagine what had happened. Had the two volunteers been shot? Had they surrendered? But why that last burst of machine-pistol fire after the Garand had fallen silent? Suddenly he relaxed. Somehow he knew that they had not been killed or taken. They had cleared the first hurdle successfully and were on their way. Under his breath the Baron said a quick prayer that the two young corporals would make it back to their own lines. Everything depended upon them now. Then, as the snow began to fall more heavily, he realized their own danger. The fire fight would have alarmed the other *Amis*. It wouldn't be long before they began searching this area. It was time to move on.

He rapped out a few orders. Wearily his young soldiers slung their weapons over their shoulders and slunk into the trees. Moments later they had vanished. Behind them the snowflakes filled in the marks of their passing.

2

THE MARCH ON LONDON

Nonsensical their schemes may have been, but there was no
doubting the solemn, ruthless purpose in the minds of the
men who planned the big breakaway from Devizes Camp.

Colonel Alexander Scotland

ONE

Knowing that the War Office was breathing down his neck for results,
Colonel Scotland and his senior assistant, Major Anthony Terry,
personally took over the interrogation of the Devizes plotters. The one-
time soldier in the Kaiser's Army had been dealing with Germans and
German POWs for half a century and he stood no nonsense from them. He
believed that German soldiers respected authority and Scotland radiated
authority. He always appeared to be in complete charge of the
interrogation and he never appeared surprised by what a prisoner told him.

But on this day, 19 December, with the snow falling softly into the
garden outside, the veteran interrogator could barely contain himself as
the plotters spilled the details of the great break-out. As he wrote later:

> No escape story of the Second World War was more daring in
> concept, more fantastic, more ambitious, more hopelessly
> fanatical than that of the prisoners of Devizes. It began with a
> bold master plan for a mass breakout of German POWs from
> prison camps in wartime Britain... It included an extraordinary
> project for an armed sweep by the escaping men through
> hundreds of miles of built-up England from the West Country
> to the Midlands.*

Scotland and Terry soon discovered that the Germans at Devizes had
set up what they called the 'traditional escape committee', which met in
the *Lagerführer's* office, where a good deal of the camp's duties were
carried out. Thus the presence of ten or more prisoners together did not
arouse suspicion. There the plotters had processed dozens of fellow
prisoners regarding their loyalty. Once admitted to the conspiracy, each

* *The London Cage,* Alexander Scotland, 1957.

107

prisoner was sworn to secrecy on pain of his life and was then given a specific task.

As Scotland wrote,

> It was a startling programme. At zero hour, the key men would begin a mass break-out. A selected handful of lorry drivers would proceed to the car park, commandeer the vehicles and drive at once to the arms store, where guns would be picked up. A second squad would make their way to the food stores, collect as many provisions as possible in a few minutes, then hurry to the trucks, where they would load the rations.*

Scotland knew that the War Office particularly wanted to know what the prisoners' intentions were once they had broken out. Knowing by this time that the attempted breakout at Devizes was not the only one and that German POW camps were seething with unrest throughout the country, the Top Brass were eager to find out what the Germans' strategy was — if they had one — so that they could take suitable defensive measures. In essence, where had the Devizes plotters thought they were going to go?

Soon Scotland discovered that the initial escape plan had envisaged the POWs marching north, collecting prisoners from other camps on the way. The goal was Sheffield's Lodge Moor Camp, with which the Devizes plotters were in touch. Here a similar escape would be made and then the whole force, using their stolen vehicles, would head east to the Wash. The Germans had already pinpointed a radio station in the area, which they would capture. Signallers among them would flash a message to one of Germany's North Sea ports, on the island of Texel, where there was a large German flotilla, or perhaps Emden or Cuxhaven, requesting a rescue flotilla to pick them up.

However, as the preparations for the Ardennes offensive grew closer to fruition, Schellenberg had ordered changes to the original scheme. At first he had been concerned only with causing disruption in Britain. As he became aware of the magnitude of Hitler's plans for the new secret offensive, however, he had thought he could add another and much more important dimension to the great escape. By the first week of December, he realized that if the German offensive succeeded in reaching its objective, the Allied supply port of Antwerp, Britain might well be forced onto the defensive, while the USA would have to bear the whole burden of continuing the war. For, at the same time, Hitler also intended to capture the French city of Strasbourg, which was second only to Paris as a symbol of French *gloire* and nationhood. If Strasbourg fell, more than

* Scotland, op. cit.

likely de Gaulle's Provisional Government in Paris would not survive long. London and Paris would be in an uproar.

So Schellenberg had decided that the plan would be modified. There would be a march on Sheffield. But once Lodge Moor Camp was liberated, the armed mobile column would head not for the Wash, but for London. Today we do not know whether there was to be an airborne drop north-east of London, as the prisoners claimed. But they believed it and it helped stiffen their resolution to break out.

It was, as Scotland characterized it, 'a wild plan'. But the prisoners had been in deadly earnest. After all, for young fanatics like Koenig it was their only hope: the last remaining chance, as they saw it, to save Germany from a crushing defeat. Otherwise their beloved fatherland would be sent reeling back to the eighteenth century. Most of them had heard of the US Morgenthau Plan, which proposed that German industry should be dismantled and that Germany should be 'pastoralized', allowed to possess an economy based purely on agriculture, as it had been two centuries before.

Listening over the concealed microphones as the prisoners bitterly discussed why their plan had failed, Scotland could almost sympathize with Koenig when he insisted that there must have been a traitor in Camp 23 who had betrayed their scheme. But Scotland's sympathy soon vanished. Schmidt, in a moment of bitter reproach, said that he might have unwittingly betrayed the plot when he told his interrogators at Devizes that 'with the help of our parachutists we could easily have taken London'. Koenig promptly turned on his comrade in a rage. In a flash Mertens and Joachim Goltz joined in, punching and pummelling the luckless Schmidt. Scotland sent in the guards. He needed Schmidt, and the rest of the plotters. He knew in general what the plan had been. He knew, too, where the main trouble spots were. What he did not know was the extent of the links between the various camps, or how information was passed from one to the other, as it had obviously been prior to the uncovering of the Devizes plot.

As Scotland saw things, it could not have been mere coincidence that the trouble had erupted this week at camps as diverse as the Italian one at Ayr and the German one in South Wales. Was there some kind of central control of what was going on? Was the IRA being used by the Germans to coordinate the troubles in the camps? Only two days before, guards at Glen Mill had spotted a civilian acting suspiciously on the hill above the camp. He had opened his raincoat twice to reveal a large swastika painted on his shirt, clearly visible to the POWs behind the barbed wire. Later, from his own informants inside the camp, Scotland learned that the POWs believed the 'flasher' was an emissary of the IRA who would guide them to Liverpool once they had broken out.

Later still, British rifles were found in the camp which were believed to have been smuggled in by the IRA, though that was never proved.

Scotland also asked himself why the Italians at Thirkleby POW Camp in Yorkshire, near the market town of Thirsk, were showing signs of unrest too. There were no Germans in the camp, which overlooked the A-19 between York and Newcastle, a key road north. In general, the Italians were classified as cooperative. Indeed, most of them worked on the surrounding farms, leaving the camp daily to go to work, returning tamely in the evening. Now he was receiving reports that the Italians were being awkward, complaining that they were not allowed to listen to the Italian radio, in some cases refusing to go to work. Twice knives had been found on POWs when they returned from the outside gangs. Why, suddenly, were they acting up?

All that evening Scotland pondered the problem. He could not return the Devizes plotters to their own camp. Nor could they be sent to a new one, where they would probably infect the inmates with their own rebelliousness. Besides, Scotland wanted to keep Koenig and the rest under better control until he learned what else they knew and whether they had told him the complete truth about the 'great march on London', as one of the Devizes plotters had called it. Somehow he had to get them to a secure place where they would feel free to 'sing like canaries' without any restraint.

While Scotland mulled over what he should do next, the authorities were still attempting to round up the prisoners who had escaped. For now they had come to the conclusion that Herzig's first escape from Devizes had been in the nature of a reconnaissance. Were these hundred-odd Italians and Germans running around all over the place conducting a similar reconnaissance, ready for a second and much stronger group of POWs to break out? They had to be caught — and soon.

In the area around Penkridge in the Midlands, which would have been on the route taken by the Devizes mobile column on its way to Sheffield, special efforts were made to apprehend the dozen or so German officers still at large. By now it was known that they had split up, dividing into groups of three and four. Some headed for the anonymity and shelter of the nearest cities. Two were recaptured at Wolverhampton and another two at Walsall. Two were caught heading north-west, intending to check out the airfields in the Derby area. Two more were taken en route for Derby itself, and four were surprised in the centre of the city by a police constable.

PC Richards had been curious about the four young men peering under the bonnet of a car. It looked to him as if they were about to steal it. Approaching the little group, he asked what they were doing. 'We are

Poles and we have no petrol coupons,' he was told. The speaker, in thickly accented English, explained that they had run out of petrol but wished to get to their 'base in Nottingham'. Richards, all sweetness and light, told them that he could help. He would show them a place where they could get a lift. Obediently the four German officers followed the constable; and it was only when they turned a corner and spotted the blue lantern with the word 'Police' on it that they realized they had walked into a trap. They tried to make a run for it, but they were too late. Richards grabbed and held onto two of the surprised Germans, yelling for aid to his comrades inside. The desk sergeant and other constables were out like a shot and the other two were taken in a matter of minutes.

Two were recaptured trying to get into Liverpool Docks and one, a merchant navy officer, who had insisted on escaping alone, was never recaught. Perhaps he died in the last hit-and-run raids of the war. Or perhaps he is still alive, an aged grandfather who speaks with a strange German-Scouse accent.

Further north, in Scotland, the Italians who had escaped first were also being recaptured in twos and threes. Some had only got as far as Belle Isle, Ayr's chief public park. Others got as far as Newton Mearns on the outskirts of Glasgow. One German-trained Italian paratroop captain and his sergeant-major had taken to the countryside and sneaked into a railway wagon near Dalrymple. But the wagon had broken down and was awaiting repairs. The driver of a passing train spotted them in it and reported them to the railway police. That same day they were recaptured.

By nightfall on 19 December Scotland knew that the first wave of escapers were safely back under lock and key. The imminent danger was over. Yet the news coming from the front in Belgium was very bad. The Germans had driven a great wedge through the American front to a depth of thirty miles by that evening. General Bradley's First and Third armies had been split from one another and he had lost overall control; he no longer even had radio or signal contact with his First Army (the saboteurs of Skorzeny's special outfit had cut the underground cable). Indeed, unknown to Scotland, the crisis on the Continent was even worse than that. At the Supreme Commander's Versailles HQ there had been a kind of palace revolution. Senior British officers said angrily that the American Top Brass was failing to react to the German threat. Something had to be done. They virtually demanded that Montgomery should be given the command of the US Ninth and First Armies and take over the northern 'shoulder' of the US defences in the Ardennes.

In view of the German success and the resultant Allied chaos on the Continent, the weary chief interrogator at the London Cage came to the conclusion at the end of that day that the Germans in Britain might well have other plans for sabotage and disruption up their sleeve. Their long-range groups under Skorzeny were roaming far and wide in Western Europe. Why shouldn't their activities be linked to further trouble on the part of the enemy POWs in the United Kingdom? He couldn't take the chance of being lulled into believing that the worst was over, as had Colonel Upton at Devizes when he had easily recaptured the first escapers under Herzig.

So it was decided that Rosterg, his man, would accompany the Devizes plotters to Comrie, the maximum security camp in Scotland. There virtually everyone was a 'black', and Colonel Scotland was quite sure that Koenig and the other ringleaders would talk more freely when they felt they were safe among their own kind in that remote Scottish camp.

That night in the little mess he discussed his idea with Major Anthony Terry, one day to be the foreign correspondent of the *Sunday Times*. Terry agreed with his chief. He knew from Captain Herbert Sulzbach, who had won the Iron Cross with the Kaiser's artillery in the First World War and who was now Comrie's political Intelligence Officer, that the atmosphere of the camp was 'ultra Nazi and horrible', with some of the occupants being 'little better than beasts'. There, he said, the plotters would feel free to talk about whatever other plans there were for using escaped POWs in Britain. But there was a danger, he opined.

'And what is that?' Scotland asked.

'Rosterg, sir.'

Scotland knew what he meant. If the 'blacks' discovered that Rosterg was working for him, the German NCO would not leave Comrie Camp alive.

TWO

Tension was acute in Belgium. The Germans had now broken through at half a dozen points. Everywhere the roads to the rear were clogged with soldiers and civilians fleeing westwards. It seemed nothing could stop the advancing Germans from reaching the River Meuse, their first objective, opposed, as they were, only by a scratch force of French and Belgium conscripts and hastily assembled US rearline troops, cooks, clerks, MPs, drivers and the like.

At the crossroads at the village of Aywaille, not far from the Meuse, the defenders consisted of a mixed bunch of white military policemen and black US service troops, all highly nervous for they had never been in combat or even handled a weapon since they had left basic training. According to Brigadier Essame of the British 43rd Infantry Division, they had already shot one American and two Belgians in their nervousness.

About midday on the 20th a jeep was seen approaching the roadblock they guarded. It contained three men in US uniform. It started to slow down as the white-helmeted 'Snowdrop' stepped into the road and raised his hand. The driver braked. There was an exchange of words. Then the military policeman asked for the password of the day. The driver started stuttering. The password of the day, buddy!' the MP rasped threateningly, as the blacks at the barrier roused themselves from their frozen torpor and stared at the jeep with more interest. The jeep driver blustered something about not having been given the password this morning. That was enough for the MP. Each soldier in the Liège district who was travelling that day had been given a password before leaving his outfit. The driver was clearly lying. The MP summoned the soldiers from the barrier and they began to check the papers of the three men in the jeep. They were Pfc Charles W. Lawrence, Pfc George Sensenbach and Pfc Clarence van der Werth. Nothing special about that. Now the soldiers started to examine the jeep. Almost immediately, hidden under the back seat, the pop-eyed blacks discovered a huge roll of one-hundred dollar notes, as fresh as the day they had come off the printing press — which wasn't surprising as they had been printed only the week before in one of Germany's concentration camps.

For a little while the Americans thought they had apprehended a group of deserting black-marketeers. At that time there were 20,000 US deserters in the Paris area alone, some of whom were living by hijacking whole supply trains for the black market. But soon the jeep was also found to contain two British Sten guns, two Colts, two German Walther pistols, plastic explosives, a radio transmitter, six US hand grenades and, most incriminating of all, cigarette lighters containing 'L' (for lethal) pills. What would black marketeers want with such items?

Now the smallest of the trio started to talk. His name was not George Sensenbach but Wilhelm Schmidt and he was, in reality, a corporal in the German Army. The American soldiers crowded around the little man as he explained that he and the other two had started their foray into US territory from Monschau on the 12th, four days before the offensive had begun. They had penetrated US lines, he explained, posing as members of the US 5th Armored Division. Their mission was 'to infiltrate through the Americans and report on the condition of the Meuse bridges and of the roads leading to their bridges'. This they had done, until they had been captured.

The MPs didn't wait to hear more. Racing for the field telephone, they contacted headquarters at Liège and told the officer at the other end what they had just heard. He told them that infiltrators were being reported on all sides. There must be hundreds of them behind US lines!

Half an hour later a fleet of jeeps filled with heavily armed MPs and members of the US Army intelligence staff came roaring up the road to interrogate the three Germans who now realized they were being regarded as spies — and for that the penalty was death.

It is not known now what methods were used on the three Germans to make them talk so quickly. American intelligence men were not particularly squeamish at the best of times. Higher HQ was screaming for information about the threat to their rear, so they applied the pressure; and soon the three Germans were spilling every detail of the scheme.

Schmidt had joined Skorzeny's special unit in November, 1944. At an SS camp at Friedenthal he underwent tests to assess his fluency in English. He passed the tests, but had to undergo a refresher course. 'For this purpose,' he told the interrogation team, 'I spent three weeks at prisoner-of-war camps at Limburg and Kuestrin where large numbers of American troops were held.' (From Schmidt's, statement, Scotland concluded later that the Germans had become past masters at infiltrating their own men into POW camps on both sides of the Channel.) Afterwards, Schmidt explained, he was posted to Grafenwöhr where he was placed in a special unit. 'Here our training consisted of studying the organization of the American army, identification of American insignia, American drill and linguistic exercises.' Now Schmidt really had his US interrogators sitting on the edge of their seats, for he told them how engineers of his group had the task of 'destroying headquarters and headquarters personnel'.

'What headquarters and what personnel?' he was asked.

Schmidt then passed on rumours which had been circulating in Grafenwöhr camp while he had been there and which he believed. He told the Americans that men of his unit disguised as POWs, with their comrades dressed as US soldiers guarding them, would dash across France and liberate the trapped German garrison at the port of Lorient; this would be the start of break-out attempts from St Nazaire, Dunkirk and many other places still in German hands. Another column would roll in from Holland in 'captured' Tiger tanks being brought back for British ordnance to inspect; in fact the tanks were to break through to Montgomery's Dutch HQ and assassinate him. A third group of agents would rendezvous in Paris's Café de la Paix for another assassination job.

'To k-kill...' Schmidt stuttered here, but he was determined to tell all if it would save his skin (it didn't), 'to kill General Eisenhower.'

Eisenhower! One can imagine the Americans' reaction to this revelation. They knew all about Skorzeny; now here was one of his men who was obviously a hired killer — why else the weapons and the suicide pills? — confessing all. Ike had to be warned at once!

The Baron's paradrop in the Ardennes, the attempted break-outs over in Britain and now one of Skorzeny's men revealing that plans were under way to kill both Montgomery and Eisenhower, the Western Alliance's leading military men, triggered off a flap which went right to the top at Eisenhower's own Supreme Headquarters at Versailles.

Colonel Gordon Sheen, Eisenhower's counter-intelligence chief, decided at once that Corporal Schmidt's story could not be ignored. He commanded that Eisenhower should be accompanied forthwith by a constant escort of armed MPs, with a Sherman tank to the front of any vehicle he used and another one to his rear. Even when he went across to the mess-hall this escort must always accompany him. Sheen reasoned that the Germans knew the set-up at Petit Trianon perfectly; after all it had been Field-Marshal von Rundstedt's own headquarters for nearly four years before he had had to flee the advancing Americans. At the same time Colonel Baldwin B. Smith, who was regarded as a perfect double of Eisenhower, was abruptly promoted to five-star general and doubled for Ike until after Christmas.

Thus it was that from 20 to 26 December, while a desperate battle raged at the front involving nearly three million soldiers, Eisenhower was a prisoner in his own headquarters, cut off from the decision-making process. As Eisenhower's shrewd secretary-mistress, Kay Summersby, recorded:

> Security officers immediately turned headquarters compound into a virtual fortress. Barbed wire appeared. Several tanks moved in. The normal guard was doubled, trebled, quadrupled. The pass system became a matter of life and death instead of the old formality. The sound of a car exhaust was enough to halt work in every office, to start a flurry of telephone calls to our office to inquire if the boss was all right. The atmosphere was worse than that of a combat headquarters up at the front, where everyone knows how to take such a situation in their stride.*

Brigadier Strong, Eisenhower's Scottish Chief of Intelligence, protested that Sheen was going too far. He was overruled. Eisenhower was to be guarded at all times by MPs carrying sub-machine guns. Once, fretting under the restrictions, he stamped out of his office, mumbling angrily to

* *Eisenhower was my Boss,* Kay Summersby, 1948

Kay Summersby, 'Hell's fire, I'm going for a walk. If anyone wants to shoot me, he can go right ahead. I've got to get out.'

Kay herself fell prey to nerves and insomnia. 'I lay awake for hours envisioning death and worse at the hands of SS agents. Sleep was impossible with the tramp, tramp, tramp of heavy-booted guards patrolling the tin roof.'

Captain Harry S. Butcher, a former vice-president of CBS, the radio network, now a kind of personal public relations man for Eisenhower, was allowed to visit the imprisoned Supreme Commander and told him of how he had been stopped by roadblocks everywhere on his return from the front. He found Eisenhower thoroughly irritable about the situation and pathetically grateful to see someone 'from the outside world'. A genial man, on informal terms with the Supreme Commander, Butcher joked with his boss just before he left: 'Now you know how it must feel to be President and always under the watchful eye of the Secret Service.'*

One wonders if, eight years later when he *was* elected President of the United States, Eisenhower remembered that quip and the circumstances under which it was made.

Now the scare had reached Paris itself. A rigorous curfew was imposed and the capital was put out of bounds for US servicemen on leave. Suddenly 'Pig Alley' (Place Pigalle) was deserted of its lounging GIs and French tarts in their little rabbit-fur jackets and cork-heeled wedge shoes. The only Americans seen in the capital's streets now were grim-faced security men on duty, searching for Skorzeny's killers.

Hemingway left his 'headquarters' at the Ritz in a hurry, telling his girlfriend (and future wife) Mary Walsh, 'They're slaughtering our boys at the front' and advising her to 'burn my papers' at once. Why he thought the 'Nazi killers' would be after his papers he never explained. General Hughes, Eisenhower's 'eyes and ears', who did a lot of private snooping for the Supreme Commander, couldn't even get into his hotel. Twice he was ejected by security guards. Another US general, the jug-eared, bear-like Robert M. Littlejohn, returned to his hotel to find it swarming with sentries carrying fixed bayonets, who hampered his every move. In despair, he turned to one of his staff officers and cried, 'Let's do away with 'em [the sentries]. If any Germans come, just send 'em to me.' He clenched his big fists. '*I'll* take care of 'em!'

Littlejohn was one of the few in authority who did not take the German threat — in whatever form it came: killers, saboteurs, parachutists, escaped POWs, etc. — seriously. Everyone else did. The whole of Western Europe was awash with rumours and half-truths. For the first

* *Three Years with Eisenhower,* Harry Butcher, 1946

time in years, people in the Allied countries were tuning into German radio stations for the 'truth', because in his first guilty panic at being caught completely by surprise, Eisenhower had ordered a total news blackout for the first forty-eight hours of the new German offensive.

Spies, saboteurs and suspected killers were spotted everywhere. Hundreds of innocent American soldiers were arrested by their own people because they couldn't answer questions like 'Who's dem bums?' and 'Who's the dame with the million-dollar legs?' And it wasn't just ordinary GIs.

Big, bluff General Bruce Clarke, currently conducting a last-ditch defence of St Vith, was arrested by his own MPs. Over and over again he insisted, 'But I'm General Clarke of the CCB' (Combat Command B).

'Like hell,' the MPs scoffed. 'You're one of the Skorzeny men. We were told to watch out for a Kraut posing as a one-star general.'

The MPs kept their furious General under arrest for five hours while the battle raged outside. In the end, when they did release him, one of them had the audacity to ask for an autograph — and Clarke was so nonplussed that he gave him it.

Clarke's senior officer, General Bradley, was also stopped. As he recorded later:

> Three times I was ordered to prove my identity by cautious GIs. The first time by identifying Springfield as the capital of Illinois (my questioner held out for Chicago); by locating the guard between the centre and the tackle on a line of scrimmage; the third time by naming the current spouse of Betty Grable. Grable stopped me, but the sentry did not. Pleased at having stumped me he nevertheless passed me on.

Thereafter Bradley ceased wearing the three stars of a lieutenant-general to which he was entitled.

Montgomery was amused by the whole business. Habitually he rode around in his Humber staff car, its bonnet flying a large Union Jack, and protected by a sole motorcyclist as his escort. But when the US Ninth Army came under his command and he started to be stopped at crossroads by soldiers of this Army, he grew annoyed. He asked General Simpson, the Ninth's commander, for an American ID card so that he could get on with his 'business of running the war'.

But Montgomery's own Second Army up in Holland was not free from the great scare either. US officers who tried to visit their girlfriends in Maastricht for Christmas were arrested by the British as Skorzeny's men and spent the festive season behind bars.

Future writer Alexander McKee, then a corporal serving with the Canadian Army HQ at Tilburg, recorded in his diary, 'Two German officers were caught in the town square, dressed as Canadians but with their gaiters the wrong way round.' A little later he recorded that a whole battalion of German parachute troops had been dropped outside Tilburg, which was manifestly untrue. 'None penetrated to the centre of Tilburg,' he noted in his diary. 'However, five German paratroops were picked up in the centre — three dressed as clergy, two in British uniform.'

Later a young Dutch journalist, picked up in the great flap and later released, told him confidentially that he had been held in a guardroom along with eight German parachutists, 'Two in regulation parachutist uniform, the rest in British uniform or civilian clothes. The two in German uniform were wreathed in smiles and telling the others of the sticky end awaiting them, while *they* were safely out of the war.'

As General Bradley summed it all up after the war, 'A half a million GIs played cat and mouse with each other each time they met on the road. Neither rank nor credentials spared the traveler an inquisition at each intersection he passed.'

Three separate operations involving only a few thousand men, the Baron's paradrop, Skorzeny's infiltrators, and the planned POW break-out, were paying enormous dividends in what today would be called psychological warfare. The British-run *Soldatensender Calais,* a supposed German radio station beamed at German soldiers in the West, reported that more than 250 of Skorzeny's men had been captured. In fact only Corporal Schmidt's three-man jeep team had been caught. Radio Nice announced that a local bank had been looted by Skorzeny's men, 400 miles away from the scene of the fighting. The London *Daily Telegraph* informed its readers, in all seriousness, that Skorzeny had had specially trained women agents dropped over Paris, where they were to seduce American soldiers. Once they had revealed all they were to be dispatched by a handy little dagger, which every German Mata Hari carried in her handbag.

The American Forces newspaper, *Stars and Stripes,* reported under the headline 'Acid-Throwing Nazi Chutists Hunt High-Ranking US Chiefs' that the 'chutists carried 'small phials of sulphuric acid which fit into matchboxes and can be thrown into the faces of anyone who tries to intercept them'. These acid-throwing German paras, according to *Stars and Stripes,* were dressed in uniforms 'from captured US officers and men who were forced to strip to their underwear and then shot'.

Rumour after rumour.

Yet beneath the rumours, the half-truths and the 'educated guesses' by armchair pundits as to the objective of these Nazi special operations was a simple military necessity: the winning of that vital battle in the Ardennes, upon which Germany's whole future depended. In particular, the Baron knew that if Klein and Bruening succeeded in reaching their own lines with the XVIII Corps plans, all the suffering and the effort would have been worthwhile. In the hands of the High Command those plans might well enable Germany to win.

THREE

The Americans of the 'Big Red One' shot Klein on the afternoon of Wednesday, 20 December. By now the men searching for German parachutists were nervous and trigger-happy. They were also angry. They had heard that a large number of American prisoners had been shot in cold blood at a place called Baugnez, above the Belgian town of Malmédy, only a dozen or so miles away from where they were now.* An unofficial order had gone out: don't take German parachutists or SS men prisoner.

Thus it was that when Klein, in the lead, emerged from the frozen undergrowth that grey afternoon, with the guns rumbling in the distance where the 12th SS were still trying to break through, he was met with a hail of fire. He was virtually at the end of his tether. He had not eaten all day and he was exhausted from his attempts to break out of the *Ami* ring. Dropping his machine pistol, he raised his hands. 'Comrade...' he said. It was the only English word he knew. But the Americans of the 'Big Red One' were too angry this afternoon to hear a plea for mercy. Besides, Klein was wearing a khaki US field jacket, taken from one of the prisoners that the *Kampfgruppe* had been holding. In American eyes that made him a spy or terrorist disguised in US uniform. The four riflemen took more careful aim, as if they were members of a firing squad. Four M-Is opened up as one. Klein was lifted off his feet and slammed against the nearest tree. He was dead before he hit the ground.

Bruening, still concealed by the undergrowth, had seen it all. A few paces behind Klein, he had thrown himself flat when the Americans opened fire. He saw them slaughter his comrade in cold blood. And still they were spraying the area with fire. Slugs ripped through the pines, chipping the bark and gouging white scars on the tree trunks, as he cowered there, hands clasped around his helmet.

* This incident, involving the 1st SS Panzer Division and an American Field Artillery Observation Battery, later became known as 'The Malmédy massacre'. See Kessler, *SS Peiper* (Leo Cooper Ltd) for details.

Slowly the firing died away. He heard the *Amis* insert fresh clips into their magazines. Someone said something in English, which he did not understand. Another voice replied in an angry tone. Then he heard footsteps, boots cracking on icy puddles. One of the *Amis* was obviously coming to inspect Klein's body. Cautiously Bruening raised his head and peered through the frozen undergrowth. He was right. An American soldier, his rifle held at the half-port across his chest, was advancing slowly to where Klein lay slumped in a pool of blood. He turned Klein over slowly with the tip of one boot. Klein stared sightless at the sky. The American, relaxing his guard, bent and started searching the body while the others rose from their ditch and began lighting cigarettes. Suddenly the cold air was flooded with the tantalizing odour of good tobacco.

As Bruening breathed it in greedily, his fear changed to a sudden rage. They had everything, the *Amis*: good cigarettes, good food, good clothing.

Kneeling by the body, the American had now found the Baron's leather map pouch which contained the vital documents. The Baron had given Klein the pouch in which to carry the XVIII Corps order. Bruening wondered how long it would take the Americans to register the importance of its contents.

Slowly, very slowly, anger pumping adrenalin into his bloodstream, Bruening clicked off the safety catch on the machine pistol. Then he wriggled forward cautiously. He wanted to be in good range of the four *Amis*. He dared not miss. If he did, they would deal with him just as they had with poor old Klein. Carefully, hardly making a sound, he worked his way to the right and slightly behind the Americans. The three of them would not be able to see him even if they did turn round, but the one bending over Klein's dead body almost certainly could, for he was standing on a slight rise. He would be the one who would die first.

Now the American had dropped the pouch for a moment. The papers it contained obviously didn't interest him. Something else did. He had spotted Klein's engagement ring. Klein had only worn it for a few days, but he had been very proud of it, boring the others with the details of how he had obtained it on the black market, because he didn't want one of the cheap nine-carat ones which was all the law approved of in war-time. It was obvious that Klein's proudest possession was destined for the *Ami's* pocket.

But there seemed to be some difficulty. Tug as he might, the *Ami* couldn't get it off Klein's finger. Now he drew out a trench knife from the scabbard attached to his boot. Bruening clenched his jaw angrily. The Yankee swine was going to cut Klein's finger off to get the ring. What a way to treat a dead man!

Bruening judged himself within range. He glanced to left and right.

The wooded marshland was empty. It was just him and the four *Amis*. He bit his bottom lip and said a quick prayer that the Schmeisser machine pistol wouldn't jam. He had not had a chance to clean it for days. Carefully controlling his breathing as he had been taught, he took aim, crooking his finger around the trigger till the knuckle whitened.

The American was sawing away at Klein's ring finger. Bruening could distinctly hear the rasp of knife on bone. It increased his rage and sense of disgust. Men like that deserved to die without mercy. He pressed the trigger. The first burst caught the American right in the back. A series of holes ran the length of his spine. He pitched forward with a muffled grunt and slumped over Klein's body, dead.

Bruening spun round. The other three Americans were grabbing at their weapons, frantically trying to unsling them. Too late. Bruening didn't give them a chance. Firing from the hip, swaying slightly from right to left, he hosed them down. They reeled backwards, clutching their shattered limbs.

Panting hard, Bruening was dimly aware of the click and the sudden end to the pounding of the machine pistol at his side. The magazine was empty. He ripped another from the leather pouch and fitted it into place with fingers that felt numb and clumsy. But there was no need for it. The three *Amis* lay sprawled out on the ground, either dead or badly wounded — he didn't care which.

Bruening spun round. There was no sound save that of the heavy guns in the distance. He was alone. There were no other *Amis* popping out of their holes and it was beginning to snow again. Visibility was falling rapidly. It was just what he needed. The *Amis* didn't like snow. They would stick even closer to the shelter of their ditches and foxholes now.

Still clutching the reloaded Schmeisser, he advanced on the Americans lying in the snow. First he picked up the pouch with the US orders and slung it over his back. As an afterthought he took off his glove and closed Klein's eyelids. He looked at the ring on the half-severed finger and told himself that he should take it. Perhaps someone could find a way of sending it back to the dead man's fiancee. But he couldn't bring himself to cut any further into the finger to get it. Instead, he looted the bodies of the Americans. He found a chocolate bar, some packs of cigarettes and, on the one he had killed first, a packet of contraceptives. Taking one last look at Klein, whose body was already covered with a thin mantle of snow, he set off again, heading towards the sound of the guns, allowing himself one small piece of chocolate as he slogged through the snow. Minutes later the snowstorm had swallowed him up.

Bruening changed his plan. The Baron had suggested they should follow the minor road which led from Eupen to Monschau and from there to the nearest German post. But all day they had been trying to get out of the forest in that direction and each time they emerged they had bumped into American positions. Now the death of Klein had convinced him to head towards the sound of the guns, which he judged was coming from the general area of the Belgian border villages of Büllingen and Bütgenbach. Here the population, he knew, was German-speaking and friendly — indeed, the two villages had been German up to 1919. If the *Amis* were in occupation of the villages, the natives would help him and show him the quickest way to his own lines. More importantly, up there the Americans would be more concerned with what was happening to their front and not to their rear. He was sure he could sneak through their positions and into the villages themselves. At least up there at the front he'd have a fighting chance of getting out; here in the forest, surrounded by a whole regiment of *Amis,* he had none.

Bruening was right about the Americans up at Büllingen and Bütgenbach being concerned about what was happening to their front. Back on the 17th the 'Big Red One' had been rushed to the area to support what was left of the battered 99th and 2nd US Infantry Divisions. By that time the Sixth SS Panzer Army had already taken Büllingen and were rolling down the ridgetop road towards Bütgenbach, the next town in the line of advance, just as the first elements of the 1st Division drove into the place.

For twenty-four hours the enemy had probed the 1st Division's defences in the Bütgenbach area. Then, on the morning of the 19th, the SS had launched a full-scale attack on the place. Twenty truckloads of infantry, plus several dozen German tanks, assaulted the Americans dug in in the fields around Bütgenbach. For four hours an intensive battle raged. It was the start of a conflict that would go on around and in the town for four days. Only then did the tide finally turn in the Americans' favour.

On the morning of the 20th, the day Bruening set off to reach the German lines, the Panthers of the 12th SS had penetrated Bütgenbach and had reached the command post of the Big Red One's 2nd Infantry Battalion. The CP had also been used as a field hospital. It had been abandoned in a hurry, with the army nurses leaving even their underclothes behind in their panic. Naturally the GIs defending the CP had looted the women's lingerie and the German panzer grenadiers who later overran their foxholes found dead *Amis* wearing bras and petticoats. The SS men didn't know what to make of it.

But they didn't have much time to ponder the matter. Lieutenant-Colonel Derrill Daniel, commanding the 2nd Battalion, signalled the divisional artillery asking for 'all the fire you can throw in the backyard'.

The artillery replied: 'We've been firing all we've got like crazy now for three hours. What in hell goes on down there?' Still, they directed the fire as requested. For another hour a ding-dong battle went on in and around the CP until Daniel sent the laconic message to divisional HQ, 'Attack repulsed. Send litters'.

For the time being the danger had been averted. Thus it was that as a weary Bruening plodded stolidly through knee-deep snow, the wind lashing his face with snow, the guns to his front went silent for a while. Of course, he had no knowledge of why they had gone silent, but he guessed that one side or the other had stopped an attack which had failed.

But Bütgenbach had now become a key objective for the Sixth SS Panzer Army, just as it was for the Americans. Indeed, on that same afternoon as Bruening plodded ever closer to the embattled Belgian town, Eisenhower, imprisoned in his Versailles HQ, called General Bradley in Luxembourg and questioned him about the vulnerability of the sector, which barred the way to Liège and the River Meuse.

Bradley, with perhaps more confidence than he felt, answered, 'The Krauts can't break through.' He chuckled. 'I've got the First Division there.'

Bradley might have had the 'Big Red One', the USA's premier infantry division, in place, but the tough young commanders of the 12th SS *Hitlerjugend* were determined to break through to Bütgenbach at last. *Standartenführer* Hugo Kras, the Divisional Commander, had been ordered personally by Dietrich to ensure that the 12th SS broke through on the following morning. The whole armoured thrust of the Sixth SS Panzer Army depended upon the capture of Bütgenbach on the morrow. As the hard-faced Kras, a veteran of the Russian front, told his staff that evening, '*Meine Herren, es ist marschieren oder krepieren*' (Gentlemen, it is march or croak).

He was right. 'March or croak' applied to everyone involved in this last great German offensive in the West. It applied to the Baron, still hiding in the swampy forest around Mont Rigi with his remaining 300 men. A new officer had just joined him, a Lieutenant Kayser, who urged him to try one last attack on the American convoys rolling south. The Baron shook his head. Attack with 300 men and no heavy weapons? Impossible!

That day they had received the first sign that they had not been altogether forgotten in these snowy wastes. A lone Junkers 52 had appeared and dropped a 'food bomb'. But it was a disappointment. Instead of the food that the weary exhausted paras had expected, they found bottles of cheap German rotgut, masquerading as *Kognak*, and some damp cigarettes.

This discovery had taken the heart out of them. Even Kayser no longer spoke of attack. Now the Baron had to make up his mind. Would they attempt to stick it out up here, although they were achieving nothing and losing men daily? Or should they try to make their way back to their own lines?

'March or croak' applied to Koenig and his comrades too, making their long train journey northwards from King's Cross to Comrie in Scotland. Angry that the great plot had been discovered, Koenig knew he must find the traitor and eliminate him. He was sure that he was among the men with him in the sealed-off, blacked-out LNER coach. That traitor had to be dealt with before he betrayed any more of their secrets. For the mass break-out of German POWs in Britain was not over yet. Time and time again the young ensign went over the events of the last few weeks, trying to think who could have betrayed them. In the corner, head resting on his pack, Sergeant Rosterg snored happily like a man who hadn't a care in the world.

Above all 'march or croak' applied to Corporal Bruening. As dusk fell that Wednesday the young para was perhaps the most important member of all the plotters, spies, saboteurs and would-be escapers. If he succeeded in reaching German lines on the morrow, the whole course of the offensive would be changed. But if he failed, all their efforts and self-sacrifice would have been in vain.

FOUR

The 12th SS Division attacked at dawn. Under the cover of a heavy snowfall, which muffled the noise of their tanks, they advanced on Bütgenbach from the south. Two companies of the defenders were caught completely by surprise. A platoon was overrun and then another. By nine that morning the SS had succeeded in doing what they had been trying to for the last four days: they had opened a gap nearly half a mile wide. Through it ran the vital road via Waimes to Malmédy. If they could maintain this gap, Dietrich could at last send his stalled armour to race for the River Meuse.

Colonel Jeff Seitz, who commanded the 26th Regiment of the 'Big Red One' which was defending the area, despaired when he heard the news. His three battalions had all suffered heavy casualties in a hundred hours of battle. He had no reserves left. There was only one thing to do; he had to plug the gap somehow with what he had at hand.

He called Lieutenant-Colonel Rippert, commanding his 2nd Battalion, in whose area the SS had broken through. 'Jack', he asked, 'how is it down there?'

'Bad, very bad, Colonel,' Rippert replied. 'We've got a gap 800 yards wide and, as far as we know, the Jerries are lousing up the whole countryside. Last report has 'em in the town between our two CPs. I've just sent out tanks to work on 'em.'

'Well, keep at it,' Colonel Seitz said, 'I'm having to pull your B Company and send them around to attack through the gap. Company A will have to fan out as well and attack as best they can. Jerry wants that road. I've got a battalion of the 18th coming down but we've got to hold on till they get here.'

Putting down the field phone, Rippert called his A Company commander, Lieutenant Charles Robertson, a tall young officer who wouldn't survive in combat much longer. Ripper told him what he was supposed to do and urged the young officer: 'Do your best, Robbie. We can't let 'em get that road.'

Robertson nodded his understanding. 'I'll work back and then around and out from my left flank. But I'll need some men to fill up the right flank.'

'God knows where they're coming from,' Rippert said. 'But we'll send what we can.'

This was the situation when a half-frozen Bruening, his eyelashes and beard white with snow, breasted a rise and saw the village of Bütgenbach below. The snow was beginning to stop and the battlefield was stretched out like a sand table, dotted with tiny black figures like lead soldiers. Bruening studied the scene. He could make out the German attack easily. He recognized the shape of the SS's Panther tanks as they tried to edge their way past Lieutenant Robertson's position. Unfortunately, the Americans had set up some anti-tank guns parallel to the road at a range of about one hundred metres; they were knocking out the Panthers one by one. Behind the wrecked tanks, the supporting infantry stalled, not wanting to risk challenging the entrenched *Amis* without the cover of their armour.

Bruening wiped the snow off his face and considered what he should do. He could, of course, make a detour around the village and try to reach the German lines further back. But he did not think he had the strength to go much further. He hadn't eaten for twenty-four hours, apart from the chocolate bar he had stolen from the dead *Ami*. Besides, the Baron had impressed on him the vital importance of getting the US orders to a German officer as soon as possible. So he had to get into Bütgenbach and contact the 12th SS. But how? He hadn't come all this way to be shot at the last, and, in the confused fighting he saw below, he was as likely to be shot by his own people as by the *Amis*.

For about half an hour he squatted there, as the snowstorm passed and the sun came out. The scene could have come straight from a Christmas card, but not for long. Soon the American artillery zeroed in on the places where the Germans had gone to ground after the destruction of their armour. Every second came the boom of a heavy gun being fired somewhere to Bruening's rear, followed an instant later by a shell screeching over his head. With frightening regularity, the shells crumped down on the trapped Germans, erupting in a thick black mushroom of whirling debris and earth.

Bruening realized that, dangerous though the *Ami* barrage was, it did present a kind of cover. As a frontline soldier he knew that during an artillery bombardment both sides usually took cover. Combat infantry knew from bitter experience just how often 'shorts' landed among them. As long as the guns fired, therefore, from whatever side, both friend and foe would keep their heads down and nobody would be looking out for someone like Bruening trying to sneak through the lines. So he started to climb down the ridge overlooking Bütgenbach.

Then the salvoes ceased for a while and he took shelter by the side of a barn. He had an eerie feeling that someone was watching him, that he was about to feel a slug bursting into his body. But no bullet came and he tried to control his imagination.

He crept past a wrecked Panther and recognized the twin skeleton keys of its insignia. It belonged to the SS's 501st Heavy Tank Company. He was coming to the German lines all right. He was getting there.

Another salvo screamed overhead. Bruening flung himself into a shell crater. It was occupied — by two dead Americans. They didn't have a mark on them. Both had been killed by blast. Now they crouched there over their weapons, eyes wide open as if they were very much alive. Bruening rifled the dead men's pockets and found a chocolate bar, which he wolfed down, followed by a quick swig from a water bottle.

He waited a while, savouring the chocolate and trying to work out how far he now was from the first German positions. His guess was about a hundred to a hundred and fifty metres. The way the shells were falling indicated that. Another three or four bounds and he would make it.

The salvo ceased and he was up again, running in a wild zig-zag to the next hole. A moment later another salvo crashed down on the field, churning up the soil yet again.

Then there was a lull in the bombardment. Back over the ridge where the divisional artillery was sited, German infiltrators had crept close to the pits in which the big 105mms were located and were sniping at their crews, forcing them to keep their heads down. For it was almost certain death for the loaders to go back to the dumps for fresh shells. Now while

126

the frustrated gunners waited for the infantry to come up and winkle out the German snipers, who in their 'spook suits' merged perfectly with the fresh snow, the guns ceased firing for a while.

Both sides took advantage of the lull. Charles Robertson and what was left of his A Company fanned out to the rear of the German attackers and linked-up with the battalion's K Company. For their part, the 12th SS sent in more Panthers and assault guns.

Bruening's heart leapt. All he had to do now was to crouch in his hole and wait for the SS to overrun the crater. He need not risk his neck any longer out in the open. But the Americans had other ideas. Suddenly the leading Panther came to an abrupt halt. For one moment nothing happened. Then a great blowtorch of flame ran the length of its deck, making the paint bubble and pop.

The Americans had brought up the last two remaining 90mm tank destroyers. Their guns were the only ones capable of destroying a Panther at extreme range. Their gunners working furiously, the two TDs poured a hail of fire on the advancing Germans. They knew that once the German tanks reached the US infantry, that would be that. The Panthers would roll over their foxholes, crushing them to death, or they would swirl round and round, filling the hole with lethal carbon monoxide gas, choking the poor unfortunates below to death.

Again the steam started to go out of the German attack. Coming on behind the tanks, the SS panzer grenadiers began to falter. Red-faced NCOs bellowed angry orders at their teenage infantry, urging them to keep going.

Bruening groaned. He knew all the signs. He had seen them often enough in attacks in Russia. It would only be a matter of moments before the young soldiers started to go to ground. He wasn't going to be overrun after all.

The great 90mm cannon cracked again. A shell shrieked across the field. Another Panther rocked to a halt. Flames started erupted from its shattered engine. The crew baled out, one of them already on fire. He staggered a few paces, then dropped to his knees in the snow, still burning.

That did it. The panzer grenadiers fell to the ground. Here and there they made some show of firing at the US positions, a hundred metres or so away, but most of them simply burrowed into the snow as deep as they could. But not all of them. Peering over the edge of his own crater, trying to make out what was happening, Bruening could just make out two shadowy figures working their way through the dead ground towards the stationary *Ami* tank destroyers.

Bruening narrowed his gaze and tried to make out what the two stealthy figures were carrying as they crept ever closer to the TDs. Then he recognized the pole-like weapon as the single-shot German missile-launcher — the *Panzerfaust*. It was a powerful piece of armament, much superior to the US bazooka, but the man who fired it had to get within fifty metres of his target to ensure that it knocked out the tank. This meant that the two men, whoever they were, would have to pass somewhere near where Bruening was hiding. Then he made a decision which was to change the whole course of his life, and indirectly that of the Battle of the Bulge. He decided that when the two men with the *Panzerfaust* came level with him, he would spring out of his crater and support them in their attack on the *Ami* TDs. Once that was achieved, they could pull back together and he would be saved at last. But it wasn't to be. Bruening watched as the two men came closer and closer. They seemed to bear a charmed life. Twice bursts of tracer hissed through the smoke in their direction; twice the tracer missed. Mortar bombs came whirling down, erupting in shards of metal. But again the two SS men came through unscathed.

Bruening tapped the magazine of his machine pistol to check if it was in place correctly. He took a deep breath. It was now or never. With a grunt, he levered himself out of the hole and stood there, machine pistol clutched close to his hip. '*Kumpels,*' he cried above the snap of the small arms fire and the thump of the big US cannon, '*Ich mache mit —*' (Mates, I'm with you).

The words ended in a shrill cry of pain as the salvo of bullets ripped into his stomach, whirling him round with the force of their impact. He had not seen the third man armed with a machine pistol who had been covering the other two from the right. He had taken Bruening, springing up from his hole like that in his rimless helmet instead of the usual German coal-scuttle type, for an American. The German had fired instinctively.

Bruening found all this out later, when they pieced the story of his little odyssey together in a series of US military hospitals, both on the Continent and in the USA, over the year it took him to recover from his severe wounds. But by then it would no longer matter. The battle had been long lost and Ernst Bruening would know that in a defeated Germany there was no future for him, the young man who had so nearly changed the whole course of the Battle of the Bulge.*

---

* Bruening was moved from the first US camp he was sent to, Camp Trinidad, when it was closed in 1946, to Camp Carson in Colorado Springs. Here he fell in love with a local girl. Because marriage between an enemy alien and an American citizen was forbidden, he escaped to Mexico, returning to the USA in 1950 or thereabouts, married his girlfriend, then dropped out of sight.

3

MURDER

Such a man as Rosterg represented an infinite danger to the fatherland. He deserved to die.

SS Sergeant Brueling at his trial, August, 1945

ONE

Predictably the murders started at Comrie in Perthshire. POW Camp Number 21, as the prison was named, just outside the remote Scottish village, was totally dominated by the 'blacks'. Anyone who harboured defeatist or anti-Nazi views at that place kept them strictly to himself, if he did not want to risk a beating or worse. Captain Herbert Sulzbach, one-time Prussian artilleryman and now the camp's political intelligence officer, hated the place and most of the prisoners too.

Now, with their comrades in the Ardennes failing to make the decisive breakthrough which would take them to the Meuse and then on to Antwerp, their mood was sombre and angry. But any attempt on the part of the camp's few 'greys' to hint that it was good thing — the quicker the war was over, the sooner they would go home — was met by open threats and sometimes by blows. The 'black' majority was not prepared to admit, even to themselves, that Germany had already lost the war.

Three days before Christmas the Devizes plotters arrived at Camp 21 and were immediately welcomed as heroes. Already the 'blacks' at Comrie knew from the inter-camp grapevine what the Devizes plotters had intended to do and wanted to hear full details of the planned march on London. But one of the men sent north to Comrie by Colonel Scotland fell foul of the 'blacks' there right from the start.

He was *Feldwebel* Rosterg who, it was later admitted unofficially, should never have been sent there in the first place. Perhaps feeling that he would be protected at Comrie by the long arm of Colonel Scotland, Rosterg seemed to go out of his way to provoke the 'blacks'. Once, for instance, they caught him reading the *Lagerpost,* the camps' newspaper which was produced by the British with German helpers. One of the 'blacks' told him: 'We have a rule here forbidding prisoners to read it. It is merely full of enemy propaganda.'

Rosterg thrust out his chin, making it clear he was not afraid of the 'black' or any of his kind for that matter, and said, '*Schon gut,* but I shall read it. What's more, I'll read the English newspapers if I get a chance.' Deliberately, it seemed, Rosterg was hammering another nail in his coffin.

On another occasion Rosterg told his fellow prisoners in Hut Four that the Ardennes offensive was a failure. It would only cause the death of more German boys. 'The war is lost,' he proclaimed defiantly. 'The man who thought up this plan' — he meant the Ardennes offensive — 'is a lunatic'

No one took up the unspoken challenge. They knew that Rosterg was a handy man with his fists and did not hesitate to use them. Besides, Comrie Camp was guarded by Polish auxiliaries, who hated the German POWs with a passion. The Poles would welcome a chance to get at the Germans.

As the hatred of Rosterg grew, fuelled by the belief on the part of Koenig and the other key plotters from Devizes that it was Rosterg who had betrayed them, the 'blacks' realized that their only chance of taking their revenge on him was during the hours of darkness and by mob violence. Their philosophy was that of the lynch mob: If everyone participates, if everyone has bloodstained hands, then there will be too many for the authorities to deal with. Naturally, however, they were aiming not to be found out.

Just before Christmas, 1944, with the fighting still raging in the Ardennes, the days were very short. By four o'clock it was dark and outside the searchlights were turned on. For the locked-in POWs the nights became even longer and more boring. But those twelve hours locked inside their huts, with no one to control their actions, were ideal for what the 'blacks' had in mind.

Two days after he had arrived at Comrie, Rosterg was startled from his sleep by a noise close to his wooden bunk. He sat up. In that instant the searchlight outside swept by and in its beam he saw Koenig on his knees near the bunk. '*Was ist los?*' Rosterg queried. 'What's the game?'

Koenig replied, 'I want these.' With a jerk of his thumb he indicated the contents of Rosterg's kitbag which he had just tipped on the floor.

Rosterg sprang out of his bunk, clad in his shirt and underpants, but before he could reach Koenig, several pairs of hands grabbed him and frogmarched him to a table in the centre of the room. Rosterg tried to shout, but someone punched him in the face and another prisoner kneed him in the groin. The shout turned into a moan of pain and he hung there limply while Koenig leafed through his diary. Finally he slammed it down on the bare wooden table and said in a cold voice, 'Bring the traitor forward. The trial can now begin.'

For the first time Rosterg realized the danger he was in. He had heard of these secret kangaroo courts at other camps, where after a sentence of guilty was passed the unfortunate victim suffered a heart attack or committed suicide. The mood of his attackers was fast approaching hysteria. They were stamping their feet and shouting wildly. It would not take much now for them to run amok.

Determined to fight back, Rosterg tried to answer the questions which were fired at him. His age...home town...political activities before the war. But all the time, with his hands pinioned cruelly behind his back, he was being punched, spat upon, kicked.

'Did you sell German arms to the French maquis?' Koenig roared at him. 'You say so in your diary.' Again when he tried to answer, he was punched and slapped across the face.

'Did you give the Tommies information about the entrance to the Elbe Tunnel so that their RAF could bomb it?'

Rosterg tried to deny the accusations. The Tommies didn't need that kind of information. It was public knowledge and had been for years just how the complicated series of car lifts at each end of the Tunnel worked. But by now they were hitting him with iron bars. His battered features were swelling quickly, with blood running from his nostrils.

Then came the final question, though it was more in the form of an accusation, for Koenig had made up his mind that Rosterg was the traitor: 'Did you give away the plot to escape from Devizes?'

But by now Rosterg was almost beyond answering. His body was caving in. His nose was broken, one of his eardrums was perforated and he kept blacking out. Suddenly the men holding him let go. He slumped to the floor, unconscious. The 'trial' was over.

Outside, the Polish guards had heard the racket, but though it puzzled them, they did not feel constrained to leave the warmth of their guardhouse to find out what was going on.

By now some members of Hut Four had sneaked out to other huts to inform the inmates of what was going on and to invite them to come and see for themselves if they wished. Naturally Koenig wanted as many prisoners as possible to be present at the final martyrdom of Sergeant Rosterg. Within the hour Hut Four was packed with all the Devizes' plotters — Herzig, the two SS men, Goltz and Brueling, as well as Zuehlsdorff and the rest.

While Rosterg still lay unconscious on the floor, the prisoners held a conference. 'There is only one punishment for treachery,' Koenig told them. 'The rope. Rosterg must hang!' In that twisted legalistic manner of the Nazis, which had made even relatives of concentration camp victims sign (and pay) for the ashes of the dead of the gas chambers returned in an urn, Koenig insisted that everything had to be done properly. Rosterg should be made to sign a paper admitting his guilt.

A rope was produced from somewhere. The scar-faced SS man Goltz threw it over Rosterg's neck and pulled it tight. Half-pulled, half-carried, Rosterg, with the rope round his neck, was taken to the *Lagerführer's* office and kicked into consciousness once more. They forced him to sit up and Koenig told him, 'You are a traitor, Rosterg. If you have a grain of honour in your body, you will go out and hang yourself.'

Rosterg was not going to do his tormentors that favour. 'I have only done what I thought right in my life,' he mumbled through swollen lips, his mouth full of blood. 'I can't hang myself ... I won't ...'

Koenig pushed a pen at him and slapped a sheet of paper on to the table. 'Sign it,' Koenig ordered. Rosterg refused, so Koenig forced the pen into his nerveless hand and guided it with his own as Rosterg signed the confession. Then Rosterg collapsed once more in a pool of blood. Someone tried to stem the blood flowing from his mouth, but it was no use. The beating had broken two of his ribs and they had pierced his lung. Without proper medical attention he would bleed to death. But the mob had no mercy. They had come to lynch Rosterg and they were going to complete the job.

Koenig, however, was becoming nervous. The *Lagerführer's* office was packed. Outside there was another mob of POWs pushing and jostling, wanting to know what was going on. It would soon be light — for they had tortured poor Rosterg all night — and the Polish guards would be moving in. So Koenig went outside and appealed for silence. He told the mob that Rosterg had signed a suicide note to say that he planned to hang himself. Soon, Koenig said, the mob could have him; but he insisted, 'We are going to do this quietly and gently.'

Of course Koenig was not going to soil his own hands as the executioner. He walked over to Zuehlsdorff. 'You are an SS man,' he snapped. 'You know what you have to do. I make you responsible — on your honour — for seeing this traitor hangs.'

Zuehlsdorff, who had lived with the dubious SS motto that 'My loyalty is my honour' for years now, snapped to attention as if it really was an honour to lynch a half-dead man. In that same moment the *Lagerführer's* office door was thrown upon and Rosterg with a rope around his neck was kicked out by a half a dozen boots into the cold snow of the dawn. He tottered and fell.

Goltz, the other SS man, fell upon the prostate man and started to beat him savagely once more, cursing all the while. The others cheered, carried away by blood-lust. With Goltz still sitting on Rosterg's chest and pounding his face mercilessly, half a dozen of them grabbed the rope around Rosterg's neck and started dragging him thus towards the wash house.

The rope dug ever deeper into his neck. His tongue came out. His eyes popped. He wet himself. Behind him, as they towed him towards the hut, he left a trail of blood on the snow. On the morrow it would be Christmas Eve, the season of goodwill to all men. But there was no goodwill present this dawn, only murder and mayhem.

Rosterg's head struck the edge of a concrete kerb. It was the final blow. His battered body went limp underneath Goltz, but still the scar-faced SS man continued to pummel him and still the mob continued their chanting.

Towing the body across the wet duckboards of the wash house, someone flung one end of the rope over a waterpipe. Half a dozen eager hands helped Goltz to haul up it, so that finally Rosterg was hanging there, his head twisted to one side, the tongue hanging out and the face battered to a bloody pulp.

A sudden hush came over the spectators now. Here and there a man pushed to the front so that he could get a better view of the corpse. Others seemed suddenly to realize the danger they were in. Rosterg was a traitor admittedly, but they had murdered him on British territory, while in British captivity. Silently they slunk away before the guards found them.

Koenig saw the cowards melting away. His lips twisted in scorn, but he knew those were the very men who might betray him if the British put pressure on them at some later date. It was time to make it clear to the backsliders that any future treachery would be dangerous. He said aloud, 'If you breathe a word of this,' his gaze swept the suddenly silent crowd, 'the same thing will happen to you.'

There was a murmur of approval from those who had instigated the crime. 'We must all stick together,' someone said. 'No one talks.'

Again the ringleaders agreed. Now it was time to move on. Soon it would be first roll-call and no one wanted to be caught outside, near that bloody monstrosity now hanging from the waterpipe. They started to move back to their huts, strangely subdued now like men who had just enjoyed the thrill of sexual gratification and were drained of all energy.

So *Feldwebel* Rosterg died. Once he had been a convinced National Socialist, but over the war years he had become a cynic and opportunist, playing both sides of the field. Obviously Colonel Scotland had made him promises for his undercover activities in Camp 23 at Devizes. But what had induced Scotland to send him with the plotters from Camp 23 to Comrie? Scotland must have known from Captain Sulzbach and others at the Perthshire camp just how dangerous its inmates were, and that Rosterg's life was at risk.

We can only assume that Scotland was prepared to take that risk because the threatened mass breakout from German POW camps in Britain justified it. One man's life was of little importance when the security of the nation was in jeopardy.

Saddened as he must have been at the loss of his agent Rosterg, whom Scotland described after the war as 'a comparatively liberal-minded anti-Nazi', the Colonel must have thought that Rosterg's murder signalled the end of the troubles in the POW camps. But for once Scotland was wrong. There were more murders to come and the escapes were not over yet, not by a long chalk.

TWO

On the same morning that Rosterg was discovered hanging in the washroom by the Polish guards, Baron Freiherr von der Heydte made his own overwhelming decision, just as his one-time subordinate Koenig had done when he decided that Rosterg should be 'liquidated'. Whereas Koenig had forfeited his life, though he did not know it yet, by his decision, the Baron on this particular freezing December morning had no intention of throwing his life away.

He lay in the best bedroom of the house of a high-school teacher, Herr Bouschery, on the outskirts of the romantic little German town of Monschau, staring fixedly at the castle ruins which crowned the hill opposite. Once Monschau had been the favourite resort of German honeymooners, set as it was in thick rugged woods, an ideal place to escape to. Now Monschau was virtually on the front line and occupied by US troops of an engineer battalion. Even as he lay there pondering what he should do, the Baron could hear the rumble of the guns coming from across the nearby frontier with Belgium.

The Baron had arrived at the lonely house the night before, exhausted and famished. He feet were frozen and his injured hand was giving him a great deal of trouble. When the frightened civilians heard his tale, they had swiftly taken him in, although the Americans had forbidden German citizens to harbour German soldiers, and had fed him. Even as the son of the house admired the Baron's parachute equipment and proudly told him, 'I'm in the Hitler Youth', he had fallen into an exhausted sleep.

For the first time in five days he had slept in a real bed and for several hours, but all the same it had been a troubled sleep. Over and over again, as he tossed and turned, he relived the events of the past four days. On 21 December he had decided that he should attempt to break through the American cordon with his remaining 300 men. It was no use attempting to carry out his original mission; he hadn't the strength.

The Baron and his paras had started by crossing the River Helle, wading through the chest-high freezing water at a spot where a little stream called 'Good Luck' flows into the river. But the name had been no favourable omen for them. Beyond, on the heights, the Americans were waiting for them. A fierce fire fight had broken out. Before the Baron was able to disengage his men, he had lost several of them badly wounded.

Trapped once more, the Baron still sent out patrols in an attempt to find a way across the heights. But each time his patrols ran into trouble. A couple of times they attempted boldly to find an exit through the firebreaks of the forest. But on each occasion an American Sherman tank or Staghound armoured car was waiting for them.

The Baron, desperate by now, realized they would never be able to break out as a cohesive unit. First, however, the burden of his seriously wounded and the thirty-odd American prisoners he had taken had to be removed. Believing, mistakenly, that he was fighting the 'Screaming Eagles' of the US 101st Airborne, which he first fought in Normandy in what now seemed another age, he addressed a letter in English to its commander, General Maxwell Taylor.

> We fought each other in Normandy near Carentan and from this time I know you as a chivalrous gallant general. I am sending you back the prisoners I took. They fought gallantly, too, and I cannot care for them...I am also sending you my wounded. I should greatly appreciate it, if you would give them the medical aid they need.

That done, the Baron left his wounded with the Americans and ordered what was left of his command to break up into groups of not more than three. In small groups he believed they might have a chance of reaching German lines.

Tensely the Baron waited till all his men had moved out in twos and threes, then he set off himself, accompanied only by his adjutant and orderly, both members of his beloved Sixth Parachute Regiment. For hours they wandered through the lonely, snow-bound forest, heading steadily eastwards, ragged, starved and shivering in the icy wind which blows up in the High Fen (Hohes Venn) even in summer.

Once they bumped into a group of his own men who wanted to join up with the Baron again. They believed that he, with his superior experience, would guide them to safety, just as he had done with the old Sixth back in Normandy when he slipped through the Allied lines 'like a Red Indian'.

But those days were over. Wearily the Baron told them to go on alone. They bowed their heads and departed, vanishing once more into the snowbound forest.

Finally they had come to the heights on the Belgian-German frontier overlooking Monschau and had stared down at the picturesque village of white, half-timbered houses clustered around the ruins of a ninth-century castle. Since the start of the operation the Baron had not eaten anything save his iron ration. He was at the end of his tether. Hoarsely, he croaked, 'I'm going straight into Monschau.'

The adjutant and his orderly protested. They didn't know whether Monschau was in German hands. It had been planned that the little town should be taken on the first day of the counter-offensive but there was no sign of a German presence down below. They suggested they should go into the place first and reconnoitre. But the Baron would have none of it. He had to find rest, food and warmth soon or he felt he would die on the spot.

So he bade his two companions farewell and staggered on by himself. Painfully he knocked on the door of the first house he came to. There was no answer save the dull echo of his knock. It was the same at the next house, a half-timbered structure perched on a rocky outcrop from the steep hill which rises in the centre of the little township. Was Monschau a ghost town, he asked himself, weakening by the minute.

At the third house he was lucky. Herr Bouschery, the schoolteacher, guided him into a blessedly warm kitchen where he told him the bad news. The Germans hadn't attacked. Monschau was still firmly in American hands. On that bad news, the Baron fell into his exhausted sleep.

Now, the morning after, he had to make his decision. He knew he couldn't walk another pace. His feet were frozen and one arm, still in the leather bandage up to his elbow, was totally useless. His lungs were on fire and he felt close to despair. What had his operation achieved, save the deaths of probably several hundred young men? Nothing. Besides, the Baron had no desire to go down with what was left of Hitler's vaunted Thousand-Year Empire. He was too much of a realist for that.

So he called for pen and paper and laboriously scribbled a formal note of surrender to the military government.

> Dear Gentlemen,
>
> I tried to reach German troops in the neighbourhood of Monschau. As I couldn't find any German soldiers here, I surrender because I am wounded and at the end of my strength. Please be as friendly as to send a doctor and an ambulance, as I can't walk. I am bedridden at the house of Mr Bouschery and await your help and orders.

Your very humble servant, Freiherr von der Heydte,
Colonel Commanding the German parachute troops in the area
Eupen-Malmédy.

The pompous note was entrusted to Eugen Bouschery who ran with it to the Hotel Hordhem, housing the US headquarters.

The surrender note was taken to Captain Goetcheus who was in charge. He sprang into action at once, for he realized the importance of his prospective captive. He whistled up a doctor and ambulance, just as the Baron had requested. Then, in a jeep, followed by a truck filled with heavily armed MPs, the Captain sped up the hill to the schoolteacher's house. At the same time an anti-parachutist alert was sounded in Monschau and the streets were filled with troops looking for the Baron's men. So to the very end the Baron's failed airdrop contributed to the Great Flap.

While the US troops were busy rounding up the hundred or so weary paras who made it to Monschau, the Baron himself was borne out of the schoolteacher's house, dressed in a borrowed nightgown and carefully shielding his face from the press photographers (though let it be noted that he immediately asked the US interpreter that he be informed if German radio announced that he had been awarded the coveted 'swords' to his Knight's Cross of the Iron Cross; he always had been one for the trappings of martial glory, but on this occasion he was disappointed).

He was then taken to US V Corps HQ at Eupen for interrogation by military intelligence. They informed Versailles of their capture of the head of the German paradrop, who had caused so much havoc behind the US lines. Swiftly Eisenhower's HQ rushed out a press release. Significantly enough, it was Eisenhower's Chief of Intelligence himself, Brigadier Ken Strong, who announced at midday on 23 December that the Baron 'has frost-bitten feet and is suffering from incipient pneumonia'. The Allied intention was clear. Every effort was to be made to play down the importance of these covert German operations being carried out behind Allied lines from Monschau to the glens of Scotland.

After his official interrogation at Eupen, the Baron was passed over to the war correspondents. Again the Allied objective was quite obvious. The widest possible coverage was to be given to the surrender of an officer who had caused such widespread disruption.

The Baron proved to be good copy. He was the highest ranking German officer captured in the offensive so far and a paratrooping Baron to boot. He spoke excellent English. Moreover, he was forthright in his opinions. The correspondents had been handed an excellent 'human interest' story. He obligingly told them how the airdrop had been a complete mess right from the start. He 'had had to fight at every stage to get things done' and he had been 'anything but satisfied with the role he had been given'. The correspondents grilled him about his pre-war life, the German aristocracy, his Carnegie Foundation Scholarship, even his favourite sport. Finally they asked him what he thought of his fellow Bavarian, Sepp Dietrich, head of the Sixth SS Panzer Army, currently locked in a life-and-death struggle with the US Army. 'Is he a great strategist?' they wanted to know.

The Baron curled his aristocratic upper lip. 'Dietrich is a cur.' That naturally went the rounds of the Allied press the following day.

But the Allied authorities knew that the Baron's capture and his cosy little chat with the correspondents were not sufficient to calm the tense agitation still gripping Western Europe. On the same day that the Baron was taken, German radio broadcasts beamed at the French- and Flemish-speaking populations of Belgium were telling them to leave their homes and flee as they had done back in 1940. 'Take shelter further inland,' the propagandists advised. 'Do not stay in your towns and villages. German armies are using terrible new weapons. Not a single human being will remain alive in the sectors where these new weapons are being used.' And because they were already panicked by the Baron's paradrop and Skorzeny's saboteurs and killers, the Belgian civilians were taking that advice and clogging the roads in the forward areas in their thousands.

Back in Britain another seven prisoners had been reported escaping from Lodge Moor POW Camp at Sheffield. Even far away in the United States, twenty-five German POWs had made a sensational escape from Papago park in Arizona, bringing the total number of POWs who had escaped from American camps to 1,152. Indeed, trying to put a stop to the escapes, the administration had decided to prosecute two women in Seattle, Washington — Mrs. Fae Burns and Mrs. Lenora Hodgson — for harbouring escaped prisoners, although the former had a husband fighting in the Pacific and was the mother of two children. It was thought that this drastic measure would help to obstruct enemy prisoners attempting to make a break for it.

But Eisenhower was determined that much sterner measures had to be applied in order to calm the public down and put an end to the Great Flap. He ordered that the first three Skorzeny Germans who had triggered off the wholesale panic in the West should be given a semi-public execution. As the Baron gave his interview at Eupen, only three miles away at the little village of Henri Chapelle, Schmidt, Billing and Parnas were led out to be shot as spies because they had been dressed in American uniform when captured. Their collective plea to Eisenhower the day before had been rejected. There was no hope for them. They were going to die *pour encourager les autres.*

It was freezing cold when the three Germans were brought out,

Schmidt meek and pale, Parnas tall and cadaverous, his black hair uncombed, and then Billing, blue eyes unblinking behind his glasses. As one who was present later recalled:

> The firing squad shuffled in the snow, their rifles at the ready. They did not like to look at one another and they seemed very white of face and when they spoke it was rather haltingly, as if something stuck in the throat...But one was more garrulous and spat from time to time and repeated, 'Why should they give us this shit?'

The three condemned men were marched to the waiting stakes, tied to them and had black masks placed in front of their eyes. White discs were attached by pins to the region of their hearts. The US chaplain stepped forward, spoke a few words and made the sign of the cross above them. All was ready now.

As the chaplain stepped back the officer in charge of the firing squad cried, 'Prepare the execution.' He was a smart young Captain of Military Police and the observer who recorded the details of the execution wondered what was going through his mind at that moment. But if the officer felt any emotion, his face did not reveal it. He raised his arm and barked, 'Ready?'

There was a few seconds' pause. The observer recorded that there was an 'awful silence'. Suddenly a 'thin piping voice' broke that silence. It was the Nazi *Oberfahnrich* Billing. He had refused the US chaplain's blessing. He would die like a National Socialist, without belief in God, only in the Führer. Evidently he had been selected by the other two to speak the last words to a world that they were about to leave.

Rigid in his bonds, as if standing to attention, he cried defiantly, his breath fogging on the freezing air, *'Es lebe der Führer, Adolf Hitler!'* (Long live our leader, Adolf Hitler.)

The MP captain waited no longer. 'Fire!' he cried.

Twelve Garand rifles spoke as one. Twelve .300 copper-headed bullets sped towards the three Germans at 2,000 feet a second. At that short range, the slugs smashed right through the bodies, breaking bone, gouging flesh, splattering blood on the ground, then crashed into the wall behind, splintering the concrete. And there the bullet fragments remain embedded to this day.

It was Christmas Eve, the last of the war. Throughout the Western Allied countries the mood was serious, muted and in some places anxious. Although the 'Victor of El Alamein', Field-Marshal Montgomery, had taken charge of the northern 'shoulder' of the American defences in the Ardennes, the front had not yet stabilized. Indeed, this day Montgomery had ordered the US troops who had been holding the key border town of St Vith since the start of the German attack to withdraw so he could commence that famous 'tidying up' of his, which he always required before he could 'get cracking'. And the seriousness of the situation was demonstrated by the fact that the Americans did not protest.

Paris, in common with most large cities behind the front, was still gripped by the great spy and killer scare. An army of German fifth-columnists, it was reported, was ready and waiting to rise 'from the sewer' at a moment's notice. At Supreme Headquarters they had baited the hook for the alleged killers. Colonel Baldwin Smith, Eisenhower's double, was openly riding back and forth between the Supreme Commander's home and his Versailles headquarters, just waiting for 'the most dangerous man in Europe', as Ike now called Skorzeny, to take a potshot at him.

In fact there was not a 'Skorzeny killer' within miles of the French capital, though reportedly several scores of suspects had joined the 1,308 American officers and enlisted men already in Paris jails, half of them charged with stealing goods from their comrades to sell on the European black markets. As Colonel E. G. Buhrmaster, Provost Marshal of the Seine Base Section, commented angrily: 'This place is getting to be like Chicago in the days of Al Capone. They hijack trucks right off the road. One major sent home thirty-six thousand dollars in a few weeks!' Thus the 'suspects' were probably harmless GIs themselves, who would now spend their Christmas Eve among the worst kind of army crooks: rear-echelon men who robbed their fighting comrades at the front. If bullets had had any saleable value, undoubtedly they would have sold them, too.*

But there must have been some truth in the rumours that there was an active force of pro-German fifth columnists in France. As we have seen, that first unfortunate 'jeep team' of Skorzeny's was carrying a fortune in

---

* At this time it was estimated that only two out of every five cigarettes shipped to France ever reached the frontline men for whom they were intended. Shortly after Christmas 1944, two officers and 272 enlisted men were brought to trial for stealing a whole trainload of cigarettes bound for the fighting troops. The latter, when they heard of it, demanded that the thieves be sentenced to death.

French and Belgian money to bribe dockworkers and hinder the flow of supplies to the troops at the front.

Now, on this Christmas Eve, the nine-hour voyage of a convoy of troopships and three escorting vessels was about to come to an end as it approached Cherbourg. Security had been lax from the very start as the 5,000 men of the US 66th Infantry Division, the last one left in the UK, prepared to board their troopships, the British SS *Cheshire* and the Belgian *Leopoldville*. Marching to Southampton, the soldiers had been wished good luck by British civilian onlookers, who had called out the division's name and its nickname, 'the Black Panthers' (after its divisional patch). As one of them who survived said long after, 'The men were labelled to friend and foe alike as so many cases of Christmas pudding.' For some 800 of the young GIs there would be no more Christmas pudding — ever.

At five o'clock that Christmas Eve, when it was already dark, the German submarine *U-486,* commanded by Lieutenant Gerhard Meyer, surfaced right in the path of the *Leopoldville*, as if the commander already knew her course. Half an hour later a lookout spotted the troopship. Then, slightly before six o'clock, Meyer gave the order to fire a torpedo. As if everything had been planned right from the start, the torpedo headed for the *Leopoldville*. Containing one and a half tons of high explosive, it struck the Belgian vessel on the starboard side and exploded in number four hold. At least 300 GIs were killed by the explosion or drowned in the water which quickly flooded two of the troop compartments. The Belgian crew immediately abandoned ship, save for four senior officers including the skipper, Captain Limbor, who was determined to go down with his ship.

A British destroyer, HMS *Brilliant,* giving up the hunt for the submarine, came alongside the stricken ship and tried to help. But the GIs found they hadn't the knowledge to lower the lifeboats. Worse, even though the GIs could see the lights of Cherbourg, the base for a whole fleet of American-crewed tugs, no one had contacted the port. Lieutenant-Commander Pringle, captain of the *Brilliant,* had no radio link with Cherbourg. He did have one with Southampton, however, so he informed them what had happened. Somehow the port authorities there failed to pass on the information.

The result was predictable: massive loss of life. As the *Leopoldville* began to drift, sinking all the time, the captain of the *Brilliant* tried to rescue as many men as possible. But there was a huge difference of height between the two ships and the trapped GIs had to jump, judging the width between the ships and the waves. As one of them said afterwards,

> It was like trying to jump on a big bobbing cork on a rough
> pond...At one second the *Brilliant* was crashing the side of our

ship some fifteen feet below me, then it was at my level but fifteen feet out. There was no telling where it was going to be at the next second.

They tried to transfer the wounded by means of lines and pulleys, but there was no way to keep the stretchers flat; even though the patients were strapped down, they slipped off into the sea between the two vessels. Others threw the wounded over the side, hoping that the British sailors on the *Brilliant* would catch them. Sometimes they did. Sometimes they didn't.

In the end, believing that help was on the way and feeling that the casualties should be rushed to the nearest hospitals as soon as possible, the captain of the *Brilliant* steamed off to Cherbourg, leaving the sinking ship to its fate. At eight thirty that Christmas Eve the *Leopoldville gave a sudden lurch. Hatch covers blew off and the ship started to go down stern first. Some men were immediately thrown overboard; others flung themselves over the side. Most were laden down with weapons, steel helmets and thick overcoats.*

Panic broke out in the icy seas as drowning men tried to find a place on the rafts, clung on to their comrades in an attempt to save them, or fought off others who were dragging them down. Even many of those who were saved would die later from hypothermia and shock.

In all, some 500 men drowned that night or died of shock, which, with the 300 killed by the torpedo, made a total of 800 or more. It was the worst disaster to befall a troopship carrying US soldiers in the Second World War.

Supreme Headquarters threw a security blanket over the whole affair (it was not until 1966 that the full details of what happened that Christmas Eve were released by Washington). But almost immediately the Germans began broadcasting what had happened, identifying the dead as belonging to the 66th Infantry Division, indicating, it seemed, that they had known all along that the troopships were on their way. Despite the security blanket which Allied HQ threw over the disaster, the *Daily Express* managed to publish some details of the sinking by quoting 'German sources' — in other words, the German radio broadcasts, a common means of circumventing censorship in those days.*

The news, when it was finally revealed by the *Express,* was not calculated to relieve the general mood of gloom which had settled on London. The seriousness of the struggle in the Ardennes was reflected in

---

* The *U-486* was sunk by the British submarine *Tapir* off Norway in April, 1945; she went down with all hands. The German U-boat files are buried in US Navy Archives, and so far there has never been an opportunity to verify whether Lieutenant Meyer knew in advance from spies in Britain or France that the *Leopoldville was coming.*

one headline in the *Daily Mail* on the day before Christmas Eve: 'Rundstedt's Panzer Thrust 30 Miles from Sedan'. Every reader of the *Mail* knew that it was at Sedan that the Germans had made their decisive breakthrough in 1940 and sealed the fate of France. It was nearly as depressing as the news that Saturday that 'there is not enough beer in some parts of the country to last over the holidays...Many public houses may have to shut down on Christmas Eve.'

But the authorities had more serious things on their minds than the lack of beer that Christmas Eve. The murder of Rosterg at Comrie, the fresh escape of seven prisoners at Lodge Moor and the puzzling fact that one of the escapers was found just outside the wire badly injured — had his comrades deliberately forced him out of the camp in an attempt to kill him? — made it quite clear that the POWs' spirit was not broken yet. It was clear, too, that the increased truculence and riotous behaviour of the German prisoners in camps throughout the country meant that they still believed in Germany's ultimate victory. Did it follow, the authorities asked themselves, that a second massed break-out was intended?

Again the authorities ordered Colonel Scotland and the fifty-odd camp commandants to increase their vigilance. Despite the fact that it was Christmas, the camp commandants were told they must not relax their guard for one moment. There would be extra rations for the POWs on Christmas Day and they could hold whatever entertainments they wanted, but soldiers on guard duty must not fraternize with the prisoners. Above all, there would be no illicit alcohol smuggled in by the guards in exchange for the toys, paintings, light fittings etc which the POWs made from odd bits and pieces for barter, and which were very popular with guards and British civilians alike.

But on that Christmas Eve of 1944, the authorities' worries were needless. For *Brigadeführer der SS* Walter Schellenberg, who was behind the Skorzeny operation, the mass break-out plan and all the other intelligence schemes in connection with the great counter-attack, had lost his faith in it. To him it was now clear that Hitler was not going to win this last great battle in the West. Schellenberg knew, too, from his intelligence sources, that the Russians were massing on Germany's eastern front. Taking advantage of Hitler's preoccupation with the battle in the West, the Red Army would launch its own massive drive into the Reich any day now.

On that Christmas Eve Schellenberg's subordinate Skorzeny was directing the operations of what was left of his brigade of pseudo-Americans (only three of his numerous jeep teams would return from behind US lines in the end; the rest were already either dead or in captivity) when he was struck in the head by a shell fragment. Skorzeny,

143

the veteran of many a wounding during his student duelling days in Vienna, had the wound sewn up without benefit of anaesthetics because he did not want to have his judgement impaired. But when the heavy bandage was put in place, he found he was temporarily blind in one eye. He was in no position to command his brigade. Indeed, six days later, what remained of his unit was relieved and Skorzeny left it for good.

The news that Skorzeny was out of action and was coming back to Berlin for treatment and a new posting seemed to make up Schellenberg's mind for him. He knew that he had no hope of convincing Hitler that the time had come to make a separate peace with the Western Allies. The Führer would fight to the end, as he had often stated, and he would drag the whole German nation down with him. Besides, Schellenberg was realist enough to realize that the Western Allies would not be prepared to do a deal with Hitler, who had started the whole bloody business.

Surprisingly enough, Schellenberg did imagine that the Allies would negotiate with Himmler, the man who had created the concentration camps. Perhaps Schellenberg reasoned that if he personally was shown to have been actively seeking peace behind Hitler's back, a very dangerous game indeed, then he would be able to curry favour with the Allies after the war was lost.

At all events, Schellenberg now went to work on his chief. As he wrote himself after the war,

> I kept on reminding Himmler how desperate the situation was and warned him that one day history would hold him responsible for his lack of decision. He replied that the Order of the SS had been built on the principle of loyalty and he could not violate this...I told him that, compared to the existence of the whole nation, the SS represented only a small minority, and after their long period of suffering, the German people would expect a release from their ordeal. They looked to Himmler, for he was a man who had not sought to profit personally from the regime. To this kind of talk, he would merely say, 'So you want to remove the Führer?' And such was his changeable nature that there were days when it would have cost me my position to have answered 'Yes'.*

All the same, while Himmler wavered, Schellenberg did start moving cautiously, putting out both direct and indirect peace feelers. He contacted Dr Musy, a former Swiss president, and, working with him and the International Red Cross, he set about arranging to have thousands of Jews brought out of German concentration camps in exchange for cars, tractors,

* *The Labyrinth,* Walter Schellenberg, 1956

medicines etc which Germany desperately needed. Schellenberg reasoned that it was Jewish organizations throughout the world which would be asked to stump up the money to buy their co-religionists' freedom and it was through these same international Jewish organizations that he would help to arrange a separate peace with the West.

Another peace move was made through Sweden. The Swedes were being subjected to increasing Allied pressure to join the war against Hitler. It was not a prospect that appealed to the Swedes, who had never fought a war since the beginning of the nineteenth century. So in the hope of postponing a decision on their entry into the war against Germany, the Swedes jumped at the chance of doing a deal with Himmler and Schellenberg on the release of certain nationalities, notably Scandinavians, held in the German concentration camps. This in its turn led to initial peace feelers with Count Bernadotte, a nephew of the King of Sweden and Vice-President of the Swedish Red Cross, who was only too eager to participate. In the end Bernadotte would negotiate with the devil himself, Heinrich Himmler, whose evil reputation concerning the concentration camps was well known to the Swedes. Anything was better than Sweden having to go to war.

Schellenberg's third peace move was to arrange the freeing of the most important US prisoner-of-war in German hands: Brigadier-General Vanamann, a former US military attaché to Berlin, who had been shot down while with an observation mission over Germany. Although the Germans had already once threatened to shoot Anglo-American 'terror fliers' and in the previous March had shot fifty RAF prisoners-of-war who had escaped from their camp at Sagan, Poland, Schellenberg now conferred with SS General Gottlob Berger, who was in charge of camps for Allied POWs in Germany and who was already stamped as a war criminal by the Allied powers. Together they worked out a plan for Vanamann and another American captive, a US colonel, to be taken to Switzerland, from where the two would fly on to Washington and meet Roosevelt. Vanamann would ask the President for improved supplies and conditions for Allied prisoners in German hands and at the same time tell Roosevelt of Himmler's sincere desire for peace. When approached, General Vanamann agreed to play his part: but by the time he was on his way to Washington, Roosevelt was dead and the new President, Harry Truman, wisely enough, would have no truck with a war criminal like Himmler.

Indeed, none of Schellenberg's attempts to arrange a peace — and in so doing to ingratiate himself with the Allies — came to fruition. But from now onwards, while he worked at the peace plan, Schellenberg wanted no part of any covert operation that might endanger him after the end of the war which he knew Germany would lose.

145

Immediately after the death sentence had been passed on Schmidt, Billing and Parnas for having worn US uniform in combat, they had written in their plea for mercy:

> We were captured by the Americans without having fired a shot because we didn't want to become murderers. We were sentenced to death and are now dying for some criminals who have not only us but also — and that is worse — our families on their conscience. Therefore, we beg the Commanding General for mercy; we have not been unjustly sentenced, but we are *de facto* innocent.

The man who had cynically manipulated those three unfortunates, along with the rest of the doomed jeep teams and those hundreds of POWs in Britain who thought their massed escape would help Germany to victory, would have felt no twinge of conscience — if indeed he had a conscience. His paramount concern was his own survival. While others, brave or foolish, carried on the struggle to its bitter end, and in the process met a violent and untimely death, Walter Schellenberg would survive to die in his own bed.

4

THE LAST ESCAPES

The point is not that we escape and fall. The point is that we
keep on trying to show you people that we are not finished yet.
recaptured German officer to British interrogator
March 1945

ONE

The start of 1945 brought bitter disappointment to those POWs in the United Kingdom who had been participants in the planned break-out. By now all the first wave of escapers had been recaptured save for two who were never found. The great counter-offensive in the Ardennes had failed and it was clear that it would not be long before the Western Allies would start their final push into the Reich itself.

But there were many still as intent upon escape as they had ever been. Some of them were SS men, who had been informed through the camps' grapevine that the SS would be treated differently from the men of the regular army. The SS, after the shooting of Canadian prisoners in Normandy and American ones in the Ardennes, was now regarded as a criminal organization. Its members could expect to spend years behind barbed wire and, if they were sent to Russia, as rumours suggested they might, then their fate was sealed; they would never return to their homeland.

Others, mostly paratroopers, wanted to escape for the sheer hell of it. For the most part they were young, barely out of their teens, with the happy-go-lucky attitude which goes with that age. They scorned their fellow prisoners who were content to sit out the war and see what would happen. They felt they had little to lose and a lot to gain by escaping. After all, even if they were caught, they had cocked a snoot at their captors.

Yet others were men who simply could not stand being behind barbed wire. They were possessed of an almost claustrophobic hatred of being imprisoned, fueled perhaps by the sexual frustration of the all-male camps. These men were natural loners, who wanted nothing more than to get out, whatever happened to them after they had escaped. Many of these loners felt that the only alternative was suicide.

The escapers at Glen Mill Camp, Oldham, however, had no intention of committing suicide. Ever since December, when some of them had hoped the mysterious 'IRA man' with a swastika painted on his shirt would help them to escape, they had been plotting alternative means of breaking out. Some were for starting a mock fight to attract the guards. Thereupon they would turn on the guards and disarm them. A modified version of this plan was eventually agreed upon. At dawn, when the night guards would be feeling the strain of two hours on duty and four hours off (which meant that they stretched out on a bunk in a smoke-filled, noisy guardroom clad in full uniform, including boots, and got no sleep), the POWs would stage their fight. The guards had long become accustomed to such rows around dawn, for this was the time that the prisoners usually held their kangaroo courts and inflicted punishment on their victims. While the racket was steadily increasing, the escapers would sneak to the perimeter under cover of the dawn gloom and cut the wire. It was hoped that at least twenty or more of them would be out before the guards were changed or came to investigate what was going on.

In early February, with British troops fighting a tremendous battle in the Reichwald Forest on the German border against the paratroopers of Student's First Parachute Army, the break-out at Glen Mill Camp began. The morning the escapers picked was ideal for their purpose. It was cold and a mist was rolling in from the surrounding moors. No one in his right mind would want to be outside on such a morning if he did not have to; and the escapers reasoned that even those Tommy civilians going to the early shift in Oldham's factories would hurry there with heads bent, intent on reaching the warmth of the shop floor.

The mock fight started. The noise of shouting and booing rose steadily as the escapers stole out into the yard and began clipping through the wire with their home-made cutters. Man after man slipped through, while the racket inside the camp continued. Everything was going as planned.

Suddenly there was a shout of alarm. A British NCO yelled an order. What he was crying, the POWs did not know or care. All they knew was that they had been spotted. In frenzied haste another couple crawled through the gap and started up the road, to be joined by another escapee who had used a plank on the wire like a springboard and had vaulted right over the fence.

By now the guards realized they were witnessing a mass escape. Ever since the Christmas alert they had been preparing for something like this. They did not hesitate to open fire. Suddenly bullets were whizzing over the heads of the would-be escapers inside the compound. Others who had come out despite the chill air fled back inside. It was obvious that the Tommies were shooting to kill. Guards were everywhere, shoving their way with bayonets fixed through groups of prisoners trying to restore order before holding a roll-call. Many of the prisoners inside refused to come out at first, then made a farce of the roll-call by moving between the ranks so that there had to be repeated recounts. And all the while the guards were jeered at and sometimes hit by cans and other missiles.

The Camp Commandant, Dennison, a careful, disciplined, middle-aged officer, knew that he had to take a firm hand. He told the POWs inside the mill that he was not interested in guessing how many men had escaped, he wanted an exact figure. If he didn't get it, and soon, drastic action would be taken. He pointed to his rear. The prisoners saw that the guards had been doubled, and up on the towers the machine-gunners had trained their Bren guns directly on them. They realized that Dennison would order his men to open fire if they did not obey him.

Once again the counting began. Now the men were checked off in batches of fifty and led from the mill yard out into a section of the main road which had been wired off. Slowly the day wore on. The POWs standing out in the open started to grow restless and defiant. They catcalled and booed any British officer who happened to pass or gave him the Nazi salute; they started to sing old Nazi marching songs. The fact that they had not been fed since the previous evening did not seem to dampen their excitement. A number of their comrades had escaped. The Tommies were in a flap. If nothing else, it was a welcome change in a dreary routine.

About three that afternoon, with a damp wind whistling across the open road, an NCO marched up the street, paused, stooped and drew a line of chalk across the cobbles. Then he turned to the sentries. 'See that the prisoners don't go over that line,' he ordered. 'If they do, challenge them. If they don't respond to the challenge, let 'em have it!'

One of the sentries, called in to help the guards, was Private John Jaffray, a gunner from Aberdeen who stood barely five foot tall. Normally it was Jaffray's job to help man the Bofors guns which guarded the Glen Mill camp against German air attack. But the only air attack Oldham had suffered since 1940 had been a V-1 which had landed on a housing estate on Christmas Eve, 1944. It had damaged or destroyed a staggering 1,050 homes over a three-quarter-mile radius, and killed or injured sixty-six men, women and children, including a whole wedding party. Jaffray had never fired a shot in anger in his life, but, although he never afterwards spoke about his role in what happened that day, it might well have been the carnage caused by the V-1 in Oldham that had filled him with such hatred. Now he was inside the wire, watching the rowdy Germans making threatening gestures and sneering at him.

Time and again Jaffray warned them to get back from the chalk mark and raised his rifle menacingly. Always they obeyed, especially as the *Lagerführer,* who was with them, added his own warning. He told his mates to stop jostling or there would be trouble — and he was right.

Then nature took a hand. It started to rain, a heavy cold downpour that drenched them all. The prisoners were cold, hungry, tired and cross. The jostling and catcalls increased. *'Es pisst, Mensch. ... Wir wollen 'rein. ... Los! Lasst uns rein, Mensch!'*

The little Scottish gunner did not understand German but he did understand the gestures. The prisoners were edging forward, inching over the chalk mark; they were coming at him. He raised his rifle and clicked off the safety catch; one little David facing a bunch of Goliaths, with the rain dropping off the brim of his helmet, holding a rifle that was almost as big as himself.

'Get back!' Jaffray cried again and again. He raised his rifle further, finger curling round the trigger. 'Get back, I tell ye!'

The more frantic he got, the more daring were the POWs. Ominously they kept moving forward.

Jaffray's orders were to fire over their heads first. But in his fear and excitement he aimed too low. He snapped back the trigger. The rifle cracked at his hip. One of the Germans slowly sank to the ground.

Abruptly the racket died. The mob halted. There was no sound now save for the soft moans of a POW behind the man who had dropped; he had been hit by the bullet after it passed through the first man.

Jaffray, still holding his rifle firmly in place, stared at the man on the ground. He lay perfectly still, blood seeping from his head.

For what seemed an age the little Scot and the mob of Germans faced each other in silence. Then there was the sound of heavy boots running into the road. The shot had brought officers and NCOs out into the compound at the double.

Jaffray was shouldered to one side. An officer ordered him to sling his rifle. An NCO told two Germans to carry their dead comrade away. He was *Soldat* Paul Hartmann, aged eighteen. Indirectly he was another victim of Schellenberg's devious schemes, just as Koenig, Zuehlsdorff, Schmidt, Billing, Parnas and the rest had been.

But the apportioning of blame would come later. Suddenly tame, the prisoners were herded back to their quarters. The alarm was called, as it was discovered that in all seven prisoners had escaped. Jaffray was told to report to the guard room and hand in his rifle. It would be needed later for the court of inquiry.

Although a brief announcement was made that a German prisoner had been killed at Glen Mill, the authorities made great efforts to keep the details secret. On the orders of the Home Office, a secret inquest was held, but the Coroner's verdict was never published. Nor was Gunner Jaffray moved away from Glen Mill, which some people thought strange. But the authorities knew what they were doing. They did not want Jaffray posted to another camp where what he had done might be revealed and inflame other POWs to further trouble and unrest.

For the mood in Glen Mill, typical of many of the camps, was still fanatical and defiant. When Paul Hartmann was buried on a stormy Saturday afternoon in the cemetery on the hill opposite the camp, the sixty POWs who accompanied the coffin under armed guard all clicked to rigid attention and gave the Nazi salute as the body was brought into the churchyard; and the pastor who preached the sermon spoke solemnly and bitterly of Hartmann's love of his Fatherland for which he had now paid the price on foreign soil.

Month after month the supporters of Sergeant Gerald Hanel continued to defy the camp authorities. Even when the war was unarguably lost they did not lose their faith in the National Socialist cause. The prisoners due for repatriation were examined by a special committee every six months as to their suitability for return to their homeland. If they were shown to be 'black', they were deferred for another six months. Many showed what they thought of the committee by entering the room, clicking their heels together and bellowing *'heil Hitler!'* at the tops of their voices. That meant immediate dismissal, and they knew it. Hanel and his fellow paras were such men. Hanel himself was not released until three years after the war ended.

But in February, 1945, the British authorities were concerned with keeping secret what had happened in Glen Mill and recapturing the seven escapers. The latter did not prove too difficult. A girl railway porter spotted the first escaper early next morning, near Castleton railway station a few miles from the camp. He surrendered tamely to the elderly railway policeman she had summoned. Two more were found at Wakefield a day later and four others in Leeds, thirty miles away. They had anticipated that the authorities would be looking for them on the western side of the country. They reasoned that the Tommies would expect them to head for Liverpool, the nearest port where they could hope to smuggle themselves aboard a ship and escape from Britain. Instead they chose Yorkshire. There were German POW camps in Yorkshire, such as the one near Hull, and they had hoped to contact fellow prisoners on working parties who might give them information on ships sailing to Belgium or even, if luck was on their side, to Sweden. But luck was not on their side.

What was much more difficult for the authorities was keeping news of what had happened at Glen Mill from spreading around Oldham. Once before, rumours had swept the town that a prisoner had been shot. In reality, the guards had merely been digging machine-gun pits to repel a supposed German para-landing to free their comrades at Glen Mill. It had been a false alarm. This time it was for real. One of the hated Jerries had been killed — and in Oldham that February the Germans really were hated. After the recent V-l attack on the city there was no love lost. between the locals and the German prisoners. Now the view was that the Jerry had deserved it; the only good German was a dead one.

Thus one night after the fatal shooting of Paul Hartmann, Gunner Jaffray went into one of Oldham's pubs with a mate. The place was buzzing with the news of the killing. One of the cloth-capped customers declared, 'If I knew which of the lads had shot the bloody Jerry, I'd buy him a pint.'

Jaffray's companion slapped the little Scot over the shoulder, much to the other's dismay, and said, 'Well, *he* did it and *he's* thirsty.' The pub's landlady did not bat an eyelid. She drew the beer and said, 'Pity you hadn't a machine gun — you could have shot a few more.'

The same view was taken by many who had had dealings with the 'blacks' in these last few months of the war. There were English people by the hundred who tried to better the lot of German POWs throughout the country by sending them food parcels and such like. But the great majority of civilians who lived around the camps hated the inmates. Now it seemed the events at Lodge Moor Camp, Sheffield, would prove them right.

TWO

The first tunnel at Lodge Moor Camp had been started at the beginning of the great plot in the first week of December, 1944. When it was realized by the bulk of the prisoners that the Ardennes offensive had failed and that Germany now had little chance of winning the war, the tunnel was betrayed to the camp authorities (one tunnel, that is; its twin was not discovered until the camp was long abandoned in 1956). The 'blacks' at Lodge Moor commenced a witch hunt for the traitor. But he was never found and as their anger ebbed the 'blacks' started a new tunnel. Laboriously they burrowed through the heavy soil, night after night, week after week. Confident that they still had a role to play in the war and that Germany was not yet beaten, the escapers worked twenty feet beneath the

152

ground with dogged persistence, trying to keep their labours secret. A second betrayal would be disastrous for morale.

February gave way to March. In Germany the Allies were lined up along the banks of the Rhine, from Holland in the north to Switzerland in the south, just waiting to cross, ready to launch the last offensive which would deal the death blow to Hitler's Germany. But in Sheffield the 'blacks' took little notice of Allied claims. They continued working, with one of them, *Feldwebel* Emil Schmittendorf, a beefy infantryman, urging his fellows to ever greater efforts. For him German victory seemed to depend on their completing the tunnel rapidly and escaping. Even though there could no longer be a march on London, Schmittendorf believed firmly that a breakout from Lodge Moor would materially help the cause of the 'Thousand-Year Reich'.

On 7 March, when the US 9th Armoured Division was beginning its assault on the railway bridge over the Rhine at Remagen, *Feldwebel* Schmittendorf was keeping watch in the hut where the tunnel started. It was his job to receive any warning from the *Schatten* (shadows) outside, who followed any suspicious Tommy in the compound and reported whenever he seemed to be getting too close to the hut from which the tunnel started.

But Schmittendorf was feeling a little lazy this March afternoon. He had been working hard the previous night and it was all he could do to keep awake. As a consequence, he missed the frantic signalling of one of the shadows who had spotted a party of armed Tommies heading straight for Schmittendorf s hut.

The door burst open. Schmittendorf sprang to his feet. There were still men below, for the escapers had been confident that they could continue tunnelling during the daylight hours. Besides, there was a great sense of urgency about the project now; they had only a few more metres to go.

The English NCO in charge of the ferrets grinned at the German but said nothing. Schmittendorf stepped back as the Tommies began a perfunctory search of the hut. Later he realized that they were simply going through the motions. They knew exactly what they were looking for and where.

After play-acting for a few minutes, the sergeant walked straight to a pile of kitbags in one corner of the room. He pulled them away and, using the crowbar he was carrying, poked around until he found what he was obviously seeking. He inserted the crowbar into a gap in the floorboards and a whole section, cut to about a metre square and nailed together, came up to reveal the entrance to the tunnel below.

In a matter of eight weeks, two tunnels at Lodge Moor had been discovered. Now the enraged 'blacks' knew they had been betrayed. Not only did the Tommies discover the tunnel, they also found the planners' stock of digging tools, food, civilian clothes, etc. The 'blacks' focused all their energies on finding the traitor.

Walking the compound with his fellow 'blacks' — the escapers would be sentenced to the usual term in the 'cooler' later on by the camp commandant — Schmittendorf voiced the opinion of the others when he remarked grimly, 'The traitor must be found and punished — *this day.*'

The others knew what he meant. By the time they returned from the 'cooler' the Tommies would have posted their '*Spitzel*' to another camp where he could start his treachery afresh. It was necessary to find and punish him *now*.

Corporal Arnim Kuehne sidled up to the *Feldwebel*. 'I have a good idea who the traitor is,' he said.

As bold and cunning as his name implied *(Kuehne* means just that in German), the eighteen-year-old Corporal had overheard another young prisoner, Gerhardt Rettig, remark to a friend that he was sick and tired of being cooped up behind barbed wire and wanted to go home, for 'the war is already lost'.

Kuehne had been brainwashed by the Nationalist Socialist creed since he was a small boy. Somehow his twisted mind had registered Rettig's remark as the words of a traitor. Now he told Schmittendorf that Rettig, and maybe his friend too, had betrayed the would-be escapers. Soon Lodge Moor Camp started to buzz with ugly rumours. There was to be a kangaroo court. Someone was going to pay for the great betrayal.

About two on the afternoon of the day the tunnel was discovered, a friend slipped furtively up to the unsuspecting Rettig and warned him what was going on. The 'blacks' were talking of revenge, trials, even execution. He told Rettig and his other friend, who was never named in the subsequent inquiry, that Kuehne and Schmittendorf and the rest were blaming them for the tunnel's discovery. He suggested the two of them should appeal to the guards for sanctuary; otherwise they might not survive the day.

Rettig protested that he had nothing to do with the tunnel's discovery. The friend warned him that the 'blacks' would not believe him. 'They want blood. Yours will do.'

Rettig considered for a few minutes. He knew his so-called comrades. They were a brutal lot. They often resorted to violence, striking out at each other mercilessly over the slightest thing — the suspicion of theft, a wrong look, a snide remark. What would they do to him if they really became enraged? Perhaps it would be best, he decided, if he asked the commandant to transfer him to another camp.

Rettig edged towards the perimeter wire, careful to keep away from his fellow prisoners. He approached the guard and asked if he would pass on a note to the Commandant. The puzzled guard asked why and Rettig whispered that he felt his life was in danger.

The guard nodded and said, 'I'll pass it on.'

Swiftly the Commandant called in the *Lagerführer* and told him he was going to have Rettig and his friend taken out of the main compound at once. The *Lagerführer* should tell them to pack their kit immediately and be ready to be taken out. The *Lagerführer* went straight to the hut which Rettig and his friend shared with some forty other prisoners. He told the two that they were being moved and must pack. Then he left.

For most of that afternoon the two POWs sat on their bunks, their kitbags between their knees, feeling the palpable hostility of their one-time comrades in the hut. Five thirty came along and with it momentary relief, for everyone had to go outside to answer their names for the last check of the day.

Roll-call didn't take long, but it was long enough for the word to be spread: Rettig and his friend were traitors, who were now being transferred to another camp to escape the just punishment which was their lot.

The POWs started to drift back to their huts, but Rettig could not face another hour of that brooding tension in the hut. He stayed outside, trying to avoid the little groups of men huddled in the compound despite the darkening sky and freezing cold. Slowly, perhaps unconsciously realizing the danger of his position, he edged towards the perimeter wire.

But he hadn't gone far when Kuehne spotted him. That's him! That's the criminal!' he cried. 'Come on, let's get him!'

Rettig had half-expected the outburst from his fellow POWs. He could see the hatred on the faces of the men. His only chance now was to make a run for the wire, but how was he to get through the line of men barring his path? He stood there undecided. It was his undoing. He should have followed his first instinct and run. Now it was too late. The others started to advance upon him, slowly and purposefully. Kuehne, however, could not wait to get his hands on the 'traitor'. He broke ranks and darted straight for Rettig.

Rettig tried to back off towards the huts, but Kuehne did not give him the chance. Just as Rettig reached the nearest hut, Kuehne struck him a blow that sent him reeling through an open door. Waiting inside, others set about him with iron bars. Rettig's martyrdom had begun.

It was the Rosterg murder all over again. In the half-darkness of the hut the POWs pummelled and beat Rettig unmercifully, slamming their boots into his ribs, lashing out at him with their fists and iron bars, while Rettig rolled from side to side, trying to keep his knees together to prevent them kicking him in the groin once more and covering his face with his hands — in vain, for it was already streaming with blood, his nose smashed and several of his front teeth gone.

Somehow he dragged himself into a corner and crouched there, gasping for breath and whimpering like a dog. But his tormentors had no mercy. Schmittendorf pushed his way through the mob and tore Rettig's arms from in front of his face. It was a bloody pulp. That didn't deter the burly NCO. He brought back his boot and smashed the steel-tipped toe right into Rettig's face. With a howl of pain, Rettig slumped to the floor. Schmittendorf called for a bucket of cold water and emptied it over him. Rettig stared up at the circle of enraged faces. He knew what was yet to happen. Catching his tormentors completely off guard, he sprang to his feet and hurtled out to the compound. His tormentors took up the chase as Rettig zig-zagged across the compound, heading for the wire. But in his panic and because he could hardly see out of his swollen eyes, he lost his sense of direction. Stumbling, blundering, he staggered into a washhouse, gasping for breath. Mutely he waited for the end to come.

The mob closed round him, chanting for his death. But Schmittendorf had a better idea. He seized one of the dying man's legs and another man grabbed the other. Together they towed Rettig through the dirt towards the camp's dustbins, while the rest cheered them on. Contemptuously they dumped Rettig there and stood back, mocking him.

While all this was going on, Rettig's friend had seized his chance to escape; he realized that he might be next. He waited until Rettig had unexpectedly given the slip to his tormentors, then he made a dash for the main gate. There he told the guard commander what the mob was doing to Rettig.

The guard commander reacted at once. He sent in a large section of the guard, all heavily armed, including one Bren-gunner. The mob heard them coming and fled. The soldiers followed the trail of blood from the washroom to the dustbins and soon found Rettig lying there like a piece of abandoned trash.

Surprisingly enough, Rettig was still alive, but barely. He was rushed to the camp hospital while POWs pressed round the stretcher party to jeer at the dying 'traitor'. Angry guards threatened them with their bayonets and they fell back. At the camp hospital the German doctor could not even recognize Rettig, his face was so disfigured by the beating he had received. The doctor did his best but in the end it was decided that he must be sent to Sheffield for emergency treatment. He died on the way. According to the pathologist's postmortem verdict, he had choked on his own blood. To all intents and purposes he had been murdered by his own countrymen.

156

Once the news of Rettig's death was released to the Press, it confirmed the general public's belief that the German POWs in their midst would stop at nothing. Clearly the war was over. On the Rhine, German soldiers were surrendering in their thousands. They knew that Hitler was finished and Germany had lost the war. But not these POWs. They seemed as fanatical as ever, as if this was still 1940, not 1945. They were beaten — so why did they still keep up the hopeless, one-sided struggle?

THREE

On 8 March, 1945, Admiral Huffmeier, commander of the German forces in the Channel Islands, who had been cut off from their homeland since the Allies had landed in Normandy nine months before, gave the signal to attack.

The Admiral, who had once been captain of the German battlecruiser *Scharnhorst,* was such a fanatic that his men called him 'the Madman of the Channel Islands'. Twice they had attempted to murder him and surrender to the British, for they were starving and wanted to end their imprisonment on the islands where food was so scarce that they were reduced to eating nettles and dandelions. Once they had tried to entice him out of his HQ with a beautiful decoy — the Admiral had an eye for a pretty female. The plan was to kidnap him and ship him to England so that they could surrender. But the plan had failed and now Huffmeier was ordering them into the attack.

With the Americans already pouring over the Rhine at Remagen, Huffmeier, 500 miles behind the fighting front, wanted to launch one of the most audacious commando raids of the whole war. From the Channel Islands, a force of the best available men would sail to the port of Granville in France. Granville had been the site of Eisenhower's first permanent headquarters in continental Europe, but had now become a quiet backwater through which supplies were run to the Allied armies. Huffmeier did not think his bold raid would change the course of the war, but he *did* think that a successful attack on the French coast so far behind allied lines would be a tremendous boost for morale back in the homeland. Like the POWs in Britain, he had no idea of the true state of German morale.

On the evening of Friday 9 March, 1945, his commando force set sail to cover the short distance to Granville from Jersey, the closest island to France, just thirty-two miles away.

For a while all went well. But unknown to the German force they had already been spotted. Lieutenant-Commander Sandel, skipper of the US *PC 564*, had seen the green blobs on his little vessel's radar screen of the enemy convoy sailing to his front. The young naval officer had taken over the torpedo boat just a few days before, and his crew was a scratch one, recruited mainly from US port offices in England. Nevertheless, he took up the challenge.

At three miles' range the young American officer ordered three green flares to be fired for recognition purposes. But even before Sandel could positively identify the suspicious outlines to his front, a German flare burst directly above, drenching his craft in its icy white light. His response was immediate.

'Open fire!' he yelled to his gun crew.

Lieutenant Klinger, in charge of the gun crew, bellowed an order. The 76mm cannon burst into action. The little vessel shuddered with the detonation. But that first shell was remarkably accurate, falling only 200 yards from the leading German ship. Again Klinger yelled, 'Fire!' Nothing happened. The brand-new artillery piece had jammed after the first round.

The American torpedo boat didn't get a second chance. With a sound like a giant piece of canvas being ripped apart, the much bigger German 88mm cannon opened up. Its first shell struck the torpedo boat directly on the bridge, killing or wounding everyone on it. Sandel and Klinger were seriously injured.

Another shell landed directly on the craft's second artillery piece, a 4cm cannon. Two further shells followed, each striking the *PC 564* so that it reeled back and forth under the impact. Drifting helplessly, its steering smashed, its radio and radar knocked out so that it was unable to report the presence of this surprise German convoy in the Channel, the little ship disappeared into the night, leaving the field to the Germans, overjoyed at the first success of their daring venture.

Half an hour later the German commandos took the little port of Granville by complete surprise. A French infantry company stationed in the port under the command of Captain St Amand, alarmed by the noise of the landing and the resultant firing, got out of their bunks. But after a few minutes Captain St Amand ordered the men back to bed. Later, when asked why, the French officer shrugged his shoulders. He thought the Americans were out on night manoeuvres and everyone knew they did things differently.

Thus, while the French defence company went back to sleep, the German soldiers and sailors swarmed ashore, the English port officer,

Lieutenant Lightholder, was felled by a burst of German machine-gun fire as he ran to his jeep to sound the alarm. The American port commander, Lieutenant-Commander Diefenbach, ran for help but he could find no one save the invading Germans.

Working enthusiastically, the German engineers blew up installations throughout the little port, cheering every time a crane or derrick came crashing down. Meanwhile, soldiers of the 'Division Kanada', as the Channel Islands garrison called itself (for that is where many of them thought they would eventually end up as POWs), roamed through the port, freeing their own men who had been working as POW labour in the harbour, rounding up Allied officers at bayonet point, many still in their pyjamas, and all the while cramming anything edible they could find down their gullets.

The audacious raid 500 miles behind the Allied front went like clockwork. The Germans took a hundred prisoners, released fifty-five of their own men, blew up four ships and captured one British coaler intact, complete with crew.

When the first American Sherman tank crawled cautiously into the port just after dawn, the birds had flown. The port was a smouldering shambles. In the Channel Islands, Admiral Huffmeier awarded several members of the raiding party the Iron Cross for their bravery. Even more welcome than the 'tin', as the soldiers called military decorations, they also received a packet of looted cigarettes and a spoonful of jam for each man.

Goebbels, far off in embattled Berlin, naturally made much of the successful raid when he heard about it the following morning. For the attack on Granville was the only piece of German offensive action on the whole of the front in the West. Radio Berlin announced that morning:

> Naval units carried out a commando raid on the French west coast at Granville. Severe casualties were inflicted on the enemy. German prisoners were liberated and brought back. Five ships of a total of 4,800 GRT and fourteen lighters were sunk; five locomotives and trucks, ten motor vehicles, one submarine shelter and a fuel depot were destroyed. The lock gates were destroyed. The steamer *Esquout* was brought back under its own steam. The town of Granville is in flames.

The news that fellow Germans, who had been virtual captives since D-Day, had carried out a successful raid on Allied territory, acted like a tonic for the German officers of Island Farm Camp, Bridgend, South Wales when they heard it over their clandestine radios that Saturday morning. Ever since the Camp Commandant, Colonel Darling, the former POW, had discovered the first tunnel back at the time of the Ardennes offensive, his men had been searching actively for the second one, for

Darling, who had escaped to Holland from Germany after three years 'in the bag', was certain that the Germans would have done what he and his comrades had done in the First World War: build another one.

But, search as they might, Colonel Darling's men could not find the supposed second tunnel. His informers in the camp had heard nothing either. With the war now entering its final phase and the defeat of the Germans quite certain, Colonel Darling started to relax his guard. Perhaps the POWs had lost their desire to escape.

Darling thought them a pretty arrogant bunch, something of a caricature of the corsetted Prussian officers of the Imperial German Army, which he remembered from the First World War. They always talked in loud voices, clicked their heels when they met senior officers and strode across the compound with their eyes fixed on some distant horizon 'like Jesus walking across the water', as Darling described them. They had comfortable quarters, originally built for the US Army when the Americans had been stationed at Bridgend before D-Day. Would such arrogant devils, living better than many a British officer, dirty their hands underground in order to escape when the war was already lost? Darling thought not.

But Colonel Darling thought wrong. The prisoners had been working on an escape tunnel for four months, virtually from the time the first officer prisoners had begun to arrive in South Wales.

Once, the tunnel had come close to being discovered. Garfield Davies, a middle-aged farmer, had been ploughing a field next to the Island Farm Camp when he noticed that the German POWs, lining the wire next to the field he was working on, were watching him intently and in total silence. Davies thought they might have been farmers themselves in civvy street and were observing how straight a furrow he was ploughing. He decided to show them just what a Welsh farmer could do. But when he started to move away from the perimeter wire, the POWs lost interest in his efforts. Then when he began the return journey they clung to the wire once more and watched with the same silent intensity — especially when he skirted a large stone not too far from the perimeter. On his next run Farmer Davies kept his tractor well away from the large stone. He reasoned they might want him to run into it and perhaps wreck his ploughshare. Indeed it seemed that way, for as soon as he steered clear of the stone, most of the prisoners lost interest in him. Finished finally, he left with his tractor, telling himself that he'd shown the Jerries just how well a Welsh farmer could plough. It was only later that he realized that he had been in a position then to stop the largest mass break-out in the history of German prisoners-of-war in the war. For the stone concealed the exit to the tunnel on which they had been working for the last four months.

Today no one knows who masterminded the great break-out at Island Farm in the second week of March, but whoever he was he did his job well. The tunnel was never discovered, despite Colonel Darling's vigilance and constant searches, and all the POWs who wished to escape that month did.

It started just before midnight of that same Saturday when Goebbels gave the details of the successful commando raid on Granville over the German radio. A middle-aged German major walked into the guardroom of the camp and told the duty officer there was something going to happen shortly in Hut Four. With that he had walked out again, leaving the surprised duty officer to call the second-in-command and tell him what had transpired.

The camp's second-in-command, who had fought in the First World War and had been too old for active duty in the Second, was nevertheless a very conscientious officer. Twice a night, at midnight and in the early hours of the morning, he did the rounds to check that all was well. Now he came hurriedly to the duty officer's room and asked what he had done about the surprise report from the middle-aged German major.

'Nothing yet,' the other man admitted.

The second-in-command didn't hesitate. 'Get a search party together,' he ordered, 'and go over to Hut Four.' It was just the sort of night, dark with no moon, when the POWs might attempt to escape.

The patrol was sent out to Hut Four. The dog-handlers were alerted and started their charges padding around the perimeter wire. Colonel Darling, roused from his sleep, was told what was happening. He in turn informed Mr. May, the police superintendent, and gave him details of the possible escape.

Mr. May already knew something of what was happening that Saturday night. A local doctor's car had been stolen and neighbours of the doctor had told Inspector Fitzpatrick that they had seen four young men pushing the little Austin down the road at a leisurely pace before trying to start it. One of the men appeared to be a German POW, they said.

Just as May passed on this news to Colonel Darling, there was the sound of shots being fired somewhere along the perimeter fence. The two men rushed towards the spot. A single sentry, rifle at the ready, was peering into the gloom. Next to him were three of the camp's inmates, their hands in the air.

The sentry then explained that by the light of a flare he had seen a head emerge from the ground. He had hit the escaper and then, to his great astonishment, found three more men emerging from the darkness near his feet. All had promptly surrendered.

After digesting the sentry's information and learning that the first POW was not dead but had been taken off to the sick bay, Darling turned to Superintendent May, who was asking the Camp Commandant whether he thought that any of his 'boys' had actually escaped.

'No, I don't think so,' Darling replied, 'but just to be on the safe side I'm having a roll-call.'

With Superintendent May and the camp's second-in-command, Darling returned to his office while the duty officer roused the POWs for an emergency roll-call.

While they were having a mug of tea the Commandant's phone rang. It was the local police station. The desk sergeant reported that he had just had a call from PC Baverstock at Llanharan. 'He says he has just caught two German paratroopers — *Leutnant* Karl Ludwig and *Leutnant* Herzler. They won't say where they're from, but we think it's likely they're from Island Farm. What shall we do with them, sir?'

Colonel Darling handed the phone to Superintendent May. Llanharan was six or eight miles from the POW Camp. They must have got out a good while before the men who had just been apprehended by the sentry at the wire. That could mean only one thing: there had been a mass escape.

The Baron's Sixth Paras were at it again.

FOUR

As Colonel Darling surveyed the escapers' tunnel that dawn, he could see at first glance that it had been a highly professional job. Indeed, it reminded him of the tunnel through which he and others had escaped back at Holzminden in 1917. This one started underneath a bed in a hut nearest to the wire and went down eighteen feet to where it joined a large natural cavern — how the Germans had discovered the natural fault Colonel Darling never did find out. Using the cavern as a base, the tunnellers had worked forward another sixty feet, right under the perimeter wire, to the large exit through which the escapers had been able to pass in comfort and without dirtying their clothes in Farmer Davies' field.

Just as in the Holzminden tunnel, air had been supplied through a series of connected tins, in this case tins of a Canadian powdered milk called Klim, supplied to the POWs through the International Red Cross, and pumped by means of a foot-powered makeshift bellows. At the last minute before the escapers had gone through, the walls had been lined with old clothes and uniforms so that their escape outfits would be clean at the other end.

Furious that all this had been going on under his nose, especially when he considered himself something of an expert at evasion techniques, Colonel Darling asked his cadaverous second-in-command how no one had noticed the spoil; the tunnel had gone through heavy clay and the top soil at Island Farm was light loam. Surely someone should have spotted that darker clay in the top soil when the POWs got rid of it there?

The second-in-command replied the clay had been buried among the flowerbeds which the POWs had started cultivating the year before. The guards had noticed the Germans working feverishly at these plots and had remarked upon the fact that they seemed to dig very deep just to plant flowers or whatever they were planting. 'We thought they knew nothing about gardening,' he said simply.

Glumly Colonel Darling nodded his understanding. The German escapers had been very professional, he realized that. Nothing could be achieved by trying to allot blame at the moment. There would be a court of inquiry, of course. After all, this was the biggest prison break-out of the war in Britain. But for the time being the most important thing was to recapture nearly a hundred German officers at present running loose in South Wales.

Superintendent May was of exactly the same opinion. He had already established an incident room for the POW operation, complete with a large map of South Wales and a supply of pins bearing a swastika. Every time a prisoner was recaptured the Superintendent would pin the spot where he was taken with a flag. In this way he hoped to establish whether there was some kind of pattern to their movements and ascertain if they were heading in any particular direction.

At the moment the map bore exactly two swastika pins at Llanharan, where PC Baverstock had caught the two German paratroop officers, whom he had first thought were burglars. But when he had shone his torch on them he found that they were dressed in the grey-green, ankle-length waterproofs of the Wehrmacht.

Now May stared at the pile of stuff taken from the two escapers in the tiny charge-room at Llanharan Police Station. Cigarettes, tins of corned beef, shaving gear and, a little surprisingly, a pair of slippers. Did they think they were going to find some cosy little refuge where they could relax in slippered comfort in front of a glowing coal fire, he wondered. He dismissed the speculation and concentrated on a large khaki handkerchief which had been made by cutting off the tail of a para officer's shirt. But it wasn't the material or size of the handkerchief which interested Superindentent May and PC Baverstock. It was the map drawn on it in clear ink by a skilled hand. It showed in detail the roads which would have helped the two lieutenants to reach any port from Penzance to Margate. It also showed all the large towns in Wales and, more significantly, the ports on the east and south coast of Eire. There, in a neutral country, they obviously felt the IRA would help them to get back to Germany as soon as possible.

The map stumped May for a while. How the devil had the Germans been able to find such a detailed map and reproduce it this way, like the handkerchief maps handed out to British aircrews, paratroops, commandos and the like? All maps were banned in the camps and ever since the summer of 1940, when Britain feared invasion, everything which would indicate the locality of a place — station names, signposts, even advertisements bearing the name of a product which was linked with a certain town — had been removed. Then it dawned on the Superintendent.

The maps had been copied from the ones that adorned every railway carriage of the Southern Railway system. Placed just above the eight seats of the average third-class carriage, they were in one of the glass-covered show cases which advertised the delights of the resorts and towns covered by that region's railway. The POWs had travelled by rail from Southampton to South Wales and they had obviously used the time locked up in their carriages to copy the map.

May shook his head. Someone had made a monumental blunder. But again there was no time to be wasted on past mistakes. With the whole of South Wales now alarmed, there was an urgent need to know what the escapers' intentions were.

Now that they were recaptured, the two para officers, Ludwig and Herzler, talked freely. They confirmed what May had guessed. The man who had been shot in the field and the three others who had given themselves up to the vigilant sentry had been the last of the escapers. They had been the most reluctant to go and had only been forced into escaping by threats of violence from the 'blacks'.

The real escape had begun as early as ten o'clock the previous Saturday night. Just after the roll-call the POWs had started a noisy sing-song, bellowing as loud as they could to distract the guards and covering any noise the escapers might make. Thereafter, at five-minute intervals, two prisoners would escape together. Looking at May smugly over the edge of his mug of tea, Herzler said that by now the camp would be almost empty. It would be a nice Sunday surprise for the Camp Commandant!

May assured him that he was mistaken. Island Farm Camp certainly wasn't empty. All the same, there were several score men now on the run that morning in an area ideally suited for escapers. The Vale of Glamorgan, with its isolated farms and large stretches of open land, had plenty of places where an escaper might hide, if he had sufficient food and water, until the hunt let up and he could make a break for one of the ports. With luck he might be able to stow away on one of the colliers plying their trade between South Wales and Eire.

That was something that Superintendent May intended should not happen. At dawn he had already put into operation what the newspapers called rather grandly 'Police Plan X'. This entailed roadblocks at strategic sites throughout the area and patrols at rail and bus stations. Constables would also patrol local war factories. After what had happened at Devizes three months before, May was prepared to believe that this was no mere escape, but possibly the start of a sabotage operation, with the German officers intent on destroying some of the many munitions factories of the Bridgend area. Until recently these factories had been guarded by the Home Guard, but now the Home Guard had virtually stood down and the authorities did not want to call them out again in case the local population became even more alarmed than it was already.

Now it was left to the Army and RAF to cover the countryside, with May's constables going into the farm communities to warn local pastors what had happened. On Sunday the country folk would congregate in their chapels and it was an ideal opportunity to spread the word before the pastor delivered his sermon.

As Army tracking dogs and light Austers carrying a pilot and an observer, usually used as artillery spotters, covered the countryside, the first sighting of an escaper reached police HQ. A German officer dressed in a light blue Luftwaffe overcoat, complete with yellow facings, and wearing jackboots, had knocked at the door of a terrace house and asked for food. It seemed that 'food' was the only word of English he knew. He had smiled at the housewife who opened the door to him and, pointing at his open mouth, repeated the word several times. The housewife, who had not heard of the escape, thought the man must be a foreign airman who had crashed on the nearby mountain. She told him that she had no food to spare and that he'd best be off before he woke the rest of the family. He fled but was recaptured shortly after.

More escapers were caught that afternoon, not due to May's careful planning but thanks to an intelligent guess by a farmer's daughter. As the Morris family at Laleston sat down to Sunday lunch they were discussing the news of the escape which they had heard while at chapel that morning. Farmer Morris was busy carving the tiny joint of mutton which would have to last them most of the week when his daughter Brenda idly commented that she knew the perfect hiding place. Where was that, he asked.

'Well,' Brenda said, 'where else but the sunken copse across the fields? I remember when I was a child it was a fine place to hide.' Farmer Morris considered the idea over lunch and then he took a stout stick, asked his neighbour, John Williams, to come with him and set out to have a look. His daughter had been right. As they approached the hidden copse, the farmers could hear voices. Carefully they edged forward and saw through the trees five Germans sitting there smoking, with open haversacks lying on the ground next to them. They appeared not to have a care in the world. It was as if they were on a pre-war picnic; only the beer was missing.

Morris noted that they didn't appear to be armed, so in the end he leapt out, waving his stick and shouting like some sheriff in a Wild West film, 'You're surrounded! You'd better give yourselves up!'

The Germans sprang to their feet. The biggest of them rapped out an order and they all turned to make a run for it.

At that instant a spotter plane came zooming in. Morris and Williams waved their sticks and indicated the way the prisoners had run. The pilot radioed to the nearest Army patrol. They came up in their 15cwt trucks and Bren-gun carriers. Hastily the two excited farmers told them what had happened and they roared away across the fields. All five escapers were captured shortly thereafter.

Another amateur sleuth was less successful. Mole-catcher Jim Jones of Merthy Mawr spotted a group of German escapers crouched in a ditch. Unobserved by them, he slipped away until he came across a platoon of British infantry deployed on a nearby hillside, training for active service in Burma. With his rattling mole traps fixed to his walking stick, he approached the platoon commander and told him what he had seen. But the young lieutenant could not be bothered about stories of German prisoners. 'We're training to fight the Japs, not the Germans,' he said sniffily. 'Now off you go.'

As the second week of that March gave way to the third, more and more of the escapers were caught all over that part of Wales. The four who had stolen the doctor's car in Bridgend were apprehended near Castle Bromwich. Cheekily one of the German officers offered to repay the doctor for the petrol they had used in their escape (the GP turned him down). Two were captured while pretending to be Dutch sailors from a ship in Cardiff docks. At Treoes an indignant farmer discovered his cows had already been milked and called the police, which led to the capture of more escapers. Six were taken at the beauty spot called The Tumbles outside Llanishen by some walkers. A group of boys spotted a group hiding in the caves outside Bridgend. A Girl Guides commissioner for Glamorgan, Miss Olive Nicholl, put another half-dozen to flight by wielding her frying pan when she and her troop came across them in a lonely wood; they were later captured.

By Monday Superintendent May's map of the area was well covered with little swastika flags for those already retaken by the police and military. Now, observing the wide spread of the places where the escapers had been captured, he had come to the conclusion that the POWs were not intent on sabotage, but merely on escaping. So far not one of them had been recaptured in a sensitive area. It seemed to him, after a hectic forty-eight hours with his only sleep hurried catnaps, that the situation was under control. It would only be a matter of time before all of them were recaptured.

That night his confidence was shattered by an excited phone call from Porthcawl, the seaside resort only a few miles from Bridgend. A woman had been shot and her husband had told the local police that she had been shot by one of two Germans to whom she had refused to give money and food.

May had believed that the German escapers were unarmed, so this news was doubly alarming. There was a tremendous anti-German mood in the area, especially as the first German concentration camps were now being overrun by the Allies and the sickening details of what had gone on there were filtering back to Britain. Many local people were armed — farmers with their shotguns and Home Guardsmen who kept their weapons at home — and May feared that the news the escapers were armed might trigger an outbreak of indiscriminate shooting. Weary as he was, he knew that he had to go and investigate the incident personally.

At Porthcawl he learned that the shot woman, a Mrs Grassley, was on the critical list. The doctors at the local hospital were fighting for her life. But her husband had been with her at the time of the shooting and he would be able to give May the details he needed. Grassley was brought from the hospital to Porthcawl police station and May took him into the interview room. From his accent, Grassley seemed to be Canadian. He repeated his account of the shooting, but May became vaguely suspicious. Dismissing him with a polite assurance that a search was under way for the German assailants, he promptly ordered that inquiries should be made into Grassley's own background.

By the next morning the local detectives had come up with a strange story. Mrs Grassley was not Mrs Grassley at all; she was Lily Griffiths, who had been living with Grassley, a Canadian soldier — who already had a wife in Canada — on and off for the last two years. Indeed, they had a son together. The two of them were spending his leave together in Porthcawl as they had done before. May also learned that Grassley possessed a revolver. He had shown it off to the son of the place where they were staying. He had told the youngster, when they heard of the escape of the German POWs, 'I'll show you what I'll do if I come across any Krauts,' and he had done a few quick draws for the boy's benefit. But though the revolver was unloaded, the boy had noted that Grassley had a clip of ammunition in his pocket.

The doctors attending Mrs Grassley had meanwhile discovered that in addition to the gunshot she had suffered in her chest, she was also extensively bruised, as if she had been beaten up. May had no time to investigate personally. He left the local detectives to get on with the inquiry, while he continued to search for the missing Germans.

By the end of the third day of the great escape from Island Farm Camp Superintendent May's map was covered with a rash of swastika flags. He could see from the way they were distributed that, although the escape had been highly organized, once the escapers had cleared the tunnel it had been every man for himself. It was clear that the Porthcawl case was the only incident of violence. Although the POWs were reputed to be very tough customers, they had all surrendered tamely enough once they were trapped. So why had violence been used only on the Grassleys?

Out on the remote farms in the area, May reasoned, POWs could easily have intimidated the elderly farmers, whose able-bodied young labourers had long since vanished into the Forces. A prisoner on the run, armed only with a home-made knife, could have found himself shelter and food for weeks in one of those places if he had threatened to use his weapon. So why hadn't the German escapers used whatever makeshift weapons they might have brought with them from the camp? And where had the revolver come from which had been used to shoot Mrs. Grassley? It was all very puzzling.

Reporters from as far away as London were also becoming interested in both the escape and the Grassley shooting. Using the usual tactics they employed when the police were slow in coming forward with information, the London hacks were suggesting that there'd be trouble in Fleet Street soon if they didn't come home with the bacon. Why had so many POWs been allowed to escape? And why hadn't they been rounded up by now? After all, they had nearly killed Mrs Grassley. It was, as May knew, a kind of blackmail. If the hacks didn't get their Mrs Grassley story, they'd highlight the failure of the South Wales police to find and round up all the escaped POWs. He told them that if they would give him until tomorrow morning he would have something to report to them then at Porthcawl Police Station.

FIVE

On the morning of the fourth day of the escape Superintendent May drove to Porthcawl to take personal charge of the Grassley case while Inspector Fitzpatrick temporarily took over the manhunt for the escapers.

At Porthcawl they informed May that Grassley had to be telling the truth about the attack by the German POWs because Mrs Grassley herself had corroborated her husband's story. But what about the bruises on her body, May objected. He was told that Grassley was a violent man, who had a bad temper when he was drunk, which was often.

May ordered Grassley brought in. White-faced and unshaven, the Canadian told his story once more. It checked perfectly with his written account that May had in front of him on the desk. But still May sensed that there was something fishy about Grassley's account of the shooting, so he tried a new tactic. He said, 'There's one thing I'm not clear about. I should like to know exactly how the German with the gun came at you. Give me a demonstration.'

Grassley went even whiter. He was rooted to his chair.

'Come on,' May urged.

Abruptly the Canadian broke. 'I can't go through with it,' he sobbed.

May knew then his hunch was right. 'Take him back to his cell and charge him with shooting the woman,' he ordered. 'And look for the gun in Grassley's lodgings, and check it with the bullet the surgeon took out of the woman. I think you'll find they match.'

They did. As if to confirm May's findings, a little thereafter he received a call from a Major Hunt of the Canadian Military Police. He had heard of the shooting at Porthcawl and now confirmed that Grassley was a deserter. The Canadian Major warned May to be careful. Grassley was armed and might shoot his way out of any trap set for him.

With the attempted murder case solved, Superintendent May returned to the business of rounding up the rest of the escaped POWs. While Grassley was being escorted away by Canadian MPs another POW was captured at Port Talbot on his way to Swansea. Three more were found by a special constable behind a hedge near the Royal Ordnance Factory at Pencoed. Another three were apprehended on a workers' bus at Glyn-Neath.

By the fifth day of the escape Superintendent May's map was almost covered with swastika flags, only a dozen escapers still remaining at large. Sightings of POWs on the run came in from everywhere. A highly nervous woman had spotted German parachutists landing to help them — the 'paras' turned out to be clouds. A golfer reported that there were Jerries crawling about on his local links, but they proved to be men of the

Royal Warwicks on a training exercise. Others telephoned to say that they thought the Germans had gone to ground in one of the many collieries of the area.

But one by one the real escapers were rounded up. Two who had hitched rides on goods trains had got as far as Eastleigh in Hampshire, 110 miles away from Island Farm Camp and a mere six miles from Southampton, where they meant to board a ship for France. They were spotted by a shunter. Another couple were arrested at another Royal Ordnance factory. Four were caught with the help of a colliery official at Nantewaeth Colliery at Cymmer. Then the first three out of the tunnel, who were the last to be recaptured, were taken by the vigilance of two women returning to a mountain farm. They heard the men speaking broken English and ran to the nearby farm of Mr John Hopkins, a burly rugby forward of nearly international standard. He tackled them without a weapon and reportedly 'convinced' them — it wasn't stated how — to give themselves up.

They were the last. Now it was over.

There would be other escapes, of course. German POWs in Britain continued escaping right into late 1947 — and returning, too. For when they finally reached Germany, they found the land they had dreamed of no longer matched up to their expectations, especially the conditions and politics of the Soviet Zone of Occupation.

But the March 1945 break-out from Island Farm Camp was the last escape associated with the planned march on London. Like all the other escapes, it had ended in total failure. Nevertheless, these German POW escapes from December, 1944, to March, 1945, had kept the whole country on constant alert. Time and again the authorities had seen a sinister purpose behind the escapes. After all, they knew what the general British public did not: that British POW camps held the equivalent of seventeen German infantry divisions, albeit without arms, who if they all broke out could create havoc throughout the land.

But now, on the day that the last three escapers were rounded up, the same day that Montgomery began his full-scale crossing of the Rhine, the time had come to pick up the pieces. Soon the POWs would start going home to their shattered country. First the 'whites', then the 'greys', and finally the 'blacks'. Britain had no intention of keeping prisoners-of-war to help build up her war-torn economy, as countries such as France and Russia would. POWs were, after all, only extra mouths to feed.

Yet before the mass exodus of the German POWs could start, there would have to be retribution and punishment of those who had transgressed against the laws of the land during the abortive march on London.

AFTERMATH

In the summer of 1945 Colonel Scotland was preparing a series of investigations on the Continent. These were all concerned with alleged atrocities against British POWs in German hands. He was to investigate the shooting of British prisoners at the village of Paradis in France by the SS; the execution of fifty RAF men who had escaped from Sagan Stalag and were retaken by the Gestapo; and the case of German Field-Marshal Kesselring, allegedly responsible for the mass shooting of Italian resistance workers in that country.

But while Scotland was still preparing to go on his European travels, which would take up the best part of two years, he was summoned by the General commanding London District and asked if he would use his influence on the Devizes plotters. Ever since the murder of Rosterg in Comrie Camp, efforts had been made to identify the killers. They had been narrowed down to five men — Koenig, Mertens and the three SS men, Zuehlsdorff, Brueling and Goltz. Three others, Herzig among them, were charged with complicity.

The five accused had been isolated in separate camps throughout Southern England to await their trial. According to the GOC, London District, the accused were now demanding to be represented in court by one of their fellow prisoners who had been a lawyer back in Germany. They flatly refused to have the services of the British barrister who had been instructed to appear for them. The General asked Scotland if he would use his personal influence with the prisoners to convince them that they could best be represented in court by a British lawyer who knew not only the language but the procedures.

After several meetings, Scotland finally managed to persuade the five accused; they agreed to accept a British lawyer. The trial could begin.

It was held in the oak-panelled drawing room of the London Cage,

171

surely the strangest place for a murder trial in twentieth-century British legal history, before a bench consisting of three colonels and three majors. The prisoners were represented by Captain Roger Willis, who one day would become a judge, and Major R. Evans, a former Welsh solicitor.

Right from the start the accused proved as aggressive as they had been in Camp 23 at Devizes. All five pleaded not guilty. Indeed, they made their position clear to Captain Willis: 'Why should we be tried for killing a traitor?'

Koenig told Willis that in a POW camp near the German (now Polish) city of Breslau, RAF officers had hanged one of their fellows who had given away an escape plan. The German authorities, on instructions from SS General Berger, head of the POW camps, had taken no action against the murderers. In Berger's view this murder had nothing to do with the German authorities.

Captain Willis, who himself had been a POW in Germany, replied that he knew nothing of the alleged murder. Besides, it was irrelevant. What happened in Germany had no bearing on a crime committed in England.

As the trial got under way the prisoners were guarded by Grenadier Guardsmen all the time, for they were still thought to be dangerous (though the bench and the lawyers were never told either that these men had broken out of Devizes camp or that, if they had succeeded with their plan, there might have been wholesale bloodshed while they fought their way to London).

But the bench must have had an inkling that there was more to the case than a murder at Comrie Camp. All witnesses, including the Intelligence officers on Colonel Scotland's staff, were referred to solely by numbers, and everyone who had anything to do with the case was sworn never to reveal the names of any of these witnesses.

One of the accused, Brueling, had confessed to taking part in the killing. However, he now said he had made his original statement under duress. During interrogation, he said, a British captain had bellowed at him, 'You rogue, you swine, you murderer. You killed Rosterg. I have fifteen witnesses that say you did it.'

It was a ploy that courts trying German war criminals would hear a lot in the next few years. Before the trial the prisoner would make an admission of guilt and then, when cross-examined during the trial, he would retract. He would state that the admission had been forced out of him by threats or by actual violence. The idea was that by this means the prisoner would overturn the prosecution's whole case. This time it didn't work. The interrogation officer denied using threats and the bench believed him.

The last witnesses were the accused themselves. They were as arrogant as ever. They gave their evidence in a brisk confident manner, as if addressing junior officers. First on the stand was Koenig who denied any part in the beating of Rosterg or in the hanging. But he did maintain that Rosterg had deserved to die. Rosterg's treason had begun on the Russian front, he declared. Then in France he had sold weapons to the Resistance and had arranged the surrender of huge dumps of German ammunition to the French after he had deserted from the Wehrmacht. The court was not impressed. They were interested in who had murdered Rosterg, not whether he was a traitor.

One after another, the accused stepped into the box and showed just how much they had lost touch with reality. All naturally denied that they had played any part in the murder of Rosterg, but all testified that it was only right and proper that Rosterg had been killed. Herzig said, 'I was in the Hitler Youth. Every decent fellow in Germany was in the Hitler Youth. We wouldn't have had anything to do with scum like Rosterg.' Brueling opined that 'such a man as Rosterg represented infinite danger to the Fatherland. He deserved to die.' Goltz believed that Rosterg had to hang, although he might have already been dead from the beating he had received, because 'I was of the opinion that a traitor should be found hanging.'

Major Hillard, the prosecutor, had little time for the blind arrogance of the accused, who were still loyal to a discredited and beaten creed. He summed up for the bench by saying,

> It is immaterial what the motive was. They had no right to kill
> Rosterg because he was not a Nazi or because he was a traitor.
> Those of the accused who with their own hands committed the
> violence were guilty of murder, as were any of the others who
> were then participating in the intention equally guilty.

In the end three, including Herzig, who had made that first reconnaissance escape from Devizes to find out the dispositions of the US 17th Airborne and 11th Armored Divisions, were acquitted. But the five others, Koenig, Zuehlsdorff, Mertens, Goltz and Brueling, were sentenced to death.

For days now the accused had been bored with the whole legal business, dozing through the lengthy translations from English to German and vice-versa. As both sides summed up, they doodled on the note pads before them, nudged each other and made little jokes as if they hadn't a care in the world.

Even when the death sentence was uttered, they did not lose their composure nor plead against their fate. Each when his turn came stood rigidly to attention; when the interpreter translated 'death by hanging' into '*Tod durch erhaengen*' each said '*danke*' politely, as if it didn't matter much that their young lives were soon to end in the hangman's noose.

Afterwards they even found time to send a polite note to Scotland, signed by Koenig, in which he stated,

> I would like, in the name of my comrades and in my own name, to express to you, sir, our gratitude. Due to your advice we asked for British officers to be assigned to us for our defence, and we have been agreeably surprised.

They would have been even more surprised if they had known that the man they had murdered had once worked for the British officer whom they seemed to regard as something of a benefactor.

There was no appeal; the Royal Warrant which had set up the court did not allow it. So in early October, 1945, that blunt Yorkshireman Albert Pierrepoint, full-time publican and part-time public executioner from Clayton, Bradford, took his usual No. 77 bus to King's Cross, changed there and headed out for the 'the Ville' — Pentonville in North London.

With him he carried the little case containing the tools of this trade: the soft leather strap; the rope; the leg strap; the copper wire; the tape measure; the pliers; and, in case one of the men to be hanged had only one arm, his own invention, the strap for the one-armed man. In due course Pierrepoint sized up the height, weight and muscular capacity of the five young Germans, made his calculations — weight of prisoner in pounds in relation to height of the recommended drop — and then went to work.

Pierrepoint had always been a quick worker. This winter he would executive twenty-seven German war criminals, including the 'Beast of Belsen', in twenty-four hours. Now he went to work on the five guilty men with his usual speedy efficiency. Each in turn he seized from the back, as they sat in their cells, facing away from the door, as was the custom, and pinioned their hands behind them with that soft leather strap. Then followed the rest of the ghastly ritual which regularly had prison officials, who were present to the end, fainting and vomiting. Within the space of just over two hours Pierrepoint had hanged the lot. Gruesome as the official hangings were, they were as nothing compared to the terrible garrotting which had been the fate of *Feldwebel* Rosterg at Comrie Camp.

Major Hillard, who had successfully prosecuted the Devizes men, now did the same with those accused of the murder of Rettig at Lodge Moor Camp, Sheffield. He made out the case that although many POWs had been involved in beating Rettig to death, Schmittendorf and Kuehne had instigated the crime.

Both men seemed completely apathetic when they were brought before the court to hear their death sentences passed. Schmittendorf, who had been in the Wehrmacht since 1934, had lost both his profession and his family — his wife and children had disappeared in the battle for Berlin in April 1945; he accepted his fate numbly. Kuehne, who was still only eighteen, had been in the Nazi youth movement since the age of nine. He had also, seemingly, lost his will to live. He accepted the sentence, '*Tod durch erhaengen*' without a flicker of emotion.

One month after the Devizes men had been hanged at 'the Ville', Albert Pierrepoint made another trip by bus to Pentonville, carrying in his hand the same little case, to hang Schmittendorf and Kuehne.

And while they were hanged, the man who had used their youthful idealism for his own purposes and then dropped them when they were no longer needed, *SD Brigadeführer* Walter Schellenberg, was making himself useful at Nuremberg to the Allied officials preparing the case against Nazi war criminals. He would appear as a key witness in the trial of major war criminals such as Goering, Ribbentrop, Keitel and other Nazi leaders.

As for his own trial, which started in 1947, Schellenberg ended up being acquitted on all but two charges: he was a member of two criminal organizations, the SS and SD. The court considered, however, that Schellenberg's guilt was mitigated by his efforts to aid concentration camp prisoners at the end of the war, whatever the motives from which he acted. Thus he was sentenced to six years' imprisonment (to run from June, 1945, when he had been repatriated from Sweden into Allied custody), one of the lightest sentences imposed by the court. It meant that he was freed after a few months, to live his remaining years first in Switzerland and then in Italy.

Schellenberg died peacefully in bed, four years after completing his memoirs which ended thus: 'For the time being my services [as a spymaster] were no longer required.' Fortunately for the world and for the sake of young men like those in Allied POW camps whom he had tricked, his services were never again required.

In September, 1946, while Schellenberg was still in prison spilling the secrets of his former masters to Allied Intelligence officers, the first of 394,000 German POWs in Britain eligible for repatriation to their homeland started to leave. Senior officers and hard-core 'blacks', however, were kept behind until they had convinced the tribunals that they no longer believed in the National Socialist creed.

By now thousands of German POWs were working in Britain clearing coastal defences, helping out on farms, dismantling their own camps when they were no longer required. Their chocolate-coloured uniforms had become a familiar sight, especially in the countryside and many of them already had British girlfriends. But while these men integrated themselves into British life and waited their turn to be repatriated, there were others who continued to defy the British authorities. Indeed, there were still some who were determined to escape and make their own way back home.

Paratrooper Gerald Hanel, for instance, who had cleaned up Glen Mill Camp at Oldham, still persisted in greeting the tribunal which reviewed his case every six months with '*Heil Hitler*!' He was finally sent home in 1947, but he did not like what he found in the ruins of Dresden, the place of his birth. Disillusioned, he returned to Northern England, married an English woman and became a chef at a restaurant on the outskirts of Derby.

Another incorrigible 'black' at Glen Mill, Hans Schaffer, escaped to Leeds. He found work in a garage which employed several displaced persons, so that his accent wasn't too noticeable, and stayed for several months before the law caught up with him. Two others got as far as Hamburg, from where they sent Glen Mill's commandant a rude letter stating that they would not be coming back to enjoy any more of his kind hospitality.

At Camp 186, just outside Colchester, three prisoners escaped and stowed away on a German cargo ship sailing from Ipswich. Once outside the three-mile limit the three men gave themselves up to the skipper, who was none too pleased with them. Indeed, once the ship reached the mouth of the Elbe, on its way to Hamburg, the skipper ordered his three stowaways to go over the side and swim for it; he wanted no trouble with the British authorities at the great port.

No one knows what happened to two of the stowaways, but one of them, Hans Mueller, made it back to the Soviet Zone of Occupation which had been his home before the war. For a while he worked on the land just outside Dresden, where his grandmother had a house. Then the Russians caught up with him and put him behind barbed wire yet again. He escaped once more and made his way to Hanover in the British zone. Here he fell in with some forgers who specialized in making false identification papers. They told him that his best bet was to return to Britain and collect some official POW release papers, which they could sell for a lot of money to war criminals on the run.

Three days later Hans Mueller was on another cargo ship but this time heading for Ipswich. There he returned to the Colchester camp, reported to the guard and asked to see the camp commandant. 'I've come back to work,' he told the commandant with a cheeky grin.

Naturally the commandant did not believe his impossible tale and he was sent to the London Cage to be interrogated by no less a person than '*Oberst Schottland*' himself.

Scotland was impressed. He cleared up the situation, obtained the proper papers for the impudent young German and sent him on his way back to Germany and the black market. Later that day a colleague asked Scotland what he had done with Hans. Scotland told him: 'Frankly, I congratulated him. In my opinion, the boy deserves a medal!'

Another POW who returned to Britain after escaping to Germany was not so fortunate. He returned to Lodge Moor Camp outside Sheffield to find the place closed up and abandoned. All his former comrades had gone home and his ex-guards had long been demobilized. In despair at finding himself in a foreign land without the security of the camp and its inmates, the escaper turned himself in to the Sheffield police. They did not know what to do with him. He had no papers and was obviously a foreigner. But at that time Sheffield was full of foreigners, Poles and DPs who were looking for work in Yorkshire because they could not return to their Russian-occupied home countries. Anyone could come along, the Police reasoned, and maintain that he was an escaped German POW in order to obtain papers and food.

Fortunately the escaped German remembered a Mr Stewart who had worked at the camp and could identify him. He thought that Mr Stewart had worked for the Sheffield Bus Company before the war. The police looked into the matter and found Mr Stewart, who duly recognized the German. He was sent back to Germany with the proper papers — thanks to a man who, a couple of years before, had been his deadly enemy.

One of the most audacious of these post-war escapers was not a German, but a renegade Dutchman who had fought with the German Army in Russia and had then been captured by the Americans in Normandy. Leo Dalderup, from Utrecht, went through the London Cage and was then sent to Toft Hall at Knutsford, which had once housed Patton's men when 'Old Blood and Guts' had been stationed in the area. This was the international camp which held non-German POWs, many of them with a price on their head. These men were desperate, when the war ended, *not* to be sent back to their home countries, for there they could expect long imprisonment — and worse. Dalderup was one of these. So he escaped, dodging out from a work party, dressed in a pair of old overalls given to him by a friendly Irishman. With some difficulty he made his way to Wales and found a boat bound for Dublin. There he told the authorities who he was and for a year worked on a farm, earning his keep as a farm labourer under the name of Leo Smith. But in 1947 Dalderup felt sure he would soon be arrested. He left the farm and went to Belfast, now using the name Vincent Gallagher, and even had the audacity to join the Royal Air Force! 'Bodies' were scarce in that year and the RAF was glad to get any recruit they could. His credentials were not checked, although he spoke with a very un-Irish accent and mumbled in his sleep *in German*! As Leading Aircraftsman Gallagher he prospered in the RAF. From Belfast he was posted to England, being based for a time at RAF Yatesbury in Wiltshire, which Koenig had hoped to seize during the great march on London.

But Sergeant Gallagher, as he was after three years, had a problem. He was too good. An excellent NCO and skilled radar technician, he was recommended time and again by his COs for a commission. Always he turned these offers of advancement down because he knew an application for a commission would entail a security check into his background. Then he would be lost.

In the end Sergeant Gallagher went on leave to Dublin and wrote a letter to his CO, telling him everything. He also told his story to a somewhat sceptical third secretary at the British Embassy there. Finally his case reached the Air Ministry. He was offered a discharge, which he took and disappeared into a new life.

Incredible as it may seem, there was, until quite recently, one German POW still at large in Britain, living illegally in Milton Keynes. Naturally the last prisoner-of-war loose in the United Kingdom had to be a para, namely Corporal Hans Teske of the 5th Parachute Regiment, who had won both classes of the Iron Cross in Tunisia — once for rescuing a wounded British soldier who was coming under fire from his own artillery. Teske was then wounded himself and sent to a hospital in Tunis, where he was captured by the British on 7 May, 1943. From there he was sent to America. In the summer of 1945 he was returned to Europe and imprisoned at a satellite camp of No. 116 at Hill Hall, near Epping, Essex, one day to be used as an open prison for such celebrities as Christine Keeler. Here Teske made himself at bit of a nuisance by escaping several times to offer his charms to the local Land Girls at Waltham Abbey; the sleek-haired East German fancied his chances with the ladies. In June, 1948, he applied to live outside the camp on a twelve-month parole basis. This was granted. Later he was allowed to move from Essex to Kent. But while the officials in Essex removed his name from their lists of parolees, those in Kent did not add it to theirs. By Christmas, 1948, all the parolees had been sent back to Germany save Teske. When he discovered that his name was not on the list of those to be repatriated, he pressed for its inclusion. His request was refused, without explanation.

The years passed. Time and again Mr. Teske, as he was now, tried to get someone to take up his case for official repatriation. Once he thought he was getting somewhere through the good offices of his MP, Mr Edward Heath. On another occasion he approached the West German Chancellor, Dr Adenauer, as he did several German ambassadors to London, including one who had been a paratroop commander himself in North Africa. To no avail.

When the West German government passed a law granting compensation to ex-German POWs still in enemy hands after January, 1949 (the bill was aimed at those Germans who would serve up to twelve years in

Russian POW camps), Teske's name was excluded, for he was not on the original list.

By 1970 he had given up. Still officially a German prisoner-of-war, he decided to live out the rest of his life in the quiet boredom of Milton Keynes.

Today, there is little that remains of the nearly one million German POWs who passed through the British camps in the Second World War. Most of those camps have long since disappeared, though some still exist. Thirkleby Camp, lying just under the white horse of Yorkshire, still has all but two of its original forty-four huts left. Today they house prime pigs, but the place still retains its old postal address — 'The Old Prisoner-of-War Camp, North Yorkshire' — and each year a dwindling number of 'old boys' come back to visit their 'alma mater'.

Not a dozen miles away, at Malton, an enterprising local businessman has turned another such camp, Eden Camp, into the 'World War Two Experience'. Here, among many other attractions, the visitor can see a reconstructed POW hut, complete with models and 'Lili Marlene' played over the sound system.

Most of the Devizes Camp, Camp 23, has vanished, but some of the original Nissen huts still exist. Now they form part of Wiltshire County Council's refuse-collecting department.

Ironically enough, there is one former German POW camp which still fulfils its original function as a place to hold prisoners, though now the prisoners are British. In part of the British Army's Correction Centre at Colchester, the once feared 'glasshouse', the inmates are still housed in the line of shabby huts which were once *'Kriegsgefangenlager Nr. 186'*

But perhaps the most poignant memorial to those many young Germans who were reluctant guests of His Majesty's Government in Britain during the Second World War is the German cemetery at Cannock Chase, Staffordshire. Here rest those thousands who never returned to their Fatherland. Innocent or guilty, they lie side by side. The victims are here: eighteen-year-old Paul Hartmann, shot by Private John Jaffray at Glen Mill: Rosterg, beaten to death by his own countrymen at Comrie, and Rettig too. Their murderers also have found a last resting place here: Koenig, Brueling, Schmittendorf and Mertens, the only one who was said to have shown any remorse before Pierrepoint hanged him.

Nowadays fewer and fewer German visitors of the wartime generation come to visit the place. The parents of the dead have died themselves. Their sweethearts and lovers have long forgotten them, married again years ago. There are few flowers on the low graves, set out in the German military fashion under shared stones. Germany's post-war generations are ashamed of their soldier fathers who lost the war. Today only an ageing few remember all their effort and suffering. By and large the young fanatics who sought to stem the tide of Germany's defeat moulder in English soil, forgotten by history.

BIBLIOGRAPHY

Alexander and Romilly, *The Privileged Nightmare* (Weidenfeld, London 1954)
Jackson, R., *A Taste of Freedom* (Arthur Barker, London 1964)
MacDonald, C., *The Battle of the Bulge* (Weidenfeld, London 1985)
Merriam, Robert, *The Battle of the Ardennes* (Souvenir Press 1947)
Nobecourt, J., *Hitler's Last Gamble* (Chatto & Windus, London 1967)
Pierrepoint, Albert, *Executioner Pierrepoint* (Harrap, London 1957)
Sanders, J., *The Night Before Christmas* (Putnam, New York 1963)
Schellenberg, Walter, *The Labyrinth* (Harper, New York 1956)
Scotland, Alexander, *The London Cage* (Evans Bros, London 1957)
Shulman, Milton, *Defeat in the West* (Seeker & Warburg, London 1947)
Tress, W. and A. Hohenstein, *Hoelle in Hurtgenwald* (Triangel Verlag, Aachen
      1991)
West, Rebecca, *The Meaning of Treason* (Macmillan, London 1949)
Whiting, Charles, *Ardennes: The Secret War* (Century, London 1985)
After the Battle
Daily Express, Der Spiegel, Jahreschronik, Rheinland Pfalz, Grenzecho, etc.